DIVULGING UTOPIA

DIVULGING UTOPIA

Radical Humanism in Sixteenth-Century England

DAVID WEIL BAKER

UNIVERSITY OF MASSACHUSETTS PRESS

AMHERST

This book is published with the assistance of a Weiss/Brown
Publication Subvention Award from the Newberry Library, as well as
a grant authorized by the Research Council of Rutgers University.

Copyright © 1999 by
The University of Massachusetts Press
All rights reserved
Printed in the United States of America
LC 98-53494
ISBN 1-55849-198-8
Designed by Steve Dyer
Printed and bound by BookCrafters, Inc.

Library of Congress Cataloging-in-Publication Data
Baker, David Weil, 1963–
Divulging Utopia : radical humanism in sixteenth-century England /
David Weil Baker.
p.   cm. — (Massachusetts studies in early modern culture)
Includes index.
ISBN 1-55849-198-8 (cloth : alk. paper)
1. England—Intellectual life—16th century.   2. English
prose literature—Early modern, 1500–1700—History and
criticism.   3. Didactic literature, Latin (Medieval and modern)—
Appreciation—England.   4. Elyot, Thomas, Sir, 1490?–1546—
Political and social views.   5. Printing—Political aspects—England—
History—16th century.   6. Politics and literature—England—History—
16th century.   7. More, Thomas, Sir, Saint, 1478–1535.   Utopia.
8. Radicalism—England—History—16th century.   9. Utopias—
History—16th century.   10. Humanists—England.   I. Title.   II. Series.
DA320.B35   1999
942.06—dc21   98-53494
CIP

British Library Cataloguing in Publication data are available.

FOR
Marcia and Abby

Contents

Acknowledgments

This book originated as a doctoral dissertation at Columbia University, where I was fortunate to have had truly wonderful mentors and teachers. David Scott Kastan encouraged and stimulated my work from its dimmest beginnings. He not only taught me how to do historicist readings of Renaissance texts, but he also introduced me to some less timebound qualities: graciousness, commitment, and resilience. Kathy Eden showed me how to do philology, and she kept me from measuring my own work with a too "leaden" rule. Anne Lake Prescott and Jean Howard gave me much advice and good cheer during the march to publication.

The publication of this book would not have been possible without a generous subvention from the Rutgers Research Council and an equally generous Weiss/Brown award from the Newberry Library. A dissertation fellowship from the Mrs. Giles Whiting Foundation enabled me to write large portions of the book.

At the University of Massachusetts Press, Arthur Kinney nurtured this project from a very early stage. No less than four readers commented helpfully on various drafts. Bruce Wilcox and Pam Wilkinson expertly guided the book through production.

At Rutgers-Newark, where I teach, I have been the beneficiary of some excellent mentoring. I especially want to thank Irwin Primer, who did the most to keep me on my toes during my first three years at Rutgers.

While writing this book, I received a jolt of much needed electricity from an NEH seminar, "The Graphic Revolution in Early Modern Europe," at the Folger Shakespeare Library. The seminar was led by Harry Berger, who is a strong presence in parts of the book. I also want to thank the librarians at the Folger Shakespeare Library, who enabled me to find all the research material I needed.

Portions of this book previously appeared in *Studies in Philology* (winter 1993) as " 'To divulgate or set forth': Humanism and Heresy in the book of the Governor" and in *SEL Studies in English Literature 1500–1900* 36, 1 (winter 1996) as "Topical Utopias." I gratefully acknowledge permission to reprint this material here.

Victoria Kahn and Jonathan Haynes first got me interested in sixteenth-century literature at Bennington College in the 1980s.

My parents, Leonard and Liva Baker, set an example of the life of writing for me. I can't imagine having become a writer without them.

Finally, this book is dedicated to my wife, Marcia, whose love and courage were my chief inspiration while writing it. The book is also dedicated to my daughter, Abby, who is teaching me how to live all over again.

Introduction
Discontented Studies

Thomas Nashe's *The Unfortunate Traveller* (1594) offers a zigzag tour of the early sixteenth century, and its distortions of temporal relations and historical sources wittily underscore the difficulties of interpreting the past. As part of his "chronicle of the King of Pages,"[1] Nashe's narrator, Jack Wilton, and his traveling companion, the Earl of Surrey, visit More and Erasmus in Rotterdam when they are on the verge of writing the literary works for which they are still best known:

> There we met with aged learning's chief ornament, that abundant and super-ingenious clerk Erasmus, as also with merry Sir Thomas More, our countryman, who was come purposely over a little before us to visit the said grave father Erasmus.... Erasmus in all his speeches seemed so much to mislike the indiscretion of princes in preferring of parasites and fools that he decreed with himself to swim with the stream and write a book forthwith in commendation of folly. Quick-witted Sir Thomas More travelled in a clean contrary province; for he, seeing most commonwealths corrupted by ill custom, and that principalities were nothing but great piracies which, gotten by violence and murder, were maintained by private undermining and bloodshed; that in the chiefest-flourishing kingdoms there was no equal or well-divided weal one with another, but a manifest conspiracy of rich men against poor men, procuring their own unlawful commodities under the name and interest of the commonwealth: he concluded with himself to lay down a perfect plot of a commonwealth or government, which he would entitle his *Utopia*. So we left them to prosecute their discontented studies and made our next journey to Wittenberg.[2]

A "King of Pages," Nashe's Wilton borrows heavily from other writers during his travels, but Wilton's use of More and Erasmus and his reference to their "discontented studies" might initially seem puzzling to modern readers of their works. For despite the implication that both Erasmus and More share this discontent, Erasmus' *Moria* figures as a "swim-with-the-

1

stream" alternative to *Utopia*. The *Moria,* however, was one of Erasmus' most controversial publications, and, although in places it seems to recommend complacency, such recommendations do not obscure the generally offensive character of what Erasmus' Stultitia says. Moreover, the reduction of *Utopia* to More's "plot" of a "perfect commonwealth" would seem to ignore the ironic framing devices that do not allow readers to assume that More meant to "lay down" such a perfect commonwealth in *Utopia.*

Nashe's inventiveness, however, does have some basis in the texts that he describes. Thus, Nashe's More, as Anne Lake Prescott has noted, is actually quoting Raphael Hythlodaeus' peroration in *Utopia* (1516) when he argues that existing governments are merely conspiracies of the rich against the poor.[3] By contrast, Nashe's Erasmus sounds a bit like persona "More" in *Utopia.* For in the Dialogue on Counsel, persona "More" had argued that the adviser to the prince must use strategies of rhetorical accommodation and a more civil [civilior] philosophy in order to sway a ruler. Such strategies of accommodation entail not mistaking the comedy of court politics for a serious drama and might even include, as the name of More's own persona would suggest, playing the fool. Like Nashe's Erasmus, however, persona "More" does not dispute the basically evil character of princely politics.[4]

Reading over the shoulders of sixteenth-century humanists, we are apt to forget the degree to which reception and the events of even relatively brief historical intervals alter the meaning of texts and make interpretive distances difficult to judge. Thus, for instance, the intervening executions of More (1535) and Surrey (1546), both victims of the violence of the same prince, might be contributing to the Hythlodaean *Utopia* that Nashe in 1594 depicted More as intending to write. At the level of language, however, English translations such as Thomas Chaloner's *The Praise of Folie* (1549), Ralph Robinson's *Utopia* (1551), and Richard Taverner's *Proverbs or Adages by Desiderius Erasmus* (1539) are interposing themselves between Nashe's readers and Latin *Moria* and *Utopia.* Indeed, Nashe's More is not only quoting Raphael Hythlodaeus, but he also seems to be making use of Ralph Robinson's translation: "[W]hen I consider . . . all thies commonwealths which now a dayes anywhere do florish, . . . I can perceave nothing but a certein conspiracy of rich men, procuringe their owne commodities under the name and title of the commen wealth."[5] Robinson's *Utopia* was reprinted in 1556 and 1597, and so readers of *The Unfortunate Traveller* might well have heard traces of Robinson's English in the language of Nashe's More.

More's Latin *Utopia* was itself part of the reception of Erasmian humanism in England, but this humanism reached a vernacular readership in the form of English translations, which do provide some basis for the "swim-with-the-stream" Erasmus of *The Unfortunate Traveller.* For instance, Nicholas Udall's edition of Erasmus' *Paraphrases* (1548) in English was one of the books that the Edwardian *Injunctions* of 1547 ordered to be placed in every parish church. This volume, which contains translations by, among others, Mary Tudor, includes a number of references to the ability of both Erasmus' writings and disseminated scriptural knowledge in general to teach "obedience of the people towardes their rewlers and governours."[6] More directly pertinent to Nashe's Erasmus, however, is Richard Taverner's amplification of the adage, "Durum est contra stimulum calcitare" [It is harde kyckynge against the gode], in his *Proverbs or Adages by Desiderius Erasmus.* For there Taverner writes that "[i]t is evil stryvyng against the streme, that is to saye, it is great folye to struggle agaynste such thynges as thou canst not overcome, or to provoke them, who if they be sturred maye do thee displeasures."[7] Here, Taverner's Erasmus castigates the "folie" of struggling against the powerful whereas Nashe's Erasmus uses the figure of Folly to make a similar point.[8]

This book will argue that translations, popularizations, and "divulgings" of humanism—beginning with Sir Thomas Elyot in the 1530s and reaching a zenith at the mid-century with the 1549 *Praise of Folie* and 1551 *Utopia*—constitute a crucial pivot upon which the politics of later English humanism and, in particular, Spenser's poetry turned. By "divulge" and its cognate, "divulgate," I mean to indicate the loss of control of audience and meaning that both early sixteenth-century print culture and the rise of the vernacular were perceived as fostering, and I will justify this usage by examining a number of texts where humanist writers confront the problems and opportunities of addressing the "vulgar" in print. The "vulgar," however, are not necessarily those at the bottom of the social hierarchy in sixteenth-century humanist writings, although the word could have this more restricted meaning.[9] Rather, the "vulgar" might also denote a mixed readership, one whose limits authors did not set. In particular, for English humanists the "vulgar" often meant an English readership as opposed to a readership versed in humanist Latin, and this vernacular readership could come from a variety of groups, including the nobility.

The debatable level of literacy in sixteenth-century England, however, would seem to militate against even an English readership constituting much of a "vulgar" audience. Yet David Cressy's relatively low estimates of sixteenth-century literacy in *Literacy and the Social Order* (1980) have been more recently challenged by Keith Thomas, Tessa Watt, and Eamon Duffy. Indeed, sixteenth-century estimates of literacy varied wildly. Stephen Gardiner thought that not a "hundredth part of the realm could read" whereas in *The Apology* (1533) More argued against the efficacy of translating the Bible into English because "four partes of all the whole dyvyded into tenne, could never rede englishe yet, and many now to olde to beginne to go to scole. . . ."[10] More's implication that over half of the English people could read a Bible in English is intriguing even though his point is to belittle the significance of this readership. For these potential readers of the Bible would presumably have been able to follow More's vernacular polemics with Tyndale and other heretics, too. In the *Apology* More envisioned the dire possibility of a "tinkar or tylar whyche could (as some there can) rede englishe" and thereby become "instructed" in the works of Wyclif, Tyndale, and Frith.[11]

Gardiner was himself one of those responsible for the 1543 Act for the Advancement of True Religion, which forbade women, artificers, and apprentices from reading the Bible.[12] This act may not prove that literacy was widespread among these groups, but it does demonstrate that the government thought that such widespread literacy existed or at least had the potential to exist if not halted. Moreover, the act also shows that the literacy of traditionally subordinate groups could engender fear. For such literacy eliminated the need for spoonfeeding from above. As More's Lutheran-influenced Messenger put it in *A Dialogue Concerning Heresies* (1529), the argument of the clergy against a vernacular Bible was that "scripture is the fode of the Soule. And that the comen people be as infantys that must be fedde but with mylke and pappe."[13]

The perception of widespread literacy or at least the possibility of its existence, however, could also provoke publications aimed at reducing the dissatisfaction of those on the bottom. Thus, Thomas Chaloner wrote that one purpose of his decision to "englisshe" *Praise of Folie* was so that "meane men of baser wittes and condicion, myght have a maner coumfort and satisfaction in theim selves."[14] How many of these "meane men" would have been able to read Chaloner's translation? This kind of question will no doubt continue to preoccupy modern social historians. Nevertheless, Chaloner clearly thought that at least some of them possessed this ability, and, for the purpose of interpreting his translation, Chaloner's assumptions about literacy are as important here as the still disputed facts of the matter.

William Caxton established the first printing press in England in the late fifteenth century, but the sixteenth century witnessed the full impact of the printing press on English life, letters, and religion. As Elizabeth Eisenstein notes, "[i]t was printing, not Protestantism, which outmoded the medieval Vulgate and introduced a new drive to tap mass markets."[15]

Indeed, Eamon Duffy has shown the importance of printing to the dissemination of English pre-Reformation manuals of lay piety, including one of Spenser's poetic models, *The Kalendar of Shephards*.[16] Given this kind of technological change and the multifarious uses to which it was put, it is small wonder that there should be no firm sixteenth-century consensus concerning the number of people who could read and the social groups to which they belonged. Nevertheless, despite this uncertainty and the anxieties it sometimes occasioned, early popularizers of humanism in England eschewed Latin and sought the broader market for humanism that the vernacular afforded.[17] Yet such popularizers of humanism had, then, to consider the possibility that, published in the vernacular, their writings could reach a heterogeneous audience, which would respond to books in ways that their authors could neither foresee nor prevent.

Problems of audience and interpretation, however, were not restricted to the early sixteenth century and the dawn of humanism in England. In particular, they informed the work of Spenser, the sixteenth-century figure who consistently published his poetry and did the most to make poetry a public and civic enterprise but who also prominently announced his fear of "misconstruction" at the outset of the *Faerie Queene*. Thus, in my final chapter the complex English reception of Erasmian humanism will serve as a point of departure for an examination of Spenser's representation of the problem of modeling a perfect world (alluded to most literally in the promised Telamond) in the 1596 *Faerie Queene*. The use of a perfect world as an Archimedean vantage point from which to critique and perhaps move the actual world is an important element of Spenser's legacy from More and Erasmus. Such perfect or Utopia-like worlds were part of humanism's claim to be exercising moral and political leadership, and their persistence as a narrative bait in *The Faerie Queene*—Telamond never does appear—indicates Spenser's own concern to raise at least the possibility of the ideal correcting the real.

But, as Spenser knew, humanism had this concern in common with a variety of sixteenth-century reformers, some of whom made Tyndale and Luther seem moderate by comparison. This overlap, in turn, makes Spenser's own representations of populist radicalism not entirely separable from the humanist elements of the *Faerie Queene*. Thus, for instance, the Egalitarian Giant, who offers a communistic vision to the "vulgar" in book 5 of *The Faerie Queene*, could be a figure of Anabaptism or Robert Kett, the leader of an infamous 1549 rebellion. But the scripture-spouting Giant might also have recalled texts such as Robinson's *Utopia* where communistic ideas are put forward not in the language of the learned but in the idiom of popular preachers and a recently vernacularized liturgy.

Indeed, by virtue of its timing Robinson's *Utopia* overlapped with the quelling of Kett's rebellion, as did Chaloner's more conciliatory *Praise of Folie.* Published two years after this uprising, Robinson's *Utopia* acquires significance from its representation of the kind of social tensions and leveling impulses that a newly reconstituted English government was eager to forget.

David Norbrook, Helen White, John King, and Annabel Patterson have done much to elucidate the importance of the social and religious upheavals of the Edwardian years (1547–53) to later sixteenth-century English literature and history.[18] Norbrook, in particular, has underscored the existence of a discourse of "radical humanism" in England that begins with *Utopia* and reaches its apex during the Edwardian years. He has fruit-fully developed this notion of radicalism as a response to poststructural-ism, which locates radicalism in the "subversion of conventional processes of signification."[19] Norbrook demonstrates the benefits to scholarship of a return to the more "conventional" model of intentionality, and his own work privileges diachronic continuities over the ruptures of language.

I will be arguing, however, that intentionality does not do complete justice to the ways in which sixteenth-century English humanists under-stood the processes of signification and the politics of their own published works. My subtitle is meant to include not only what texts such as *Utopia* meant to their authors but what these authors feared they might mean to their readers. My usage of "radicalism" encompasses radicalizations and even preemptive authorial strikes against such radicalizations. Applied as an exclusive standard of meaning, intentionality too narrowly defines the scope of authorial responsibility. By contrast, the protestations of More and Erasmus against certain readings of their published works indicate that they felt at least accountable (albeit perhaps unfairly so) for inter-pretations they might not have intended.

My notion of "radical humanism" also includes a recognition of the difficulty of separating "religious" from "secular" humanist radicalism during the sixteenth century.[20] As we shall see, Gilbert Burnet, the second English translator of *Utopia* (1684), effectively made such a separation in the late seventeenth century when he distinguished between what he regarded as More's serious advocacy of proto-Protestant religious ideas in *Utopia* and his less serious presentation of communism.[21] Burnet, who went on to become a defender of the Glorious Revolution of 1688, was himself a protoliberal and a "possessive individualist" in the Macpher-sonian sense, but his attempt to differentiate More as religious reformer from More the social and political reformer will prove to be of only limited validity for the sixteenth century. The two kinds of reform were often indistinguishable, as More himself emphasized when he accused Tyndale of, among other things, giving the people "corage and boldenesse to resiste theyr prince and disobey their prelates."[22] Challenges to political and ecclesiastical hierarchy go together in More's critique of Tyndale.

More's castigation, however, of Tyndale's seditiousness is also tendentious since in 1533, when *The Apology* was published, More had resigned the Chancellorship of England and both the king and Parliament were in the midst of what would become a broad attempt to nationalize and hence subjugate the English Church to the monarch. *The Apology* was More's response to St. German's *Treatise concernynge the Division betwene the Spirytualitie and Temporalitie* (1532), which attacked the jurisdiction of ecclesiastical courts and was brought out by Thomas Berthelet, the king's printer. Unlike Tyndale's works, German's *Treatise* did not have to be printed abroad and then smuggled into England. More's linking of royal and prelatical authority in *The Apology* is an attempt to show that the two support and therefore should not oppose one another at a time when Henry seemed determined to prove that he could strengthen his rule by weakening the clergy.

Secular governmental support of radical religious change was nothing new in the sixteenth century. We have only to recall the kind of high-level encouragement that Wyclif received in the fourteenth century to realize that English rulers had long been less than certain of what More was trying to argue in the *Apology*. Yet fourteenth-century peasant revolts (1381) also underscored the connection between religious ferment and social upheaval from below. If John of Gaunt gave support to Wyclif, the firebrand preacher, John Ball was also part of the climate of controversy that helped to make rebellion thinkable. Responding to the threat of incendiary preaching, a 1382 statute was enacted against wandering preachers whose heresies were not only undermining the Church but also causing "dissention . . . entre diverses estatz du dit Roialme," both spiritual and temporal.[23] In 1401 *De Heretico Comburendo* enjoined the punishment of Lollard heretics by secular authorities, and legislation following the revolt of Sir John Oldcastle in 1414 clarified the link between treason and heresy.[24]

In the wake of Lollardy, canon law, too, included its own recognition of the need to attend more closely to what the populace was reading and thinking. The 1408 Constitution of Archbishop Arundel, which forbade translations of the Bible not approved by the clergy and targeted the Wyclif Bible in particular, was a key part of the reaction to Lollardy in England. As More put it when defending this constitution in the *Dialogue Concerning Heresies,* the purpose of the constitution was to protect the "people" from the "harme" that they might take from the "translacyon prologes and gloses of Wyclyffe."[25] This "harme" was not merely that of religious error. For discussing Wyclif's other "yll bokes," More wrote that their transportation into Bohemia and inculcation there by Huss was the "occasion of the utter subversyon of yt hole realm."[26]

The perception, however, of the link between secular and religious dissention provoked attempts to distinguish between them well before Burnet. For instance, Langland's *Piers Plowman* combines scathing critique of the Church with, as Helen White puts it, "social conservatism."[27] *Piers Plowman* even blames friars motivated by Envy for preaching communism and citing Plato and Seneca in its defense.[28] The itinerant friars were rivals of Lollard preachers, and communism accordingly functions as a smear in *Piers Plowman.* Significantly, the sources of the communism of the friars in *Piers Plowman* are the pagan writers—Plato and Seneca—rather than the Bible.

The difference between secular and religious reform as well as radicalism was a distinction in the making during the early modern period. We need, then, to be wary of any neat separation between the two but also willing to acknowledge the efforts to demarcate their boundaries. Henry VIII, for example, did succeed in strengthening his own position at the expense of the clergy. But the possibility of a radical Protestant critique of the English Church undermining the monarchy as well as other social and political structures plagued Henry's successors up to the revolution of the next century. Along with the English government, English humanists, too, attempted to distinguish between radical reform of the Church and radical reform of social relations. Yet this distinction was often problematic because both kinds of reform had a Christian basis. For as is conveniently omitted in Langland's castigation of communistic friars, the Bible as well as Plato and Seneca contains passages in favor of communism.

The sixteenth-century Bible, in particular, problematizes any easy distinction between secular humanism and religious radicalism. For Erasmus' editions of the Greek New Testament as well as his *Annotations* (1516, 1519) showed that humanist philology and textual criticism had much to offer scriptural studies. Building on the work of Lorenzo Valla, Erasmus disputed the Vulgate translation at numerous points, and these disputes did not involve abstruse linguistic issues alone. For as Jerry Bentley has argued, even in the scholarly *Annotations* Erasmus frequently "suggested what might be called a moral application of scripture: he established New Testament teachings as a standard against which he measured his own times, usually finding them wanting."[29] In so doing, Erasmus provided a model for the empowerment of the individual interpreter of the Bible.

Erasmus dedicated his 1516 edition of the Greek New Testament to the pope, but Erasmus' well-known influence on nearly every major Protestant reformer gave his scriptural philology more of a charge than its dedication to the pope would suggest. Luther, for instance, made extensive use of Erasmus' New Testament for his 1522 translation of the New Testament into German. Tyndale's 1526 English New Testament was also indebted to Erasmus. Nor was Udall's use of Erasmus in his government-sponsored edition of the *Paraphrases* an entirely easy one. Thus, although Udall claims Erasmus as an advocate of obedience to princes, he also includes a somewhat anxious defense against the charge that reading either Erasmus or the translated Bible leads to sedition. An "adversarie to Erasmus wrytynges," wrote Udall in his prefatory letter to Katherine Parr, Henry VIII's last wife, is an "enemie to the ghospell." Yet the "comon faulte that malignaunt persones dooe allege against the publishyng of Goddes woorde in the mother tongue and against the setting foorth of holsome and godly exposicions upon the same" is "that suche bookes cause sedicion."[30] Udall circumvents this allegation by arguing that the word of God does not cause sedition but acts as a "perfeict touchestone whereby to fynde out and to trye suche cancarde stomakes as would fain rebelle and move sedicion."

Including a chapter on Erasmus in a book on "radical English humanism" is not, then, merely a gesture toward the cosmopolitanism of this humanism. To be sure, some of English humanism's most radical ideas were Erasmian in origin or at least a function of Erasmus' labors on the Bible. But perhaps even more importantly Erasmus' career as, to use Lisa Jardine's designation, a "man of letters" offered the most illustrious example of a problem that would preoccupy English humanist writers from More to Spenser.[31] How could they use print to discuss, at times, radical reform of church and state and not become confused with what they perceived to be more anarchic and dangerous versions of their own ideas? Furthermore, Erasmus' own apparently contradictory attitudes toward divulgation, especially the divulgation of the Bible in the vernacular, provided a model for English humanism's not always consistent aspirations both to write for a broad public and yet retain the exclusive right to determine the significance of these writings. For Udall's cankered readers were a threat to any humanist text that addressed potentially incendiary political and religious questions.

The solution to these problems, however, was not necessarily a tepid centrism, the middle course between Scylla and Charybdis that Luther accused Erasmus of always following.[32] Rather, Erasmus' writings generally include *both* Scylla and Charybdis instead of avoiding either of them. That is, cautions and risks alternate throughout the same text without eliminating one another, and such alternations provided yet another model for English humanism's efforts at religious and social critique. Indeed, cautions arguably enabled Erasmus and later English writers to take certain chances, and they could even have the effect of underscoring an author's daring. Thus, Nashe's "swim-with-the-stream" Erasmus is both a response and testimony to the existence of a far different Erasmus, one whose own "discontented studies" helped to give birth to the Hythlodaeus-like More of *The Unfortunate Traveller.*

II

Renaissance humanists could not be sure of the hypothetical status of what Harry Berger has termed their "second worlds."[33] Rather, sixteenth-century England lived with the fear that humanistically conceived "second worlds" would, in the form of Anabaptism and later levelers such as Robert Kett and Martin Marprelate, burst violently and chaotically into political actuality. Contemporary historicist criticism of the early modern period would do well to take such fears seriously. Thus, in the essay, "Murdering Peasants: Status, Genre, and the Representation of Rebellion," Stephen Greenblatt, like Merritt Hughes before him, rightly criticizes what he sees as the romantic tendency to discover that artists sympathized with the exploited masses, and Greenblatt links the search for such sympathy to Albrecht Dürer's "utopian" project of creating a monument to celebrate the defeat of rebellious peasants.[34] Nevertheless, Greenblatt's argument suggests that, despite sixteenth-century fears to the contrary, texts such as *Utopia* and *The Faerie Queene* constituted a relatively unproblematic part of "official" culture and that such "official" culture could only be read in an official way.

Greenblatt's radical/official binary is symptomatic of a larger problem affecting the "revisionist" approach to humanism—a tendency to confine the scope of humanism to school and state.[35] This tendency, in turn, owes a good deal to Paul Oskar Kristeller's grounding of the meaning of the word "humanist" in the professional activities of teachers of the humanities in secondary schools and universities as well as secretaries to princes.[36] Kristeller's focus on humanism as a collection of such activities rather than a putatively coherent philosophical program has proved useful to all subsequent scholarship, but the more recent work of Jardine and Kristeller himself has emphasized humanism's professional connections to the book trade, too.[37] Nor was the humanist involvement in this trade and use of the printing press as a tool of dissemination entirely separable from the humanism of the schools and the court. As Erasmus and More both knew well, rivalries within universities between those who professed the *studia humanitatis* and more conservative theological faculties could lead to vituperative printed polemics.[38] One effect of such polemics was precisely to extend potentially circumscribed academic disputes beyond the province of the universities.

My emphasis on printed divulgation is meant to indicate the ways in which humanism offered much more of an interpretive problem than its supposedly more confined ideological role would allow. This emphasis highlights the Erasmus who, among other things, worked as a proofreader for Aldus Manutius, and it entails a reexamination of figures who might otherwise seem politically complacent. Thus, for instance, Anthony Grafton and Lisa Jardine have presented a fascinating account of Gabriel Harvey as would-be member of the "Tudor Establishment" and have made his annotations of Quintilian their primary evidence.[39] But what about the Gabriel Harvey who, supported by the London printer John Wolfe, participated in a public and published quarrel with Nashe and Lyly during the 1590s and was even accused of being Martin Marprelate?[40] In 1599 an order of the English bishops enjoined the burning of the satires of both Harvey and Nashe. Harvey's life extended beyond the bounds of school and state, and the Nashe-Lyly-Harvey controversy showed that Harvey did not have as much interpretive control over his own politics as his annotations of Quintilian would suggest.

From Erasmus and More to Harvey and Spenser, sixteenth-century humanists read their own and one another's works in the way that Greenblatt argues is postromantic. To be sure, such readings were often objects of fear and trembling rather than of revolutionary triumph, as is evident, for instance, from More's frequently quoted remark that he would rather see some of his works burned than translated into English and become exposed to "misconstruction."[41] But this kind of self-reading, often defensively termed a "misconstruction" in the sixteenth century, does indicate that the interpretations dubbed anachronistic by Greenblatt were scarcely inconceivable in the early modern period. Such interpretations were in fact frequent, and they are evidence of English humanism's sense of its own political ambiguity. Indeed, this humanism mediated the radical/official binary as well as reinforced it.

An example from Taverner's *Adages* will illustrate what I mean. The adage that came first in Erasmus' *Adagia* was "Amicorum communia omnia," a virtual call for a return to the community of goods that characterized the primitive church as described in acts 2 and 4. There, Erasmus argued that communism harmonized Christianity and Platonic thought.[42] Erasmus himself qualified this adage slightly in 1526 after the humanistically educated leader of revolting German peasants, Thomas Muntzer, was said to have confessed under torture that his goal had been the institution of such an apostolic community.[43] Later developments such as the rise of Anabaptism during the 1520s and 1530s and, in particular, the Anabaptist community at Munster (1534–35) supplied an ever more radical contemporary referrent for the adage, and, as Margerita Isnardi-Parente has shown, Erasmus' disavowals of apostolic communism eventually became quite pronounced.[44]

Taverner's 1539 translation of this adage demonstrates the interpretive problem that it presented for humanism, that is, that of distinguishing Erasmian communism from Anabaptism at a historical moment when such a distinction was particularly necessary:

Amonges frendes al thynges be comune. The authur of thys proverb is Pythagoras an auncient philosopher. Neither dyd he only speak it but also brought in, such a certayne communion of lyfe and goodes as Christ wolde have used amonges al Christians. For as many as were admitted of him into the felowship and companye of his doctrine, al the money & substaunce they had: they layd it togither, which thyng not only in worde, but also in dede was *coenobium*. Certes, this communion of those Hethen Pithagorians resembled moche better that communion used in the primative churche amonges the Apostles, than doth either our Monkry at this day, or the wycked Anabaptistical secte, which will have no Rulers, no order, but whiche go about to disturbe the hole world with horrible confusion.[45]

Taverner's interpolations concerning "monkery" and Anabaptism might well gloss his advice not to "swim against the stream," for they exhibit a high degree of confluence with the kind of *via media* that the Henrician Reformation attempted to implement during the 1530s. Taverner had been a client of Thomas Cromwell, and Taverner's translation shows his desire to distance himself from the more radical kind of reformation with which Cromwell had become tainted before his fall and execution in 1540.[46] Cromwell, of course, was no Anabaptist, but Anabaptism arguably functions as a code word for extreme Protestantism here. Indeed, the repudiation of Anabaptism continued to be a way of denoting the *via media* between radical Protestantism and Rome that remained the policy of Henry's Protestant successors. Thus, the Thirty-Nine Articles (1563), which took religious reform farther than Henry had envisioned, nevertheless still represented a middle road, and such moderation entailed an article attacking the Anabaptist doctrine that the "riches and goods of Christians" should be "common."[47]

But Taverner's interpolations also represent a reading of "Amicorum communia omnia," one that articulates the very misconstruction they are designed to prevent. During the 1520s and 1530s, Erasmus was ever in danger of being interpreted as a proto-Lutheran figure, and Taverner addresses an extended version of this problem by defending the adage against a proto-Anabaptist reading. Taverner's claim that the adage does not endorse the anarchy of Anabaptism may resemble a dismissal, but it highlights a genuine interpretive problem, that of reconciling Erasmus' communistic pronouncements with the necessity of order and rule. Nor does Taverner fully erase the potential unruliness of the adage, for he includes the point that, like Pythagoras before him, Christ would have the "communion of lyfe and goodes, . . . used amonges al Christians." Likewise, Taverner uses the adage to redefine *coenobium,* which no longer denotes "our Monkry at this day" (as it generally did) but rather a communion of deed as opposed to word. The nature of the communion of deed that will replace a corrupt monasticism remains an open (perhaps dangerously so) question in Taverner's translation.

But if humanism blurs Greenblatt's overly stark binary between radical and official culture, the politics of sixteenth-century humanism are not necessarily or essentially radical either. Thus, my attention to the reception of humanism is meant to complicate J. H. Hexter's notion—to which Norbrook and, more recently, Margo Todd are indebted—that *Utopia* inaugurates a tradition of "radicalism" that in Hexter's distinctly anti-Marxist formulation extends to the French Revolution but not to modern socialism.[48] For there is a danger of slipping from *Utopia* as a radical text to humanism as an essentially radical development or to More himself as a political radical. Yet, writing from the vantage point of modern socialism, Karl Kautsky has underscored at least one area—More's reaction to the German peasant uprisings of the 1520s—that presents problems for any attribution of radicalism to More. For all his wide-ranging intellect, More was ultimately a "man of order," argues Kautsky, and thus he was horrified by rebellion.[49]

Nevertheless, Hexter's approach to Utopian radicalism is quite useful because, in addition to defining this radicalism as a "window" to the future, it also adumbrates a less teleological way of addressing the question of what sixteenth-century radical humanism might be:

The idea of eradicating, deracinating, pulling up by the roots—the starting point of radicalism—is not only implicit in *Utopia,* it is sporadically explicit. To attain

13

justice, property must be utterly cast down. . . . In Europe pride is too solidly fixed in men to be ripped out easily . . . but the Utopians have extirpated the roots of ambition. . . . *Subferre, evellere, radicibus extirpare* . . . the vernacular equivalents of such terms are the standard coins of intellectual commerce with the modern radical.[50]

Hexter's account of radicalism here has the advantage of having a sixteenth-century basis, that is, the language of deracination in *Utopia,* and of being applicable to a number of aspects of Utopian society. Thus, for instance, in addition to attempting to uproot ambition, the Utopians are also literal deracinators of whole forests, which they transplant to convenient places. Moreover, the Utopians are aggressive founders of "coloniae," an etymologically agricultural word, and, when they deem it necessary, they expel other peoples from their land.[51] Indeed, Spenser's own colonialist *A View of the Present State of Ireland* could arguably be read as a work showing the dark side of radical humanism. In this dialogue between a moderate and an immoderate reformer, the zealot is said to want to "beginne all as it weare anewe and to alter the whole forme of the governement."[52] The desire to begin anew and the refusal to continue "patching up one hole to make manye" also distinguishes Raphael Hythlodaeus from more temperate reformers.

Most important, however, Hexter's notion of humanist radicalism is applicable to a number of sixteenth-century English or Englished texts, from Erasmus' *Adagia* to Elyot's *The Governour,* that in different ways entertain, even if they do not fully endorse, the possibility of uprooting religious, social, and political structures. Thus, in my own usage, humanist "radicalism" is not a consistent program, nor were humanist "radicals" consistently radical. Rather, humanist "radicalism" refers to the tendency of early modern literati to demolish existing structures and then build perfect worlds, or, Telamonds, on the printed page, even as they remained unsure of who they wanted to have access to these worlds. A perfect world might look different to Spenser than to Erasmus, but the texts of humanist radicalism do share certain features. Thus, for instance, communism, whether as an ideal of social justice or the perversion of such an ideal, is nevertheless generally an issue for such texts. Unable to be ignored, communism must either be made a part of perfection or conspicuously excluded from it.

The Erasmian adage, "Ut fici oculis incumbunt" [as piles lie on the eyes], suggests that early modern readers of *Utopia* were conscious of the language of deracination that Hexter has underscored, but this adage also shows that humanism was wary of its own radicalism, too. For in "Ut fici oculis incumbunt," which first appeared in 1517, one year after the first edition of *Utopia,* Erasmus, like Raphael Hythlodaeus, vehemently critiqued a number of social ills, including tyrannical princes. Unlike Raphael, however, Erasmus then went on to argue that these "rooted" ills [actis radicibus] should be tolerated rather than plucked away {avelli]. Such language constitutes a response to Raphael's radicalism, but Erasmus' modifications of the adage show how the Reformation exacerbated his sense of the danger of this radicalism. Thus, in 1517 the Swiss republics constituted Erasmus' example of how eradicating social evils could be worse than tolerating them. But in 1526 Erasmus removed the Swiss from the adage and substituted for them the revolting German peasants, a far more threatening challenge to the rule of princes.[53]

Erasmus' alterations provide an interpretation of both "Ut fici incumbunt" and *Utopia,* one articulating links between humanist radicalism and the social agenda of the radical Reformation.[54] Indeed, his alterations of "Ut fici" show Erasmus, like Jack Wilton, traveling in history and doing so in a retrospective or backward way. That is, Erasmus views the 1517 "Ut fici" through the lens of 1526 just as Wilton reads *Utopia* and *Praise of Folly* via intervening translations and historical events. In particular, although he goes to Wittenberg after meeting More and Erasmus, Nashe's Jack Wilton travels to the Anabaptist community at Munster prior to meeting them. Nashe, a participant in the Martin Marprelate controversy of the 1590s, makes the Anabaptists proto-Puritans ("Hear what it is to be Anabaptists, to be puritans, to be villains"),[55] but Nashe's Anabaptists are also proleptic of aspects of the figures of More and Erasmus that Wilton encounters later in the text of *The Unfortunate Traveller.* Thus, the Anabaptists' comically grotesque battle against imperial troops provides a salient referent for More's remark that great "principalities" are maintained by violence and that the "chiefest-flourishing kingdoms" are merely a conspiracy of rich against poor.[56] Such historical conflations are further complicated by what R. B. McKerrow has shown to be Nashe's reliance on an account of the defeat of the rebels led by Thomas Munzer in 1526 for his depiction of the conquest of the Anabaptists in the 1530s.[57]

Nashe, however, may not be so much expressing a subversive sympathy for Reformation radicals as suggesting that the discontent of humanists such as More and Erasmus and that of the Anabaptists do overlap. This area of overlap, moreover, was a product of social origins as well as a willingness to oppose principalities. Thus, Nashe's Anabaptists vaunt that "there was not a pease difference betwixt them and the apostles," and they are of "base trades"—tailors, cobblers, and curriers.[58] But More, the grandson of a baker, and Erasmus, the bastard son of a priest, were themselves not so far removed from the baseness that Nashe ascribes to the Anabaptists. The same can be said of Spenser, the poor scholar at the Merchant Taylors School who only as a colonizer in Ireland was able to occupy a castle. As Guyon's Palmer puts it when distinguishing between two different kinds of fountains, "some were so from their sourse indewd / By great Dame Nature" and "other some by gift of later grace, / . . . Had vertue pourd into their waters bace" (FQ 2.2.6). More, knighted in 1521, was himself a fountain of the latter kind, and, along with Erasmus, Spenser, and Nashe, he mediated the radical/official binary socially as well as intellectually. This social mediation helps to explain how the *studia humanitatis* could in the *Unfortunate Traveller* become Erasmus and More's "discontented studies."

An identifiably humanist figure even becomes apparent during Nashe's lengthy critique of "cynical reformed foreign churches" in general:

Because the poverty of their provinces will allow them no proportionable maintenance for higher callings of ecclesiastical magistrates, they would reduce us to the precedent of their rebellious persecuted beggary—much like the sect of philosophers called Cynics who, when they saw they were born to no lands or possessions nor had any possible means to support their estates, but they must live despised and in misery do what they could, they plotted and consulted with themselves how to make their poverty better esteemed of than rich dominion or sovereignty. . . . Diogenes was one of the first and foremost of the ringleaders of this rusty morosity—and he, for all his nice, dogged disposition and blunt deriding of worldly dross and the gross felicity of fools, was taken notwithstanding a little after very fairly a-coining money in his cell.[59]

We shall see that Diogenes and, more generally, the Cynic or "dog" philosophers were an important point of reference for sixteenth-century humanism, but for now it is enough to note that Diogenes is the persona adopted by Robinson in the preface to his 1551 *Utopia*. Here, on the other hand, Diogenes derides the "gross felicity of fools," and thus he seems to play a part opposite to that of Nashe's Erasmus, who praises folly and thereby swims with the stream. The "plotting" of the "cynics" may be a poor person's response to the "conspiracy" of rich against poor that Nashe's More identifies, but it also looks ahead to the "perfect plot of a commonwealth" that this More is said to be proposing in *Utopia*. Indeed, encountered after developments such as Anabaptism and puritanism, the commonwealth of Utopia could seem to be a conspiratorial "plot."

Radicalism can best be described as a "vulnerability" of sixteenth-century humanism. I find Thomas Greene's term quite useful because it mediates between the notion of an entirely recuperable intentionality and a deconstructive anomie, but I want to extend its range beyond the realm of literary history to which Greene largely confines it.[60] Greene's analysis of Erasmus' "Festina lente" as a vulnerable text leads Greene to make a number of richly suggestive claims about Erasmian humanism, the chief of which is that the "profession" of humanism was "divulgation." Erasmus saw himself as using "literae communes," which Greene translates as "ordinary writing," rather than a medium of "semiotic perfection"—that is, the hieroglyphics favored by the ancient Egyptian priesthood. Moreover, such "ordinary writing" put Erasmus, according to Greene, in the position of being an "antipriest."[61]

But, although Greene notes that Erasmus' 1526 additions to "Festina lente"—a castigation of primarily German printers—are devoted to the "risks of divulgation," he does not sufficiently situate them in the context of the religious and political history that concerned Erasmus as much as its literary counterpart.[62] To be an "antipriest" in 1508 was quite different from being one in 1526 when the radical Reformation had led to widespread violence. In the 1508 "Festina lente" Erasmus could celebrate the humanist printer Aldus Manutius as a Herculean hero for his ability to make a library extend beyond its own "domestic" walls and encompass the world, but Reformation controversies over the availability of scripture and other religious works in the vernacular gave a potentially radical inflection to Aldine dissemination.[63] That is, if Aldus is the heir to the emperors Augustus and Vespasian in the adage, the threatening swarm of German printers are the heirs to Aldus, who in fact died in 1515.

In his 1526 *De Lingua,* an anatomy of linguistic monstrosities and a rather copious praise of brevity in speech, Erasmus makes the connection between divulgation and rebellion clear:

No mercy is shown to benefactors, or to age, . . . no mercy is shown to the rank of princes or bishops or the supreme papal authority. . . . And as if this devilish tongue [diabolica lingua] were too ineffectual, we find defamatory caricatures in addition; scandalous pamphlets are disseminated, and this abominable livelihood supports many printers. The man who picked up a painted clog is torn limb from limb as an instigator of rebellion [seditionis autor]. But is there anything left unsaid by the pictures which are spread at random [passim evulgantur]? Once upon a time the man who disclosed his name and published [evulgasset] a scandalous pamphlet ran the risk of prosecution; now men amuse themselves.[64]

The painted clog, a symbol of peasant rebellion, indicates a decidedly contemporary referent for this passage, and indeed the subtitle to *De Lingua* asserts that it is a work "most apt" [aptissimum] for these times. As in the 1526 additions to "Festina lente," Erasmus engages the "risk" of divulgation here, but he gives a more concrete idea of the social and political character of this risk. Yet even the additions to "Festina lente" mention the way in which print undermines the authority of princes and ecclesiastical officials.[65] For although these additions are somewhat vague as to how this undermining works, a skeptical reference to those who detect in "Holy Scripture" points "which escaped the notice of Jerome or Chrysostom" suggests that Erasmus is alluding to what he saw as the excesses of Lutheran *sola scriptura* and the interpretive authority that it gave to each reader.[66]

"Festina lente" shows that the communism of material goods was not the only political "vulnerability" of sixteenth-century humanism. A communism of what I would term "interpretive property" was its other site of overlap with Reformation radicalism, and thus the "literae communes" of "Festina lente" are "common" as well as, in Greene's translation, "ordinary letters." As exploiters of the power of print and the burgeoning democracy of learning, humanists did act the part of the "antipriest," making more widely available (albeit often in Latin) learning that was either buried or sequestered in some way. Erasmus' 1516 New Testament and his *Paraclesis* are religious texts that exemplify this tendency. Defending Erasmus' scriptural labors in his 1520 Letter to a Monk, More defined Christian communism as extending beyond material goods and including an end to factionalism and the attempt to monopolize certain religious beliefs and traditions.[67] Although living outside a cloister, Erasmus, as a practitioner of such communism, proves the true monk in More's letter.

But Erasmus, as we shall see, qualified the message of the *Paraclesis* before Luther began to occupy his attention, and even in the 1508 "Festina lente" Erasmus includes an admonitory example whose function is to keep the power of print from becoming abusive. Thus, Achilles, who represents the hastiness of "make haste slowly," is shown abusing his king, Agammemnon, verbally and even drawing his sword against him: "But that in itself was an indication of a lack of mental control, to pour out such abuse and revilings in the full assembly of princes against the holder of supreme power."[68] The haste of Achilles is represented in the Aldine motto by a dolphin wound around an anchor, but, despite the universal and rapid circulation of Aldus' books, such celerity does not lead to rashness because it is symbolically at least held in check by the anchor. In 1526, however, this haste is largely unchecked, and thus the books of the German printers are said to fly through the world [provolant] in much the same way that the dolphin was described earlier as being able to fly past ships [transvolare].[69]

Like Taverner's modifications of "Amicorum communia omnia," the 1526 additions to "Festina lente" offer a reading of the 1508 version of the adage. That is, Erasmus is guarding against the possibility that his own stance of "antipriest" in the 1508 "Festina lente" could be confused with the communism of interpretive property that was a hallmark of the Reformation in both Germany and England. From our own historical perspective such a proto-Lutheran reading of "Festina lente" would be both legitimate and illegitimate. It would be legitimate because Erasmus clearly sees its possibility and even its plausibility. We would not be imposing an anachronistic set of values on a Renaissance text. But such a reading would also be illegitimate because the 1526 "Festina lente" shows Erasmus trying to defend himself against it.

The context for understanding Erasmus' reservations about print, however, includes classical texts as well as sixteenth-century religious controversies. In particular, Plato's *Phaedrus,* whose provocation is the *biblion* or speech on love of Lysias (228b), is the crucial subtext to what figures in both "Festina lente" and *De Lingua* as the challenges of the common, antipriestly letters of print. In the *Phaedrus* Socrates applies the ambiguous metaphor of the *pharmakon* [drug or poison] to the Egyptian *daimon* Theuth's invention of letters (274e). The question that Theuth raises is one of divulgation: Should these letters be given [diadidomi] to the other Egyptians? This question then provokes the god Ammon's distinction between a *pharmakon* of memory and one of reminding. But the initial question—whether Theuth should or should not impart his discovery to the rest of the Egyptians—recalls the kind of antidemotic writing, that is, hieroglyphics, for which the Egyptians were famous. Nevertheless, Socrates' critique of writing indicates the degree to which Theuth's invention has, whether for better or for worse, triumphed in democratic Athens (275d–e). For according to Socrates, writing circulates everywhere [kulindeitai] and does not know to whom to speak and to whom not to speak. As Derrida has argued, writing in the *Phaedrus,* "at the disposal of each and all," is "essentially democratic."[70]

Erasmus modeled aspects of the *Antibarbari, Convivum Religiosum, De Lingua,* and, as Arthur Kinney has recently argued, the *Moria* itself after the *Phaedrus.* Indeed, the *Moria* even contains an account of Theuth's invention of letters as well as the disciplines of learning.[71] (In the *Phaedrus* Theuth is said to be the inventor of geometry, astronomy, and dice in addition to letters.) In the 1515 Froben *Moria,* Stultitia dubs Theuth a "humano generi infensus genius" [a demon hostile to the human race], and she extends (and wittily perverts) Ammon's critique of letters to all "disciplinae," albeit giving some credit to those disciplines that rely upon common sense. Yet the first such commonsensical discipline that Stultitia mentions is medicine—which raises in a literal sense the problem of the *pharmakon.*[72] In *De Lingua,* which opens with a reference to the *Phaedrus,* language itself figures as both a "poison" [venenum] and a "drug." As a health-giving drug, the resources of language should be made common [communicare] to all, but the lethal capacities of these same resources need to be carefully guarded.[73]

Eisenstein has emphasized the empowering effect of the fixity of print and the ways in which this fixity made possible a number of important intellectual transformations, including the democratization of learning.[74] The *Phaedrus,* on the other hand, gave sixteenth-century humanists reason to distrust anything that enhanced the fixity of writing, for such fixity paradoxically entailed more instability, a greater loss of control over the meaning of one's words and ideas. The 1515 Listrius commentary on the Froben *Moria* explicates Stultitia's reference to Theuth by rearticulating the question of whether Theuth's various arts ought to be distributed [distribui] to the rest of the Egyptians. The conclusion of the Listrius commentary is that Plato's having made Theuth the inventor of both "pestiferous" games of chance as well as "humanae scientiae" was no less of a serious point than a joke. We may infer that such sciences, too, are a gamble.[75]

The *Phaedrus* ends with the adage "koina ta ton philon" [279c]—that is, "common are the things of friends"—but the "friends" of the *Phaedrus,* whose discussion takes place beyond the walls of Athens, are a small group, situated at a distance from the democratic *polis.* As a model for Erasmus' own writing, the *Phaedrus* suggests that the ideal community of humanist readers to which the *Adagia* and other Erasmian texts appealed was a relatively closed one, and that, even as Erasmus exploited the printing press, he located himself and his readers at a distance from the democracy of learning. Indeed, throughout *De Lingua* Erasmus suggests that the laconicism of Sparta (not coincidentally, an oligarchy) may be a better model for the republic of letters than democratic Athens, which he dubs the "most talkative city of all."[76]

But *De Lingua* is itself a flagrantly garrulous text, and it also reveals Erasmus' own affinities with the Athenian loquaciousness that he condemns. The contradictions of *De Lingua* and other Erasmian texts have allowed Erasmus' oscillation between secrecy and publicity to be read in opposed ways. Thus, while Greene makes Erasmus into a divulgator, Edgar Wind has assimilated Erasmus to the kind of Neoplatonic mystification and secrecy practiced by Ficino and others.[77] Indeed, the publisher Aldus Manutius was himself involved in numerous attempts to found "academies."[78] Yet, even when Erasmus' writings suggest secrecy most strongly, they generally leave open an avenue to a broader public. Thus, the *Antibarbari* takes place in a closed orchard—"sed pomarium prius occludatur, ne quis nos videat" [let the orchard first be closed, lest somebody see us]—but the presence of the "Erasmi stilus" [pen of Erasmus] renders the preservation of this sequestration unlikely just as the plane tree [platonos] hovers over the conversation of the *Phaedrus*.[79]

In the *Republic*, on the other hand, the adage, "Common are the things of friends," gives rise to Socrates' vision of sexual communism and, more generally, it encapsulates the virtually complete absence of private property among the elite Guardians.[80] This sexual communism was something of a scandal in the Renaissance. But, because it was restricted to a carefully circumscribed social group, even the Guardian's lack of other forms of private property did not harmonize with Christian communism to quite the degree that Erasmus claims in the first adage. For as described in Acts 2 and 4, the early church was a rapidly growing community, absorbing masses of new converts, and it did not require nor could it sustain the kind of careful exclusions that separated Platonic friends from everyone else. This tension between two forms of an idealized community, one relatively open and the other closed, informs Erasmus' career as a writer and religious reformer, and it also extends to other humanist perfect worlds such as More's Utopia. For such worlds suggest and resist the possibility of their divulgation.

As a vulnerability of humanism, then, radicalism meant reading sixteenth-century humanist texts as if an ideal community designed for a few friends could apply to everyone. Yet Erasmus in places encouraged just such a reading of his own works so we cannot simply label it a "misconstruction." Rather, we must examine how Erasmus mediated between Platonic and Christian ideal communities and the historical forces that made this kind of mediation increasingly difficult for him. Not surprisingly, Erasmus' primary strategy of mediation will prove to be rhetorical, but it was not limited to the relatively contained rhetoric of the grammar school. For Erasmus attempted to make the rhetorical and ethical standard of decorum a means of addressing the dangers of the written word at a time when the technology of its dissemination had undergone tremendous enhancement. Chief among these dangers was the inevitability of this word's becoming common to friends and enemies.

ONE

The Vulnerabilities of Hercules

Erasmus and the Divulgation of the Logos

Nicholas Udall's point that an adversary of Erasmus' writings was also an enemy of the Gospel depends upon a connection between the divine *logos* and human words that Erasmus' life and work did much to establish.[1] For a number of otherwise quite different texts by Erasmus share a faith in both the efficacy of the divine speech and its broader Erasmian corollary, the power of language, or, as he translated *logos* in 1519, *sermo.* Thus, the *Paraclesis,* which prefaced Erasmus' 1516 translation of the New Testament into Latin, offered a Christian counterpart to Ciceronian eloquence, urged the vernacular translation of scripture, and exhorted ordinary women and ploughmen to make the Bible a part of their daily lives.[2] The 1523 preface to Erasmus' Paraphrase on Luke, on the other hand, was addressed to Henry VIII, but it also advocated what Marjorie O'Rourke Boyle has termed "logotherapy," the ability of the Bible to heal social ills.[3] Even in a ludic work such as the *Moria* Erasmus claimed to be pursuing by other means the aims of his more explicitly religious books,[4] and, likewise, Doctor Logos helps to cure the ailment of Nosoponus, a kind of paganism, in the *Ciceronianus.*[5]

Doubts, however, continued to accompany Erasmus' faith in language's ability to heal all ills. One problematic historical development, in particular, that separated Erasmus from earlier users of rhetoric, both sacred and secular, was the advent of print, and this development has yet to be made a part of rhetorical criticism of Erasmus.[6] Rhetorical criticism, nevertheless, provides the basis for its own extension to the technology of mechanical reproduction. Most provocatively, Terence Cave has used *De Copia* to articulate a poststructuralist version of Erasmian rhetoric, and he has even applied poststructuralism to Erasmus' accounts of the difficulties of scriptural exegesis.[7] On the other hand, Kathy Eden has argued that Erasmus' understanding of scriptural exegesis was also indebted to a rhetorical tradition that provided at least a tentative answer, that is, decorum, to the problem posed by the *Phaedrus*.[8] Thus, for Eden the rhetorical principle of "decorum" was the "first rule of Erasmian hermeneutics," as developed in later works such as the *Ratio Verae Theologiae* (1519). That is, Erasmus advocated a method of interpreting the *germanus sensus* of such master rhetoricians as Jesus and Paul by attending to the circumstances and historical moment of these words and, in particular, to the "changing audiences" to which these words were addressed. For, as Erasmus argued in the *Ratio,* neither Jesus nor Paul said the same thing to all people. Rather, they accommodated themselves to different audiences, ranging from the apostles to the still "rude" populace.[9]

The views of Eden and Cave, albeit quite different, nevertheless serve to define Erasmus' dilemma as a rhetorically astute man of typographical letters. Even in case of the *Moria,* indeterminacy per se was never quite the Erasmian desideratum Cave claims it was. But the burgeoning of the printing industry in sixteenth-century Europe and Erasmus' own gener-ally enthusiastic participation in that burgeoning made the principle of decorum an increasingly difficult one to apply to his own works and words. The printing industry had a financial interest in making books available to as many readers as possible, and Erasmus was himself not above exploiting the new medium for pecuniary gain. Yet, even as the pos-sibilities of the new medium militated against the kind of decorum that Erasmus emphasized in the *Ratio,* they also underscored its importance.

This dilemma necessarily qualified the meaning of the Erasmian *sermo,* which could include copiousness as well as a laconic secrecy. For as Mar-jorie Boyle has argued, Erasmus' trinity of Father, Son, and Holy Spirit was one of "humanists all: writing, publishing, advising."[10] Accordingly, in his *Apologia de in Principio erat Sermo* (1520), Erasmus' defense of *sermo* over *verbum* as a translation of the second person of the Trinity hinges on the difference between a continuous revelation and a single, discrete one.[11] The Son as *logos* does not manifest himself only in the form of an incarna-tion, a solitary event, but rather he endlessly proliferates and is always being born, as it were, from his father [semper a patre nascens].[12] Neither *sermo* or *verbum* fully captures what Erasmus sees as the "polysemousness" of the Greek *logos,* yet since *verbum* is generally restricted to a single word, *sermo* is the better translation.[13]

But if Erasmus' version of the filial *logos* is a humanist publisher of sorts, ever manifesting the will of his writer father, this *logos,* nevertheless, should do so with caution. As C. A. Jarrott has noted, even before the full effects of the Lutheran Reformation had begun to be felt, Erasmus was already modifying the message of the *Paraclesis.*[14] Thus, the temporal proximity of the 1520 *Apologia de in Principio erat Sermo* to the 1519 *Ratio* is no coincidence. For addressing the problem of a "rude" audience in the *Apologia,* Erasmus argued that his New Testament was never meant to supplant the Vulgate but rather to be read at home by the learned, who would engage in the favorite humanist hermeneutical activity, the *collatio* of texts. But, Erasmus complained, carping preachers vulgarize [evulgare] Erasmus' translation among women, tanners, and weavers, the kind of readership for scripture that Erasmus had advocated in the *Paraclesis.*[15] In the *Apologia,* however, such divulgation of scripture leads not to a restoration of Christianity but rather to the possibility of sedition.

Translated as *sermo,* the divine *logos* acquires plurality, but Erasmus did not think this plurality should be an unlimited one. Or at least by the time of the *Ratio* and *Apologia,* he had begun to consider the desirability of circumscribing the dissemination of both the Bible and his own writings. As a model for Erasmus' own writing, the Scripture of the *Ratio* suggests the need for discretion and prudence. For a sixteenth-century writer who, as Erasmus did, chose print or, in some cases, had it chosen for him could not expect to be addressing only the select few, a loyal readership of disciples and apostles. Rather, this writer would most likely be addressing a perhaps still rude and certainly heterogeneous public. Indeed, in the case of Erasmus, this public included not only theologians such as Martin Dorp but also a lay audience that did not necessarily read Latin. Both, vernacular translation and preaching provided a means of disseminating Erasmus' words to those who did not know Latin.

The problem of exercising discretion in print became even more acute when Erasmus addressed Luther's fulminations against the papacy.[16] Thus, writing in 1520 to Albert of Brandenburg, also the dedicatee of the *Ratio,* Erasmus claimed that Luther's greatest sin was imprudence rather than impiety,[17] and, criticizing Luther in a 1521 letter to Jodocus Jonas, Erasmus argued the necessity of selectively publishing controversial views:

What therefore was the point of dealing in paradoxes, and putting some things forward in language that was bound to give even more offence at first sign than when regarded steadily at close quarters? What was the point of a savage torrent of invective directed against men whom it was unwise to treat like that if he wished to make them better, and impious if he did it to provoke them and set the whole world by the ears? Furthermore, when a prudent steward [prudentis oeconomi] will husband the truth [dispensare veritatem]—bring it out, I mean, when the business requires it and bring it out so much as is requisite and bring out for every man what is appropriate [accommodum] for him—Luther in his torrent of pamphlets has poured it all out at once, making everything public [nihil non evulgans], and giving even cobblers a share [cerdonibus etiam communia faciens] in what is normally handled by scholars as mysteries reserved for the initiated.[18]

The pressure of events is evident in this passage. Luther had just refused to recant at the Diet of Worms (1521), and books such as *The Babylonian Captivity of the Church* (1520) and *The Freedom of a Christian* (1520) were threatening to set the "whole world by the ears." Though Luther emphatically supported obedience to secular authority well before the German Peasants' Revolt, the limits of his own defiance of authority were by no means clear in 1521. Luther's refusal to recant meant defying the Emperor, and even his 1523 *Temporal Authority: To What Extent It Should Be Obeyed* would combine a legitimization of the temporal sword with some rather vehement denunciations of contemporary princes.[19]

In Erasmus' 1521 letter, however, most revealing is the contrast between rhetorical terms such as "prudens oeconomus" and "accommodum" and locutions denoting the uncontrolled dissemination of language, that is, "evulgans" and "communia faciens." *Oikonomia* is a technical word referring to the rhetorical accommodation of an audience,[20] but here the prudent "oeconomus" is, more literally, a "steward," someone who knows when and to whom to dispense certain truths. Divulgation, on the other hand, emerges as the opposite of a rhetorically astute stewarding of the truth.

But Erasmus did not always espouse such rhetorical stewardship. Christ, Erasmus writes elsewhere in the letter to Jodocus, is "communis omnium," and Erasmus, too, seem to have, intermittently at least, aspired to a comparable universality.[21] Thus, in the same letter Erasmus notes that Plato recognized the need for dissimulation on the part of the philosopher-rulers of his ideal republic, but he also states that such dissimulation hardly befits [decet] a Christian. Nevertheless, at times the truth must be hushed [tacetur veritas] just as doctors do not at once employ extreme measures but rather first try less onerous drugs.[22] Erasmus here implicitly acknowledges the truth of Luther's criticisms of the church, and he even expresses a Christian repugnance for the dissimulation recommended by Plato. Nevertheless, Erasmus' own metaphor of the doctor who knows when to dispense certain treatments and drugs is a decidedly Platonic one.

An author as well known as Erasmus, however, was not always able to choose between dissimulation and exposure. Appropriated by an intermediary, Erasmus' 1520 letter to Albert of Brandenburg was itself published [vulgata typis] and circulated as evidence of Erasmus' Lutheranism, even before it reached its recipient. This letter, Erasmus later claimed, was intended to be secretly read, not widely disseminated.[23] Similarly, in the letter to Jodocus Jonas, Erasmus complains that certain "odious" excerpts from his books have been translated and published in German because they could seem proto-Lutheran [quae viderentur affinia quibusdam Lutheri dogmatibus]. Additionally, public preachers are now expounding the "congruent" teachings of Erasmus and Luther.[24] In 1521 Eberlin von Gunzberg translated and published in Basel Folly's critique of mendicant friars and the superstitious veneration of saints, topics that would lend themselves to Lutheranism. In 1520 the *Enchiridion,* too, was translated into German.

But, although he did not ever fully master the press or see himself as having done so, Erasmus was hardly its victim either. At least, Erasmus was quite canny when it came to maximizing the potential profits of his own books. Thus, for instance, the early-sixteenth-century printer Jodocus Badius complained that Erasmus was wont to follow the first impression of his works with endless revisions, which made the first impressions worth little but allowed Erasmus to sell virtually the same works to different printers.[25] Even Badius' complaints, however, are couched in polite terms, and John Froben is equally deferential to Erasmus.[26] Erasmus' works were evidently good investments, and his correspondence with figures such as Badius and Froben indicates the competition among publishers to acquire those works.

This correspondence also reveals Erasmus' keen desire to work with publishers to retain control of his writings. Thus, for instance, a letter from Bruno Amorbach asks Erasmus to respond by letter to the threat of a Parisian printer whose intention was to "imitate" Erasmus' edition of Jerome's *Opera.*[27] Erasmus' swift compliance with this request demonstrates in a rather concrete way his sense that his works belonged to him and those whom he had selected to publish them even as they were becoming "communis omnium."[28] Indeed, to rephrase Udall's point about Erasmus' writings and the Gospel, Erasmus' status as a best-selling author and the promoter of a Gospel-based Christianity were one and the same.

There are two kinds of authors, claims Stultitia in the *Moria.* On the one hand, the "erudites" appeal to the judgment of the few whereas Stultitia's followers write for a "mass audience" [plurimi].[29] Yet, this binary does not hold for the erudite Stultitia as it did not for Erasmus. Stultitia mockingly claims that the goal of popular writers is to be praised vulgarly [vulgo laudantur] when they stand among the booksellers or when others point to them in a crowd with their fingers [ostenduntur digito]. But, according to the 1515 Listrius commentary on the *Moria,* Stultitia herself resembles such a widely read author. For the commentary notes that at the outset of her oration she points to herself [seipsam digito ostendat], and indeed by 1515 her declamation, one of Erasmus' most lucrative works, had gone through several editions. Such self-reference highlights the degree to which Stultitia and her author are creatures of the popularity she satirizes. As one seventeenth-century English epigrammist put it, "Stultituam non tu laudasti solus Erasme; / te laudant multi, stultitiamque tuam" [You alone did not praise folly; many praise you and your folly].[30]

In her appeal to the entire human race, Stultitia also resembles the Gospel described by Erasmus in the *Paraclesis*. Yet the reservations expressed in the *Phaedrus* about the written word—it says the same thing to all readers—continued to haunt Erasmus, ever conscious of the need for rhetorical decorum, particularly as he became more drawn into Reformation conflicts. Thus, the Erasmus-Luther debate over the freedom of the will, which included Erasmus' *De Libero Arbitrio* (1524), Luther's *De Servo Arbitrio* (1525), and Erasmus' *Hyperaspistes* (1526), casts a somewhat different light on the problem of popularizing religious texts than does the *Paraclesis*. Yet Erasmus' position on divulgation in *De Libero Arbitrio* and *Hyperaspistes* does not so much represent a repudiation of an earlier belief as the unfolding of contradictions that had been present in his writings all along. Not surprisingly, the ludic Stultitia figures as one of the more prominent examples of Erasmus' attempt to discover a rhetorically sophisticated mode of divulgation.

MASKING AND UNMASKING: ERASMUS AND LUTHER

In his *Answer to a Poisoned Book* (1533), Thomas More criticized the anonymous author of *The Souper of the Lorde* for hiding behind a mask:

suche as walke in visours, have mych the lesse fere and shame, bothe what they do and what they saye, bycause they thynke theym selfe unknowen: so these folk oftentymes lytell force what they write, that use to putte out theyr bookes, and set not theyr names unto theym. They thynke theym selfe unsene . . . and therfore they fere not the shame of theyr foly. As some have I sene ere thys, full boldely come daunce in a maske.[31]

Masks could serve as a protection against public exposure, the "shame" of "foly," but the rhetorical disguise that More terms the "visour of dyssimulacion" (*dissimulatio* is the Latin word for the Greek *eironeia*) could also constitute a spectacle of its own.[32] Thus, responding to his anonymous opponent, More turns him into "Mayster Mummer" and "Master Masker," designations that effectively locate the masker on a stage of sorts. Indeed,

More's labels also indicate the difficulty of distinguishing between a mask and its wearer. The writer who dons a mask risks being identified with the mask or, in the case of More's opponent, reductively defined as a masker.

Protestant heretics, however, were scarcely the only early modern writers to don a visor of dissimulation before entering print and undergoing the risk of being shamed for their "foly." Indeed, both More and Erasmus were well versed in this kind of dissimulation. Thus, writing to Martin Dorp in 1515, Erasmus had described himself as not exposed in the *Moria* because he had donned the "Stultitiae persona" just as Socrates had covered his face when reciting the strictures of love in the *Phaedrus*.[33] Masking provided Erasmus with one way of rhetorically mediating between secrecy and divulgation, but it was not a secure or even an entirely stable form of mediation. In Erasmus' own writings his personae receive numerous reconfigurations, and these reconfigurations are generally the product of controversy or at least its threat.

The personae of Hercules and Stultitia, in particular, show Erasmus responding to opponents, both perceived and actual.[34] The important point of origin for Hercules was the 1508 adage "Herculei Labores," where Erasmus described the adagist and, more generally, the restorer of classical literature as a Hercules figure battling the Lernean Hydra of carping critics. The Hydra symbolizes the obstacles facing scholarly writers who want to deserve [bene merentur] well "de vulgo."[35] Indeed, Erasmus goes so far as to compare such a writer to a good prince, who, while regarding only the "communis utilitas," reaps ingratitude as his only reward.[36] This notion of the "common good," in turn, informs Erasmus' discussions of the nature of an adage in the introduction to the 1508 *Adagia* and the adage, "Culicem colant." These discussions also recall Erasmus' vision of a Christ who is "communis omnium." In "Culicem colant" the "vulgarity" of the adage becomes analogous to the central Christian mystery, Christ's assumption of human flesh.[37]

Although a prince of the "republic of letters" and a relentless toiler on behalf of the common good, the Herculean scholar is, nevertheless, himself subject to powerful and unruly democratic forces. These forces in turn become more tumultuous in later Erasmian texts. Thus, for instance, in his *Apologia de in Principio erat Sermo,* Erasmus subtly alludes to the adage when he castigates preachers and theologians for assailing him publicly. These preachers are attacking someone who, by virtue of his huge expense of labors [impendio laborum], deserves the best treatment from them [de ipsis optime merens].[38] In the *Apologia,* the unappreciated scholar-adagist of the 1508 "Herculei labores" has become the unappreciated biblical exegete, and this lack of appreciation now involves charges not only of inaccuracy but of impiety, too.

In his 1526 *Hyperaspistes,* however, Erasmus used the figure of Hercules to castigate another famous biblical exegete. For there he described Luther as wont to don a lion's skin, the emblem of Hercules, and to manage his affairs with a club, a Herculean attribute, too.[39] In addition to Hercules, this jibe also contains a reference to the story of the Cumaean ass, who by putting on a lion's skin passed as a lion, but the club is Erasmus' addition to this story.[40] The immediate point of the mock Herculean Luther is to indicate Luther's presumption. Luther is an ass, a figure of folly playing the hero. Yet Erasmus seems here to be also invoking "Clavam extorquere Herculi," an adage denoting those who try to take for themselves the belongings of a more powerful person [potentior].[41] This adage can refer to literary imitation and appropriation, for instance, Vergil's use of Homer; and in *Hyperaspistes* the adage is meant to suggest that Luther is copying Erasmus' style of argument during parts of their debate.

In a more than stylistic sense, however, the evidence of his own influence on Luther was one of Erasmus' chief worries. Donning the lion's skin recalls Erasmus' own figure of folly, Stultitia, and her assumption of this disguise before describing Christian ecstasy: "But now that I've 'got on my high horse' [the Latin has 'put on the lion's skin'] I want to take the next step and argue that the happiness after which Christians strive so passionately is nothing but a certain kind of Folly."[42] For Stultitia, whose favorite exclamation is "me Hercles,"[43] is also a figure of Herculean powers of the printing press, or, rather, she demonstrates the ability of the press to give momentary authority and a kind of pulpit to those members of society who conspicuously did not enjoy a place in the ecclesiastical hierarcy.

As a woman, Stultitia represents the entire "vulgus" that Erasmus would elevate over theologians in the 1516 *Paraclesis,* and, because her gender makes her an outsider, Stultitia is also an exaggerated version of Erasmus' own relative lack of theological credentials.[44] For the press provided Erasmus with a plausible, albeit not always successful, way of bypassing the authority of university theological faculties and reaching a lay public. Writing to Albert Pio in 1526, Erasmus described himself as someone who, if he were to try to pass as a great philosopher or theologian, would deserve to have his lion's skin removed.[45] However disingenuous, this comment indicates Erasmus' sense of his own kinship, as an amateur, to Stultitia. Like Erasmus, Stultitia compensates for her lack of credentials and authority with numerous quotes from the Bible as well as other religious, poetic, and philosophical texts.

In *De Libero Arbitrio,* however, Erasmus invokes Stultitia to satirize Luther's rejection of the interpretive authority of the Church and its theologians. Such a rejection, Erasmus sardonically writes, entails preferring the judgment of *nepioi,* that is, "simplices et juxta mundum stulti," to that of philosophers. Indeed, *nepioi* is a Greek word that Stultitia lifts from the *Odyssey* as well as from the New Testament and applies to herself in the *Moria,* but in *De Libero Arbitrio* it no longer serves as a way of redeeming Stultitia from opprobrium.[46] Instead, the exaltation of fools offers a critique of what Erasmus saw as the leveling tendencies that Luther may not have entirely foreseen but to which his attack on the Roman Church gave rise.

In contrast to such leveling, the Stultitia of the *Moria* and the Herculean adagist of "Herculei labores" have in common a ruler's aggrieved sense of the ingratitude of their beneficiaries. Stultitia's charge that her followers refuse to acknowledge her and even sometimes malign her is reminiscent of the afflictions of the princely scholar who braves the Lernean Hydra of print. More broadly, however, the problem is one of being misunderstood. Both Stultitia and the Herculean adagist present themselves as attempting to correct a vulgar misunderstanding. "Utcumque vulgo mortales de me audiunt": so Stultitia begins her declamation with a reference to her widespread, bad reputation.[47] Like Erasmus at the outset of so many of his works, Stultitia is immediately on the defensive.

Defensiveness forms a thread connecting mid-career Erasmian writings such as the *Moria* to the debate with Luther. But, by the time of the debate with Luther, the nature of the vulgar misunderstanding had become much more threatening, both to Erasmus and to the stability of the social order. For the peasants that Erasmus had, along with women, exalted as the ideal readers of scripture in the *Paraclesis* were in revolt, and thus the club that Luther brandishes in *Hyperaspistes* may be an emblem of literal force as well as literary imitation and borrowed ideas. For despite Luther's vehement attacks on the peasants, the revolt owed much to the provocative potential of Luther's writings and, in particular, his 1522 German New Testament. But, since Erasmus' own *Paraclesis* and scriptural exegesis had inspired Luther's translation, Erasmus' criticisms of Luther's dissemination of scripture could also double as a mode of self-protection, too.

Given the need for such self-protection on both sides, the Erasmus/ Luther debate not surprisingly contains a good deal of masking, unmasking, and sheer pretense. Such theatricality, however, does not obscure the existence of real disagreements between the two antagonists, particularly on issues of language and its interpretation. The "sermo dei," wrote Luther in *De Servo Arbitrio,* was meant to transform the world [mutaturus et innovaturus], and thus this "sermo" inevitably entailed a certain amount of uproar [tumultus].[48] In *De Libero Arbitrio,* on the other hand, Erasmus had employed the Pauline dictum—"omnia mihi licent, sed non omnia expediunt" [all things are permitted to me, but not all are expedient]—to argue for the application of a standard of rhetorical decorum even to the Word of God. In *De Libero Arbitrio* Erasmus uses a number of locutions including "evulgari," "publicare," and "haec vulgo prodita vox" to castigate the dissemination of language without any attention to this principle of decorum.[49]

Scripture, according to Erasmus, rhetorically adapts [attemperare] itself to human sense, and thus those whose task it is to dispense the "divinus sermo" should be equally careful not to act any "fabulae" in the theater of the promiscuous multitude. Rather, some topics are best left to the "colloquia eruditorum" and the theological schools. As Luther knew, however, Erasmus was qualifying the message of the *Paraclesis* in their debate. Thus, Luther responded to Erasmus by arguing that Christian "doctrina" could not be bound to "personae" and "tempora," but rather must be divulgated to all [invulganda] as, Luther added, Erasmus himself had argued in the *Paraclesis.*[50] But in *Hyperaspistes* Erasmus retorted that in the *Paraclesis* he had never meant for the dissemination of Scripture to lead to "in utramque partem" debates over the meaning of particular passages "quovis modo" [in any manner] or "apud quoslibet" [among anyone].[51] Only if he can be said to be a good doctor who offers any drugs [pharmaca] to anybody, then will he be a good theologian who "provulgat" the "verbum dei" without any regard of time, place, or person. In other words, "logotherapy" is not for all patients.[52]

Victoria Kahn has argued that humanists extended to reading the realm of deliberative oratory, entailing the ability to argue both sides of a question [rhetoric in utramque partem], as well as the prudential faculty that such oratory required in a reader. She makes the case that in *De Libero Arbitrio* Erasmus is trying to preserve this prudential realm against Luther's assaults upon the efficacy of human reason.[53] But the reverse of her argument is also valid. For when opposing Luther in their debate, Erasmus is also opposing rhetoric *in utramque partem* debates over the meaning of Scripture, at least in certain contexts. Rather, as Erasmus sees it, Luther is relying too much on the prudence of ordinary readers of the Bible. Such reliance for Erasmus is the greatest imprudence.

Erasmus argued in *Hyperaspistes* that Luther saw no difference between criticizing a bishop or prince "privatim" or attacking such authority figures "seditiose" among the "populus." In other words, Luther and his adherents had actually wreaked the kind of havoc that Erasmus, in *Apolo-*

31

gia de in Principio erat Sermo, had accused his conservative theological critics of potentially inciting. In particular, by making available his doctrine of "Evangelica libertas" to the laity [idiotae] in German, Luther had contributed to the climate of revolt. Such doctrines "suo loco, sobrieque praedicata, fructu non carent: sic praedicata, quid fructus attulerint, vides" [in their place and soberly preached do not lack fruit: thus preached, what fruit they have brought you see].[54]

The connection between theological and civil disruption is also evident from a work of Erasmus' published in the same year as *Hyperaspistes— Praestigiarum Libelli cuisdam Detectio.*[55] Erasmus' *Detectio* was itself a response to a recently published book whose title contained both Erasmus' and Luther's names as the prelude to the argument that Erasmus and Luther had the same opinion on the Lord's Supper. But the book's opening apparently went beyond strict theology to make a somewhat different charge. This charge was that, as Erasmus repeated it in the *Detectio,* Luther was merely achieving more openly [fortius & apertius] what Erasmus had already accomplished in the *Moria, Adagia,* and other works—that is, the complete refutation of all "humanae constitutiones." Such refuted "constitutiones" included not only the papacy but also "leges civiles."[56]

The defensiveness of the *Detectio* indicates that the contrast between Erasmus and Luther was not as evident as Erasmus would have wished. The risk of readers confusing the two helps to explain Erasmus' insistence on the impossibility of disseminating doctrines of evangelical liberty without causing sedition. For even as he was accusing Luther of having attacked bishops and princes in too public a manner, Erasmus was himself vulnerable to the stigma of having articulated no less radical views, albeit less openly. Not only the *Paraclesis,* then, but the *Moria* and adages, too, were liabilities for Erasmus when he wanted to distinguish himself from Luther. In the *Detectio* Erasmus claimed that if he had foreseen the Lutheran "tempestas," he never would have written the *Moria.*[57] Nevertheless, Erasmus also admitted to having warned and reprehended princes, bishops, and monks quite freely [multa liberrime] in all his books.[58] Thus, the *Moria* would be only the most flagrant example of a general tendency.

The implication of the *Detectio,* however, is that Erasmus' satirical writings combine an extreme freedom with discretion. Thus, in the *Detectio* Erasmus insisted that he had never displayed "timiditas" but rather "prudentia aut religio,"[59] although he did not fully explain the nature of this prudence. But Erasmus' claim to have joined prudence and a liberty of reprehension constitutes a retrospective reading of the *Moria* and the 1515 "Utopian" *Adagia,* which contained some of Erasmus' lengthier criticisms of bishops, princes, and monks. For if Erasmus is to be taken at his word, these works provide both a precedent and a model for the supposedly unseditious form of social criticism that Erasmus wanted Luther to adopt during the 1520s. Following the course of Erasmus' own rereadings of his earlier writings, we must then turn to the *Moria* and *Adagia* to examine how they perform this feat of bringing together radical critique and a cautious prudence.

PRUDENT CRITICISM

The 1515 Froben *Moria* and the Gerard Listrius commentary, which first appeared with this *Moria,* exemplify Erasmus' prudence and his concern to exert some control over the meaning of his most caustic words. The commentary, which Erasmus wrote in part, offers an authorized reading of the *Moria,* a reading that in general attempts to define carefully the scope of Stultitia's satire.[60] Thus, in addition to explaining learned allusions, the Listrius commentary provides frequent qualifications of Stultitia's message: for instance, she is not attacking all theologians, only the bad ones. Yet the Listrius commentary was added to one of the most pointedly critical editions of the *Moria.* In 1514 Erasmus had inserted several lengthy castigations of the Church hierarchy and theologians into Stultitia's declamation, and thus the frequent cautions of the commentary are themselves a response to the intensification of the satire.[61]

Erasmus, to be sure, in his own prefatory letter to More, had claimed not to be uncovering the Juvenalian "sewer of hidden crimes."[62] He did not, however, fully explicate this claim until his 1515 letter to Martin Dorp, which was first printed with the 1516 Froben edition of the *Moria:* "We all know how many things could be said about bad popes, scandalous bishops and priests, corrupt princes—if, like Juvenal, I had not been ashamed to write down [ea mandare literis] what many are not ashamed to act out."[63] Erasmus also highlighted his own prudence in the letter to Dorp: "Oh, friend Dorp, if you could only enter silently into my thoughts; you would understand only too well how many things I am leaving prudently unspoken in this place [prudens hoc reticeam loco]." "I preserved the same caution everywhere," Erasmus continues, "not to write anything indecent, nothing libellous or seditious [seditiose]."[64] Thus, long before Luther became a problem for Erasmus, the possibility of sedition formed one limit of Erasmian satire.

The Listrius commentary, however, not only proposes specific interpretations of various passages of the *Moria,* but it also proposes, more generally, a way of reading the satire of the *Moria,* one that combines classical rhetoric and biblical hermeneutics. Thus, in response to the possibility that someone might blur the identities of Erasmus and Stultitia, the Listrius commentary specifies a scriptural model for understanding Stultitia's attacks on secular and ecclesiastical authorities—that is, the Apocrypha:

Nullus igitur opinor erit tam iniquus, ut siquid dictum videbitur in principes, aut sacerdotes, aut in alios offendatur, cum non taxentur ulli, nisi leniter & iucunde magisquam acriter. . . . Postremo cum stultitiae personam loquentem fecerit, non convenit et imaginari personam, autoris, id dicere quod sub persona Moriae dictum est. Non hercle magis quam siquis diabolum faciat disputantem cum Michaele de corpore Moysi quemadmodum est in Apocryphis, quidquid diabolus dixerit, hoc ex autoris persona dictum videatur. Aut Siquis Phalaridem loquentem inducat sensisse videatur quicquid Phalaridem loquentem fecerit.[65]

[No one will be so unfair that if something will appear to be said against princes or priests or as an offense against some other group (since not any are reproached, except softly and pleasantly). . . . At last since he made the persona of Folly speaking, it will not be suitable to imagine the person of the author to say this thing which under the persona of Folly has been said. No more, by Hercules, than if someone should make the devil disputing with Michael concerning the body of Moses as it is in the Apocrypha, whatever the devil said should seem uttered by the person of the author. Or if someone should bring forward a Phalaris speaking, he should be thought to have said what Phalaris said.] (my translation)

This passage creates an equivalence between the rhetorical skills of Lucian, whose *Phalaris* contained the self-justifying oration of an infamous tyrant, and an excerpt from the Apocrypha. While Erasmus invokes numerous classical and postclassical precedents for the form of the mock encomium in his own prefatory letter to More, this passage offers a distinctly biblical exemplum of such rhetoric. To be sure, the reference to Michael and the devil is found in the Epistle of Jude, a canonical part of the New Testament: "Yet in like manner these men in their dreamings defile flesh, reject authority. Yet Michael the Archangel, when contending with the devil he disputed about the body of Moses, durst not bring against him a railing accusation, but said, The Lord rebuke thee."[66] But, as Erasmus explained in his annotations of Jude, the canonicity of Jude was itself somewhat suspect because the story of Michael and the devil is not found in any canonical book of the Old Testament but seems to derive from a lost Apocryphal text.[67]

The reference to Jude, however, does not seem entirely applicable to the relation of the "persona" of Stultitia to her author in the *Moria*. Thus, in Jude, Michael's eschewal of a railing accusation exemplifies respect for the princes of the world, even the devil himself. But the *Moria* would not appear to contain such devil's advocacy, or, as it was dubbed in the Renaissance, rhetoric *in utramque partem.* Erasmus' fear was of Stultitia's being deemed seditious, not a supporter of princes. (But he was himself vulnerable to the charge of fawning flattery as well as of attacking authority figures.)[68] Nevertheless, Michael's silence might be one model for what Erasmus saw as his own reticence in the *Moria.* To refrain from saying all that one could against the devil arguably constitutes a kind of advocacy. Yet, Michael is not entirely quiet in Jude either: he indirectly rebukes the devil by calling on the Lord to do so.

The Listrius commentary clarifies certain things and leaves others deliberately vague. The commentary uses the Apocrypha to prohibit the identification of Stultitia and her author, but this prohibition also underscores the difficulty of distinguishing between them. In his 1515 letter to Dorp, Erasmus even compared the *Moria* to "vulgares" comedies, where invectives are hurled against monarchs and other potentates without any damage being done. For the object of attack merely "prudenter" dissimulates that he has been assaulted, and thus general satire does not translate into the potentially seditious recognition of the culpability of a specific king or priest. But the flaw of this argument, which Erasmus would later emphasize when critiquing Luther's imprudence, is its assumption that the spectators are not drawing their own conclusions.[69]

In a broader sense than the local reference to Jude implies, however, the Apocrypha provided a way of responding to this problem of readers drawing unauthorized conclusions from the *Moria,* and thus the status of the Apocrypha as a whole will help to illuminate the Listrius commentary's proposed hermeneutics of reading Stultitia's satire. We might begin by noting that the comparison between a Lucianic text and an apocryphal story is not entirely far-fetched. For the Apocrypha were the most Hellenistic part of the Old Testament. The basis of their authority was the Greek Septuagint, not Hebrew manuscripts, and thus Jerome included them in his translation of the Bible "ad aedeficationem plebis, non auctoriatem ecclesiasticorum dogmatum" [for the edification of the masses, not the authority of ecclesiastic dogmas]. But, despite this caveat, the Apocrypha were dispersed throughout the Vulgate Bible.

In contrast to Jerome's inclusion of the Apocrypha for the edification of the masses, the name Apocrypha denotes "hidden" or secret books—that is, the opposite of what should be divulged. Indeed, Protestant translators of the Bible segregated the Apocrypha because their ambiguous authority made them an obvious affront to the Protestant insistence on the infallibility and lucidity of scripture. Thus, in his 1534 translation, Luther grouped the Apocrypha together and glossed them as "books not to be esteemed as part of the Holy Scripture, but nonetheless profitable and good to read." Similarly, in England the Coverdale Bible (1534) separated the Apocrypha and prefaced them with a warning that the Apocrypha contained "dreams, visions, and dark sentences." To get through the Apocrypha the reader had to eschew such darkness and adhere to the "plain text."[70]

The dubious status of the Apocrypha, however, rendered them an ideal paradigm for the problem of interpreting the religious messages of humanist personae such as Stultitia or Raphael Hythlodaeus, whose first name also comes from the Apocrypha. The language of both these personae has powerful religious resonances, but neither Raphael or Stultitia speaks with the voice of complete authority, nor do they speak necessarily with the voice of their authors. The first biblical text that Erasmus deployed against Luther in his *De Libero Arbitrio* was from the apocryphal Ecclesiasticus. Nevertheless, in defense of this book, which Stultitia also quotes when she plays the part of a theologian, Erasmus separates Ecclesiasticus from the rest of the Apocrypha, and he disparages the latter as a class of "hagiographia" that, for good reason, are not canonical.[71]

Despite this disparagement, however, Erasmus' decision to begin his scriptural *collatio* with an apocryphal text is an important one, and in *De Libero Arbitrio* Erasmus does indicate a way of applying the Apocrypha to scriptural reading in general:

Quaedam voluit nobis esse notissima, quod genus sunt, bene vivendi praecepta. Hic est sermo dei, qui neque petendus est e sublimi conscenso caelo neque e longinquo importandus transmisso mari, sed prope adest in ore nostro et in corde nostro.[72]

[He wanted certain things to be most familiar to us—precepts of living. Indeed, this is the word [sermo] of God, which is neither to be sought by scaling the sky, nor carried from far away across the sea, but is near in our mouth and in our heart.] (my translation)

That is, we should approach the "sermo" of God for the purposes of moral edification rather than adjudicating vexed doctrinal disputes—the very claim that legitimized reading the Apocrypha. On the other hand, this exclusively moral reading of scripture yields uncertainty. The Bible no longer provides a way of resolving vexed doctrinal issues, and its own authority lessens. Erasmus' application of the apocryphal model to the scripture here produces a form of scriptural interpretation that is not too far from the way in which the humanists read Cicero and other pagan authors. The Apocrypha provide Erasmus with a bridge between the divine *logos* and human *sermo,* and such bridging may help to explain Erasmus' prominent deployment of an apocryphal text in his debate against Luther.

As a model for the *Moria,* however, the Apocrypha do not necessarily entail reveling in indeterminacy or the license of readers. Rather, just as the very dubiousness of the Apocrypha generated attempts to circumscribe the limits of their authority and significance while retaining their moral efficacy, so the 1515 *Moria* shows the Listrius commentary performing a similar function. The marginal commentary acts as the literal and figurative boundary to what Stultitia says. If her speech did not have such affinities with Lucian and the parts of scripture most akin to Lucian, such a boundary would presumably not be necessary.

Stultitia herself indicates the crude extreme to which the guidance of interpretation can be taken. As part of her claim to be responsible for civil concord, she cites a long list of figures, including the infamous Menenius Aggrippa, who manipulated their audiences through apologues. Menenius Aggrippa kept the Roman plebeians from rebelling against the senate, and, in conjunction with him, Stultitia also lists Minos and Numa, both of whom used religion-based deceptions as a way of establishing and maintaining civic order.[73] She thus suggests that revolt is one possible consequence, of allowing large groups of people to form their own conclusions. She also makes the case for the ability of religious deception to uphold civil authority.

A manipulative apologue in the tradition of Menenius Aggrippa represents the ultimate victory of a persona/author over her/his interpreters, but the history of Erasmus' later polemics concerning the *Moria* show that he was not always able to achieve this victory. He often failed to separate his own persona from that of Stultitia, and, as Clarence Miller has shown, even passages from early editions of the *Moria* erase the difference between Erasmus and Stultitia.[74] Nevertheless, the Listrius commentary prominently offers the persona as a kind of lightning rod for criticism as well as a check to those who think that Stultitia's assaults upon worldly potentates are completely authorized by Erasmus. The Listrius commentary, like later Protestant warnings concerning the Apocrypha, urges the reader to beware because all parts of the *Moria* are neither equally authoritative nor clear.

In addition to the Listrius commentary, the text of the *Moria,* too, reveals the dangers of interfering with the masking process. For instance, Stultitia argues that all human things constitute a Silenus figure, that is, the opposite of what they seem, and that it is imprudent to open the Silenus and reveal what it contains. Such imprudence resembles the actions of "someone in a theater" who tries to "strip the masks [personae] off the actors in the middle of the play [fabula]." If this were to happen, among other things, a powerful king might appear to be the most "abject slave" and the "actor who before appeared as a woman would now be seen as a man"—a possibility that could apply to the masked Erasmus as well. The reader who unmasked Erasmus would be acting as imprudently as the wiseman in the theater and would deserve the same fate as the latter—expulsion from the show. But prudence protects the king as well as Erasmus from exposure.[75]

Erasmus, however, was not always himself so prudent. Thus, in the 1515 adage "Sileni Alcibiades" Erasmus played the part of the wiseman that he adumbrated in the *Moria*. Princes, priests, and bishops are all exposed as "reversed" Sileni, who are not nearly as magnificent on the inside as they are on the outside. On the other hand, pagan figures such as Socrates and the Cynic philosopher Diogenes as well as Christ himself and the *sermo humilis* of Scripture are Sileni who present a veneer of poverty to the world but possess great inner riches. The Folger Shakespeare Library has an anonymous English translation (154?) of "Sileni," whose title emphasizes its criticism of the "Spiritualitie how farre they be from the perfite trade and lyfe of Christe." Just as the truth of the various social orders is revealed in "Sileni Alcibiades," so Erasmus in this adage seems to drop the protective mask that shielded him in the *Moria*.[76]

In 1515 Erasmus showed himself capable of acting a "fabula" on stage that resembled the one he would in 1525 criticize Luther for playing before the promiscuous multitude. Yet, even in the "Sileni" adage, Erasmus exercises a certain amount of discretion and Michael-like silence before the princes and prelates of the world. The "prudens lector," Erasmus writes, must understand how much he keeps silent [tacere] and within himself [apud me] while appearing to lambast virtually all levels of political and ecclesiastical hierarchy. One area of silence, as in the *Moria,* is the names of individuals. Thus, Erasmus notes that no one ought to be offended [offendere] by his Sileni because his criticisms are general and their objects anonymous.[77]

But the most important clue to Erasmus' discretion in "Sileni" is what Erasmus terms the reader's unspoken thought [tacita lectoris cogitatio]:

What are all these disgusting remarks leading up to? Do you want the prince to be like Plato makes the guardians of his republic? Do you want to rob priests of their power, dignity, glory, and riches?[78]

Erasmus' reply is that he is not "robbing" them but rather "enriching" them with "greater possessions," and he is not "turning" princes "out of their domain" [dejicio de possessione] but "calling them to better things." In other words, Erasmus, although acting the part of the imprudent wiseman and stripping the "personae" away from princes, has not taken this part to the point of sedition. The "Sileni" is an exhortation to reform from above, not a call to arms or rebellion, and the absence of such a call is an important part of its silence.

One sign of reticence is the figure of the Cynic philosopher Diogenes that Erasmus introduces as an example of a good Silenus. The Diogenes of "Sileni Alcibiades" is a muted version of the normally obstreperous philosopher, whose willingness to say anything at any time would make the Cynics almost a byword for abrasive and inflammatory language. For instance, in Erasmus' *Convivium seu Lapithae,* a Latin translation of a Lucianic satire, the arrival of a Cynic philosopher at a "convivium" turns the feast into a reenactment of the battle between the Centaurs and Lapiths. In the Listrius commentary on the *Moria,* Diogenes even gives Demosthenes the finger.[79] But in "Sileni" Diogenes, although vulgarly considered to be a dog, is merely said to be someone whom Alexander the Great would want to be if he were not Alexander the Great. Indeed, the "bark" of the Cynic philosopher proves to be only the illusory outside of the Silenus figure.[80]

By contrast, the beetle of the 1515 adage "Scarabeus aquilam quaerit" presents a more threatening version of the Silenus topos. The beetle is, despite its lowliness and plebeian character, a powerful creature, and the story of the adage shows the beetle more than holding its own against the eagle, symbol of both the might of ancient Rome and the contemporary Holy Roman Empire. The beetle is contemptible and lowly, but "anyone who opens this Silenus-image and looks at this despised creature more closely will find it endowed with so many unusual qualities that he would decide that he would rather be a beetle than an eagle."[81] Part of the reason, however, for this preference is that the unusual qualities of the beetle are ones of military as well as moral superiority.

The beetle has features resembling Diogenes as well as Silenus. Thus, the statement that anyone looking closely would rather be a beetle than an imperial eagle recalls Alexander's wish to be Diogenes if he were not Alexander. The beetle's habit of rolling balls of dung, its home, up and down a hill is reminiscent of the famous story of Diogenes rolling his tub, also his home, up and down a hill outside of Corinth. But Erasmus also links the Greek name of the beetle, *cantharos,* to "centaur," and he thus connects the beetle to the obstreperous guests at the battle of the Centaurs and Lapiths.[82]

The 1515 "Scarabeus," whose conflict between plebeian might and imperial power virtually adumbrates the Peasants War of the 1520s, is perhaps where Erasmus comes closest to displaying the lack of caution that he ascribed to Luther in 1525. Nevertheless, even in the "Scarabeus"

Erasmus gives the prudent reader some indications that he has not said all that he could have. Humor is one such clue, for it undercuts the beetle as well as his opponent. Thus, for instance, as part of his opening of the Silenus-image in "Scarabeus," Erasmus undertakes a lengthy encomium of manure, the beetle's home and element. But this encomium will not prove easily assimilable to a Bakhtinian reading that highlights the regenerative properties of the lower body and lower classes.[83] For, as Erasmus points out, the beetle does not mind the smell of excrement because it lacks a nose, the traditional organ of satire. Possessing neither any satiric nor olfactory sense, the beetle not surprisingly finds its habitat delightful. But we cannot attribute this same lack of a sense of satire to Erasmus.

CHRISTIAN FOLLY AND FEASTING

Erasmus' confusing willingness to take the part of those whom he seems to be attacking reaches a zenith in Christian Folly. I want, however, to address the social rather than Neoplatonic or ecstatic importance of Folly's apparently sudden religiosity at the end of the *Moria*. Indeed, this religiosity is not as sudden as the label of "Christian Folly" makes it seem. The Christian significance of Stultitia should be clear long before she dons the lion's skin or acts the part of a theologian at the end of her declamation. Rather, this garment arguably makes her more of a theologian and less of an Erasmian Christian than before.[84]

The point of Platonic Christian ecstasy may be to demonstrate that Platonism and Christianity do not entirely mix. To be sure, as M. A. Screech has shown, Platonizing patristic writers such as Origen exerted a powerful influence upon Erasmus, and thus the abstruse Neoplatonism of Ficino was not Erasmus' only model for assimilating Plato to Christianity. Nevertheless, whether it is ultimately indebted to Italian or patristic models, Stultitia's Platonic Christian ecstasy represents a withdrawal from what Erasmus so frequently emphasizes in his writings—the social importance of the Gospel message.[85] For this message, however masked at times, pervades the earlier parts of the *Moria,* and thus it constitutes the necessary preliminary to understanding the significance of Stultitia's final ascent.

Stultitia's leveling tendencies, as we have seen, have a distinctly Christian analogue. Christ, as Erasmus put it in the letter to Jodocus Jonas, ideally should be "communis omnium," and Stultitia, too, claims to offer all things to all people [una omnibus largior omnia].[86] Significantly, Stultitia takes credit for the "amicorum charitas et consuetudo," and indeed asserts herself to be the glue that holds all human society together.[87] In 1515 Stultitia's use of the "charitas" of friends would have recalled the

Erasmian adage, "Amicorum communia omnia," which inaugurated the *Adagia* and suggested that the community of its readers formed a radical alternative to existing societies. Indeed, Stultitia's usage of "charitas" alludes to the Christian rather than Platonic basis of the ideal community of readers of the *Adagia,* and thus she suggests that her version of this community is an open one.

Stultitia can neither be divided nor defined [meipsam finitione explicem, porro ut dividam, multo minus] in the usual dialectical manner because her divinity [numen] extends to all of humanity.[88] Here "division" and "definition" are terms with a technical significance, but they also indicate the all-inclusiveness of Stultitia. Given such inclusiveness, it is hardly surprising that her usages of "vulgus" refer to a wide range of social groups. Thus, while making "vulgus" a synonym for plebeians, she will also refer casually to the "vulgus" of optimates or orators. Although Stultitia alludes disparagingly to the vulgarity of others and does divide her followers into numerous categories, as a preacher who ultimately places all members of her audience at the same level, she is also a vulgarizer par excellence.[89]

At her most radical, Stultitia represents the possibility of a return to apostolic Christianity and charity. This possibility becomes clearer if we further examine Jude as a source for understanding the *Moria.* For the subject of Jude, as Erasmus noted in his annotations of this letter, is the corruption of the apostolic church and the Gospel by "cupiditates," desire and greed, and thus this letter is pertinent to much of Erasmus' writing. Such corruption ought not to seem strange, claims Erasmus, since it was predicted by the apostles, yet the purer members of the flock have no choice but to bring the others to their senses through scolding and admonition. Otherwise, they must separate themselves and await the advent of Christ. Erasmus' "argumentum" highlights his sense of the pertinence of Jude to his own time.[90]

One philological note, in particular, gives an indication of the nature of Erasmus' interest in Jude. Translating *agápe,* the Greek word denoting Christian love, charity, and the communal feasts of the early church, the Vulgate has Jude complaining of "in suis *epulis* maculae" [blots in your feasts]. Annotating this passage in 1516 and again in 1522, however, Erasmus argued that the blots should be "in dilectionibus vestris" or "inter charitates vestras" [in your love feasts]. In defense of his translation, Erasmus distinguished between feasts that could occur for any reason and "convivia quae pauperibus refocillandis exhibebantur" [feasts for the purpose of refreshing the poor] and which were therefore called *agapai.*[91] In other words, Erasmus was concerned to make clear the basis of the feasts in

Christian charity and sharing with the poor, a basis that the Vulgate translation obscures.

Erasmus' interest in the early Christian *agāpe* provides a revealing contrast to his failure to commit to a definite position on the truly controversial meal of the 1520s, that is, the Eucharist. For despite the defensive attempt to clarify his views in the *Detectio,* Erasmus was a disappointment to both sides of the Eucharistic controversy.[92] He never made a firm doctrinal statement concerning the real presence, or at least one to which he consistently adhered. This omission may have been the product of typically Erasmian evasiveness, but it was also a consequence of Erasmus' interest in evolving Christian community rather than in vexed theological disputes. Thus, *agāpe,* although it contributed little to the debate over transubstantiation, was an important paradigm for Erasmus' understanding of "religiosa convivia."

Nevertheless, Erasmus recognized that even in the times of the early church the *agāpe* had undergone corruption. Annotating in the 1520s 1 Corinthians 11, a text crucial to eucharistic controversies, Erasmus uses Paul's castigation of the corruption of the "coena dominica" to distinguish three phases of Christian feasting and to trace the deterioration of Christian charity and society. Paul, according to Erasmus, wanted to castigate the "inaequalitas convivii" [the inequality of the feast] and show, by contrast, "qualia debeant esse vere religiosa Christianorum convivia" [the true kind of Christian feasts]. Erasmus goes on to note that in the beginning of the church, "erant omnia communia" [all things were in common], but the church gradually slipped from this "summa charitas." The next stage of Christian feasting retained a "pristinae communionis vestigium" [vestige of the original communion], and it entailed the institution of certain feast days when rich and poor would eat together. Finally, the poor were excluded from the feast, and each ate with their own [quisque cum suis epulabantur] as the feasts began to resemble pagan orgies of drunken behavior. The middle stage, however, of Erasmus' description of the decline of church communism and community corresponds to the *agāpe* of Jude. The *agāpe* represents an implicit link between perfect Christian unanimity and the fragmented and corrupt church of Paul's day and Erasmus' as well.[93]

The model of the early Christian *agāpe* informs the *Moria,* too, although Stultitia does initially invoke a number of pagan examples of conviviality as precedents for the hilarity that she promises.[94] Most importantly, Stultitia is a Diotima figure, and her ascent to Christian folly is reminiscent of Socrates' use of Diotima in the *Symposium.* Diotima, however, was an absent presence at that feast, for it was closed to women. On the other hand, the early Christian *agāpe* offers a kind of conviviality that resembles the promiscuous character of the banquet that Stultitia proffers. Rich, poor, women, and men are all part of her festivity; its and her vulgarity recreate in ludic form the *agāpe* of the apostolic church.

The *Moria* reveals Stultitia to be an advocate of apostolic charity and an upbraider, like Jude, of those who pollute it. Thus, Stultitia describes theologians complaining that Paul did not define or divide "charitas" in a sufficiently dialectical manner in Corinthians.[95] The joke is that these theologians do not understand that charity or *agāpe* is meant to overcome divisions and boundaries as Stultitia herself does. Similarly, monks are supposed to have professed "apostolica charitas," but, as Stultitia enumerates the various trivialities that divide one order of monks from another, they reveal themselves to be no different from theologians, determined to mince themselves to bits.[96]

Indeed, the ultimate image of such divisiveness is the need to split open the theologians' heads in order to deliver them of their Minerva-like progeny.

They [the theologians] also like to invent new worlds, just as fancy suits them, and adding when they choose another one of their own, the largest and finest of all, so the happy inhabitants won't lack space to take a stroll, arrange a picnic [*convivium* agitare] a game of ball. With these freaks and thousands of others, their heads are stuffed so full that I expect Jove's brain was just as cramped when he was about to give birth to Pallas and had to borrow the use of Vulcan's axe to get her out. So don't be surprised if at public disputations you see the heads of scholars swathed in bands; it's necessary, or their brains would pop out. (my emphasis)[97]

Here, the theologians are unable to hold their own brains together, much less any sort of Christian community. The "convivium" that the theologians imagine enjoying in their "new world" [novus orbis] would presumably resemble the public disputations of the old world, and thus it would represent the opposite extreme of the *agāpe*, whose meaning Erasmus was so concerned to elucidate when annotating Jude. Indeed, the Listrius commentary on this passage compares the theologians and their fabrication of new worlds to the archheretic Basilides and the Abraxians, who, according to Augustine, fabricated three hundred and sixty-five worlds.

Stultitia's ascent to the third heaven in her peroration is another version of what the theologians are doing when they fabricate new worlds. Her subject in this peroration is the "felicitas" of a small group of fools, who, like the theologians playing ball, try to remove themselves far from the "vulgus hominum."[98] We should thus take her claim to be acting the part of a theologian seriously and not necessarily assume that this ascent is supposed to represent her at her most Christian. For one of the points of the *Moria* is to show how far theology has drifted from the origins and significance of Christianity.

Stultitia's vision of Christianity ecstasy owes much to Platonic attempts in the *Phaedrus* and *Symposium* to distinguish different kinds of *erōs* and elevate some over others, but it has little to do with the kind if *agāpe* that Erasmus elucidated in his annotations on Jude. Indeed, in her peroration Stultitia is ready to dispense with "charitas" altogether. The vulgar [vulgus], she claims, make much of "charitas in liberos, in parentes, in amicos" [charity toward children, parents, and friends].[99] The pious, however, attempt to eradicate these "affectus," too, unless, for instance, "amor" of a parent is really contemplation of the deity as reflected in that parent. Instead of the Stultitia who fostered the mutual charity of fools scratching one another's back, Platonic Stultitia dissolves social bonds.

Throughout the *Moria* expressions such as "me Hercules" had served to associate Stultitia with Hercules, but when she finally dons the lion's skin, it transforms her. Thus, on the one hand, the Herculean Stultitia, like Erasmus, usurps in print the authority of theologians in the interests of a Christianity that is evangelical rather than full of dialectical subtleties. Hence, in 1526 Erasmus could see Luther as folly dressed in a lion's skin; for Luther had merely carried to an extreme Erasmus' own evangelical Christianity—to which, in retrospect, not only the *Paraclesis* but the *Moria,* too, could seem to have lent themselves. But once she truly takes the place of Hercules, Stultitia begins to act like a theologian, and the vehicle for such behavior is Platonism. Her true followers no longer include everybody, but rather a small group that has been separated from the "vulgus."

Erasmus' own moves, however, in the direction of a Platonic withdrawal from Christian agape did not always lead to such extremes. Erasmus' 1522 "Convivium Religiosum" explicitly recasts the *Phaedrus* as well as Christian feasting. In doing so, "Convivium Religiosum" maintains a precarious balance between a religion of withdrawal and what we have seen to be a primary concern of the evangelizing Erasmus—that is, rebuilding the Christian community in the image of the apostolic church. The "Convivium Religiosum" features a gathering of laymen in the country retreat of Eusebius, and the model for this gathering is the colloquy of Socrates and Phaedrus: "How many wonderful things did your Socrates teach to Phaedrus in their rural resting place and learn from in return!"[100] urges Eusebius, and the suburban character of Eusebius' retreat makes it an apt analogue for the situation of Socrates and Phaedrus beyond the walls of Athens in the *Phaedrus.* Moreover, the communal spirit that prevails in this retreat provides an implicit contrast to the behavior of priests and monks, who, as Eusebius puts it, have failed to follow the Pythagorean and Platonic dogma of communism, and thus have remained in the city to pursue profits.[101]

The apparently secular nature of the feast does not, however, last long. For in the "Convivium Religiosum" the Bible replaces the *biblion,* that is, the speech of Lysias, as the primary, albeit not sole, subject of discussion, and passages from the Old and New Testaments as well as from Cicero are interpreted with an equanimity and civility unusual for the time. Despite the anomaly of such civility in 1522, however, within the confines of Eusebius' home, interpretation is a collective and collaborative rather than contentious activity. The collation of scriptural passages, a method of interpretation that Erasmus favored but would employ to no avail against Luther in *De Libero Arbitrio,* makes possible the elucidation of even the most obscure parts of the Bible.

Agāpe prevails in the "convivium," but it does so within carefully circumscribed limits. Thus, Eusebius tells his guests that his home belongs to them as much as to himself: "Tota domus haec mea est, simulque vestra [i.e., my home is yours],"[102] and his hospitality is a version of the adage "Amicorum communia omnia." Similarly, Eusebius has a public [publicus] garden whose gates are almost never shut. Thus, anyone can pick its flowers or drink from its stream at virtually any time.[103]

In addition to *agāpe,* however, Eusebius' feast also recalls the restrictiveness of the third and least charitable stage of Christian conviviality as described in Erasmus' annotations of 1 Corinthians 11. Thus, within Eusebius' public garden is an immured "cultior" garden, which is not open to the public, and within that more cultivated garden is still another enclosure, Eusebius' house. It is within the house that discussions of Scripture take place, and, although Eusebius orders some of the leftovers to be sent to a poor neighbor, he does not invite her to partake of the feast. The feast is not even open to all the inhabitants of the house. Significantly, Eusebius' wife is not invited to partake, and the model for this exclusion is that of Socrates' wife, Xanthippe. Comic violence—Xanthippe overturned the table at a Socratic symposium—constitutes her threat. Clearly Stultitia herself would not be welcome either at this highly Platonized convivium.[104]

Other threats of violence, too, serve to define the boundaries of the feast. Thus, at the end of the convivium, Eusebius leaves the enclosure and goes to resolve a quarrel between "two men, not bad fellows at heart—but both stubborn."[105] He is afraid that if he does not resolve the quarrel, it will turn into a "gang fight." These two men (Luther and the pope? Luther and the emperor?) are said to be friends, but clearly the spirit of friendship that animates Eusebius and his guests does not animate them. Similarly, the walls of the room where Eusebius and his friends eat contains some admonitory images—Alexander the Great murdering his best friend at a feast and the battle of the centaurs and Lapiths. One of the galleries in Eusebius' garden even has a picture of an eagle devouring a rabbit while a beetle, the "scarabeus" from "Scarabeus aquilam quaerit," protests in vain. In that adage, the eagle's devouring of the rabbit had inaugurated the war of the beetle and the eagle.[106]

A remarkable coexistence, however, of liberty of speech and peacefulness characterizes Eusebius' home, which is also described as a palace [regia] and where he is said to reign [regnare] by living as he pleases [Et si regnat, qui libere vivit ex animi sententia, hic plane regno].[107] This freedom extends beyond criticisms of corrupt monks and the superstitious veneration of the sacraments to include the doctrine of evangelical liberty that Erasmus had accused Luther of disseminating irresponsibly rather than cautiously and under the right circumstances. For while explicating Proverbs 21:1–3—"the king's heart is in the hands of the Lord"—Timotheus argues that such a king is not literally a monarch but rather a perfect man [vir perfectus] who has subdued all his affections and is therefore not bound by human laws. Instead, like the "homo spiritualis" of Romans 14, this "king" judges all things.[108] Such freedom must have had strong Lutheran resonances in 1522. Thus, a year after the "Convivium" was published, More's *Responsio ad Lutherum,* argued against what More perceived as Luther's desire to eliminate all law and to substitute for it the judgment of the individual.[109]

Eusebius is himself a likely candidate for the kind of kingship described by Timotheus, and the "convivium" allows a group of rather spiritual laymen to judge a number of things independent of church authority. Nevertheless, checks on such judgments are included in the "Convivium." Thus, expounding the Pauline dictum—"omnia mihi licent, sed non omnia expediunt"—Eulalius argues that "Evangelica libertas" must be qualified by considerations of "charitas." That is, one person's evangelical liberty must not lead another astray.[110] Similarly, Eusebius' interpretation of the verse from Proverbs—"the king's heart is in the hand of the Lord"—suggests that Christian liberty should not turn into an assault upon temporal authorities: "It's not that kings don't sin against their people and do them great harm, but that no man is authorized to condemn them [cuius auctoritate condemnantur]—though of course no man, however powerful, can escape the judgment of God."[111] In other words, the scarab must merely watch rather than try to prevent the eagle's rapacity.

In addition to being a layman's answer to the corruption of monastic orders,[112] Eusebius' home is also a giant Silenus image whose interior is not meant to be exposed to the outside world, which can penetrate only as far as the public garden. Indeed, the enclosure of the "convivium" illustrates the kind of environment Erasmus meant when he described his New Testament as designed to be read "privately" at home rather than divulgated. Privacy, however, clearly does not mean isolation or solitude for Erasmus, but rather it evokes the intimate world of an idealized community of humanist readers. Sequestered in Platonic fashion from the many, this humanist community owes something to the isolation of the pious from the "vulgus hominum" at the end of the *Moria*. Nevertheless, Eusebius and his friends do not eliminate charity entirely as the ecstatic Christians do. Rather, the piety of the "convivium" restricts the scope of charity, and thus it enables charity and evangelical liberty to coexist.

Eusebius' community of friends is a carefully circumscribed perfect world, and its sequestration comes close to matching that of More's Utopia. Indeed, the "convivium" that Eusebius and his friends enjoy may owe something to Utopian conviviality as described by Raphael Hythlodaeus in 1516. Eusebius, however, offers a revealing contrast to More, the religious controversialist of the 1520s and 1530s. For as we shall see, More was skeptical of the possibility of successfully mediating between Utopia and the arena of Protestant-Catholic polemic. At least, More wanted to keep the two realms separate. Reviewing *Utopia* during the 1520s and 1530s, More will prove to have more in common with the Erasmus who wished that he had never written the *Moria* than with the optimistic Eusebius.

TWO

Heresy and Utopia

The 1566 Louvain edition of More's Latin works begins with the epitaph that More wrote for himself. Among other achievements this epitaph lists the following: "neque nobilibus ... invisus neque iniucundus populo furibus autem, homicidis, heretisque molestus" [neither hateful to the nobility or unpopular; to thieves, homicides, and heretics, however, harmful].[1] This triad of thieves, murderers, and heretics defines the limit of More's ability to be what Erasmus termed an infinitely agreeable "omnium horarum hominem," or, as it was translated into English, "man for all seasons." This infernal triad also indicates the two kinds of law, both secular and religious, that concerned the English humanist whose course of honors led him to become the first lay chancellor of England and its most accomplished writer against Protestant heresy.

The author of *Utopia,* however, is difficult to discern in More's epitaph, although its reference to theft and murder might have recalled Raphael's discussion of the punishment of these two crimes in *Utopia.* The Louvain edition of More's Latin works contains *Utopia* and More's other prereformation writings as well as his *Responsio ad Lutherum* and the Tower work, *De Tristia Christi.* More's epitaph, however, seems to make only a passing allusion to literary works such as *Utopia* or the *Epigrammata.* The epitaph describes More as "in litteris utcunque versatus" [in every way versed in letters], but it does not detail his accomplishments in this recognizably humanist field of "letters."

The purpose of the epitaph, however, was not to celebrate these literary accomplishments but to enable More to get the last word in his fight against heresy. Thus, the 1533 letter from More to Erasmus that originally included the epitaph describes More's need to defend himself against the rumor of his having resigned the chancellorship unwillingly. Not for his own sake, however, does More claim to defend himself but because he is the author of books in the vernacular against the advocates of contentious dogmas and must therefore maintain the "integritas nominis mei."[2] More writes to Erasmus of an ambitious willingness [ambitiose] to display his hatred of heresy,[3] and this ambition extends to More's need to protect himself even after he has abandoned his "cursus honorum." Thus, the epitaph will provide a counterargument [redargueret] if anyone tries to taint More or, through him, orthodoxy itself.

More's epitaph and letter to Erasmus offer salient reminders that he, in contrast to Erasmus, was officially and unambiguously involved in the battle against Protestant heresy. In addition to More's defense of Henry VIII against Luther in the 1523 *Responsio ad Lutherum,* More may even have played a role in determining the shape of the King's own *Assertio Septem Sacramentorum* (1521), for which Henry earned the title, "defender of the faith."[4] More became a noted vernacular controversialist, too. In 1528 Cuthbert Tunstal, Bishop of London and a minor character in Thomas More's *Utopia,* praised More as England's answer to Demosthenes, and he gave More a license to read heretical books in order to refute them in the vernacular.[5] During the 1520s, More oversaw the burning of Tyndale's New Testament, interrogated heretics in his Chelsea house, and in accordance with Tunstal's commission, wrote polemical works in English such as *A Dialogue Concerning Heresies* (1529) and *The Confutation of Tyndale's Answer* (1532). Even after his resignation of the chancellorship in 1532, More continued to debate heretics and defend his reputation, not only on his tombstone, but also in works such as *The Apology* and *The Answer to a Poisoned Book.*

The correspondence of More and Erasmus during the 1530s reveals the continued keenness of More's commitment to this debate. Thus, in one letter More complains to Erasmus of a "hereticus" Tyndale who is nowhere and everywhere, "nusquam et ubique," and he associates Tyndale with the "secta" of Wyclif.[6] More also laments the work of those who, by badly translating and interpreting the Bible [male vertendo scripturas et deterius interpretando], were introducing into England every variety of heresy from the Netherlands [omne genus haereseos e Belgica].[7] More's reference to the Netherlands as a source of heresy targets Tyndale, who, at approximately the same time as More received a license to examine and refute heretical books, settled in Antwerp and began using its considerable printing resources to provide further material for More's scrutiny.

Despite More's apparently passing reference to humanist "litterae" on his tombstone, however, religious controversy did not allow More to forget humanist "letters" as completely as he might have liked. In particular, *Utopia* and Raphael Hythlodaeus were crucial vulnerabilities of the public More of the late 1520s and early 1530s.[8] For like Erasmus, More feared the possibility of his own words being turned against him in the writings of his opponents. In particular, *Utopia* is a subtext to More's debate with Tyndale, as More's remark about Tyndale being both "nowhere" and everywhere would suggest. Indeed, the careers of Tyndale and the author of *Utopia* overlapped in some intriguing ways. Most importantly, *Utopia,* whose discussions are set in Antwerp and first place of publication was Louvain, made the Netherlands a point of origin for what we will see to be a "heretical" version of Christianity, although it did so in Latin, not the vernacular. Nevertheless, albeit sequestered in Latin, this Utopian Christianity might have retrospectively seemed to anticipate some elements of the heresy that Protestant heretics were disseminating into England from the Netherlands and other Continental locations during the 1520s and 1530s.

In the *Confutation of Tyndale's Answer,* More wrote that in "these days in which men by their own defaute misconstrue and take harm of the very scripture of god," he would burn the *Moria* or some unspecified "works" of his own if anyone would translate them into English.[9] More does not mention *Utopia* by name here, but the passage would certainly have brought *Utopia* to mind since it was so closely associated with the *Moria.* Writing to Erasmus in 1532, More gave some indication of what he meant by "misconstruction" in the *Confutation.* In this letter, More reiterated and elaborated upon a point that Erasmus had himself made in the *Detectio:* according to More, if Erasmus had earlier known what pestilent "haereses" were going to arise, he would have "more gently" [mitius] proposed certain things in his pre-Reformation writings. But, More hastens to point out, Erasmus is in good company as far as heretical misconstructions of his own works are concerned. For the "ecclesiae doctores," the apostles, the evangelists, and Christ himself were also subject to the same fate of being heretically misinterpreted in ways that they did not foresee.[10]

Erasmus' work on the editing of the New Testament and doctors of the church such as Jerome, however, makes More's analogy a particularly close one. For not only were Protestant heretics using scripture to make their points, but they were also exploiting Erasmus' work on scripture to do so. Likewise, More's implied equivalence between misconstructions of his own works in translation and the "very scripture of God" may also be more than a convenient parallel. For *Utopia* is also indebted to Erasmus' efforts to use the Bible and the model of the early church as a tool of reform. This debt may be in part a function of timing: More wrote his letter to Martin Dorp defending Erasmus' life and scriptural labors at approximately the same time as he was composing Book 2 of *Utopia* in the Netherlands.[11] In particular, the apparent heterodoxies of Utopian religion and society will become clearer if measured against the scriptural standard that Erasmus did so much to establish.

But the misconstruction, or, to put it more benevolently, reception of *Utopia* was an issue that More addressed even prior to entering the lists against heretics, and he did so most evidently in *Utopia* itself. The marginalia of the Latin *Utopia* may not explicate the text to the same degree that the Listrius commentary on the *Moria* does, but, since *Utopia* is a dialogue and more generally a text that endlessly comments on itself, the interaction of its speakers and parts serves the function of a more elaborate marginal apparatus. Yet, as with Erasmian texts such as the *Moria,* the self-commentary of *Utopia* does not necessarily yield a middle way between extremes. Rather, cautions often serve to highlight rather than eliminate the risks of radicalism.

SHOUTING FROM THE ROOFTOPS

The center of Utopian society is Erasmus' first adage writ large. *Utopia,* however, does not merely combine Christian and Platonic communism, but it also provides an elaborate depiction of a society that, unbeknownst to itself, replicates several features of the early church underscored by Erasmus' scriptural exegesis. Nevertheless, *Utopia* also critiques, primarily in the character of Raphael Hythlodaeus, the reckless religiosity of those who preach their message without any regard to time, place, or circumstances. This critique cautions readers of *Utopia* that the passage from Utopian institutions to those of a particular time and place would be more difficult than Raphael imagines, and such a critique would later prove useful to More in his castigations of heretics, too.

Utopian society itself warns against an imprudent Christian zeal. Thus, while the Utopians are said to be far more tolerant of other religions than the Europeans, the one person who is identified as having been prosecuted for religious beliefs in book 2 of *Utopia* is guilty of inciting a riot rather than of any particular religious offense:

Only one of our company, when I was there, was interfered with. As soon as he was baptized, in spite of our advice to the contrary, he spoke publicly of Christ's religion with more zeal than discretion [prudentia]. He began to grow so warm in his preaching that . . . he condemned all the rest. . . . When he had long been preaching in this style, they arrested him, tried him, and convicted him not for despising their religion but for stirring up a riot among the people [excitati in populo tumultus].[12]

The Utopians are less concerned with what this preacher says than the potentially tumultuous consequences of his harangue. Despite their recent conversion to Christianity, the Utopians still follow their eponymous lawgiver, Utopus, who instituted religious toleration primarily in order to preserve peace. Utopus is the kind of moderate skeptic that Luther would later accuse Erasmus of being. Utopus dares to define rashly nothing concerning religion [religionis . . . de qua nihil est ausus temere definire], and he forbids the followers of one religion to impose their beliefs on others, lest struggles be decided by "arms and riots [tumultus]" and the best religion be lost, "like grain choked by thorns and underbrush" (an allusion to the parable of the sower). The truth, as Utopus sees it, will emerge as the result of harmonious social conditions rather than dogmatic insistence.[13] The Utopians, in turn, require even Christian preachers to submit to certain standards of behavior and to exercise "discretion" [prudentia] in public.

Although narrated and endorsed by Raphael himself, the Utopian prosecution of an overly zealous Christian preacher, nevertheless, serves as something of a corrective to Raphael's own ideal of Christian preaching, as described in book 1. Raphael expresses this ideal during the Dialogue on Counsel after his triumphant conclusion that there is no "locus" [room] for his philosophy at court—a pun that anticipates the description of a country whose name means "nowhere." "More," on the contrary, urges a "civilior" [more practical for the statesman] philosophy, and he enjoins Raphael to play his part at court "cum decoro" [appropriately] and to act "ea fabula quae in manibus est" [the play in hand]. "More" encapsulates his "civil" philosophy in the phrase "obliquus ductus" [indirect approach], which will supposedly be able to lead the monarch more effectively than the direct approach advocated by Raphael.[14]

Raphael, however, goes on to reject the advice of "More" and, more generally, the rhetorical strategy of accommodation:

Truly, if all the things by which the perverse morals of men have come to seem odd are to be dropped as unusual and absurd, we must dissemble [dissimulemus opportet] almost all the doctrines of Christ [pleraque omnia quae Christus docuit]. Yet he forbade us to dissemble them to the extent that what He whispered in the ears of His disciples [quae ipse in aures insurasset suis], He commanded to be preached openly on the housetops [palam in tectis iusserit praedicari].[15]

Here, Raphael is making use of Matthew 10:27, Luke 12:3, and the Erasmian adage, "In angulo," which opposes "whispering in a corner" [in angulo susurrantem] to preaching from the rooftops, to argue that apostolic Christianity was a less decorum-conscious religion than its sixteenth-century descendant.[16] In contrast to the open preaching of the apostles, Raphael goes on to say, "[P]reachers, crafty men that they are, finding that men grievously disliked to have their morals adjusted to the rule of Christ . . . accommodated [accommodaverunt] His teaching to men's morals as if it were a rule of soft lead."[17] In Raphael's view, such dissimulation on the part of preachers provides the model for the kind of deceit or "obliquus ductus" that the humanist must practice at the courts of princes.

The "rule of lead" symbolizing such accommodation can be traced to the "Lesbian rule" that Aristotle, in book 5 of the *Ethics,* uses to distinguish between the flexibility of equity and the rigor of strict justice. There, Aristotle argued for the necessity of an equitable accommodation of the universal rules of law to particular cases and circumstances. On the other hand, Erasmus in the *Adagia* made the "Lesbian rule" a way of denoting corruption and, in particular, the lax morals of courts. Thus, princes, according to Erasmus, "preposterously" make their behavior suit the "mores" of the people they govern rather than forcing the people to conform "ad principis arbitrium." Furthermore, these princes may have ceased measuring their own behavior by any real rule of conduct. Although, as Kathy Eden has shown, Erasmus is in favor of equitable accommodation as a principle of scriptural hermeneutics, nevertheless, in the adage, "Lesbia regula," Erasmus, like Raphael Hythlodaeus, emphasizes the tendency of excessive accommodation to erode moral standards.[18]

Raphael seems to stand on at least some of the ethical high ground when he and "More" discuss the virtues and vices of accommodation and decorum, but the Utopian punishment of an overly zealous Christian preacher suggests that shouting on the rooftops should not be taken to the point of popular tumults. At the very least, the Utopian banishment of this zealot indicates that the Utopians are more attuned than Raphael to the often intractable consequences of religious upheaval. In this case, the Utopians may reveal as much about the authorial More as Raphael and "More" the character, and even in 1516 More had reason to fear the consequences of religiously inspired popular tumults. By 1516, Lollard preachers had been a problem in England for over a century, and the death (possibly murder) of the Lollard Richard Hunne in 1514 had caused such a powerful reaction in London that More continued to feel the need to engage it in his later combats with Lutheran heresy.[19]

Raphael's name further qualifies the reception of his message.[20] For this name, which denotes the healing of God, promises divine salvation, but, since Raphael's instrument of healing is his speech, his name would also have suggested the duality of language, both medicinal drug and poison, to a humanist audience. (Indeed, the word *pharmaca* appears in book 2 of

Utopia as a potential synonym for the Latin *venena,* i.e., "poisons.").[21] Thus, Raphael offers a form of logotherapy to a diseased Christian Europe, and, as we shall see, he even suggests that, without his brand of healing, the sickness is incurable. Nevertheless, his brand of healing may also be lethal.

As a promise of divine salvation, the name Raphael necessarily evokes its source, the Book of Tobit. There, Raphael is the angel responsible for curing Tobit's blindness, guiding his son to a wife, and finally reuniting son and father. But Raphael Hythlodaeus is no angel, and he is not even a priest. Consequently, the religious basis of his own authority as healer and guide is less clear than that of his biblical namesake. Moreover, Tobit was itself a part of the Apocrypha, which, as we saw in the Listrius commentary on *Moriae Encomium,* were not only of doubtful authority but could also pose the same exegetical problems as the rhetorical sophistication of Lucian. That is, to understand the Apocrypha readers might have to be able to recognize devil's advocacy and not mistake such advocacy for the word of God.

E. H. Gombrich has noted that the Book of Tobit is the only place in the Bible where the angel Raphael discloses his name and nature to mortals.[22] This revelation occurs near the end of Tobit when Raphael, hitherto disguised as a mortal, doffs this disguise and shows Tobit and Tobias his angelic nature. Raphael also makes manifest to them, in Jerome's translation, the "occultus sermo" between Raphael and God concerning the long-delayed remedying of Tobit's plight. The Book of Tobit takes place during the Assyrian captivity of the Jews, and thus Raphael's revelation shows that God is not only still with Tobit during his own tribulations but with the Jewish people as well. Indeed, the angel Raphael does offer something of a justification of the ways of God to man in Tobit, and this theodicy may help to explain the importance of this angel in Milton's *Paradise Lost.*

In Erasmus' *Encomium Medicinae* (1517), on the other hand, the medicinal powers of Raphael give him an explicitly Christological significance:

. . . the most convincing commendation of all: that the same Christ when still unknown to the world, gradually worked his way into the minds and hearts of men, not by gold, not by authority, but by healing the sick? What he, being God, could do at will the physician strives to imitate as far as his human powers allow. They too participate in the divine nature of healing, by virtue of the powers conferred by God to this end. Did not the great Apostle Paul, in prescribing for his follower Timothy a little wine to fortify his weak stomach, openly play the role of physician? But why should this be remarkable in the case of the Apostle, when the angel Raphael cured the blindness of Tobit, and thus even found fame among students of the apocryphal scriptures? O heavenly and truly sacred science of medicine, whose name does honour to holy minds such as these![23]

Erasmus underscores here the rhetorical efficacy of Christ's medicinal powers. Christ's healing of the sick was not only good per se, but it was persuasive: through healing Christ was able to work his way into the minds and hearts of potential converts. So too Raphael finds "fame" through his medicinal powers. Thus, Erasmus' encomium, even as it links Raphael, Paul, Christ, and human physicians in the "divine" undertaking of medicine, also raises the problem of the easily misused *pharmakon*, which haunts Erasmus' discussions of language, writing, and rhetoric. Nevertheless, we have seen that in the *Ratio* and elsewhere Erasmus used Paul and Christ as figures of the potential and (for Erasmus) necessary compatibility of Christian logotherapy and the classical standard of decorum. As he appears in the *Encomium Medicinae*, Raphael, too, is suggestive of the benign efficacy of such logotherapy.

Like Erasmus, however, More in *Utopia* not only celebrates logotherapy, but he also underscores its dangers. Thus, for instance, the Utopian priests and magistrates exhort [hortantur] the incurably sick to seek a voluntary death,[24] and those persuaded ("[h]aec quibus persuaserint") either starve themselves to death or are put to sleep. Here, the ability of the word to heal becomes paradoxical. For on the one hand, the Utopian priests combine religion, medicine, and rhetoric, as do the angel Raphael and Christ in Erasmus' description. On the other hand, Utopia's religious leadership takes this combination to an extreme that, albeit perhaps not so shocking to modern sensibilities, was abhorrent to orthodox sixteenth-century Christianity. Indeed, in the seventeenth century John Donne would see *Utopia* as a supporting text when he attempted to wrestle with the question of suicide in *Biathanatos*.

But the full import of this kind of persuasion becomes clear in comparison to Raphael's rejection of palliative responses to political problems in book 1:

Special legislation might be passed to prevent the monarch from being over-mighty and the people overweening; likewise, that public offices should not be solicited with gifts, nor be put up for sale . . .

By this type of legislation, I maintain, as sick bodies which are past cure [deploratae valetudinis] can be kept up by medical treatments [assidua fomenta], so these evils, too, can be alleviated. . . . There is no hope, however, of a cure and a return to a healthy condition as long as each individual is master of his own property. Nay, while you are intent upon the cure of one part, you make worse the malady of the other parts.[25]

Here, communism, which Raphael has just proposed as the only solution to social ills, constitutes a repudiation of conventional medicine in favor of something far more drastic. Raphael could be understood as exhorting the political counterpart to voluntary euthanasia. That is, he would be urging the death of European politics as they were then constituted and a move to something entirely different. But, as "More" recognizes, the danger of Raphael's cure is that he may simply kill the body politic and leave no basis for any kind of social or political order. Thus, in response to Raphael's elaborate medicinal trope, "More" argues that communism would remove any "locus" [place] for the authority of magistrates and leave instead only perpetual slaughter and "seditio."[26]

Raphael's own favorite maxims concerning death are also pertinent to an evaluation of his credibility as an interpreter of Utopian society. Thus, according to Peter Giles, Raphael is himself not full of cares [curiosus] concerning his grave, but instead he is always repeating two aphorisms: "Caelo tegitur qui non habet urnam" [he who has no grave is covered by the sky] and "undique ad superos tantundem esse viae" [From all places it is the same distance to heaven].[27] Raphael uses these maxims to express his own indifference to death, burial, and earthly geography, and he also emphasizes heaven as the only place that matters. Given Raphael's professed inability to see any differences between terrestial locations, his attraction to a best form of republic that exists "nowhere" makes sense. But Raphael's preoccupation with the way [via] to heaven then raises the question of whether his discovery of a nowhere republic constitutes a detour from this upward journey or perhaps a dangerously attractive shortcut.

The old name of Utopia is suggestive of heavenly (albeit perhaps spuriously so) qualities. For before Utopus' conquest, the name of Utopia was Abraxia, and, as we have seen from the Listrius commentary on the *Moria*, Abraxia was the name of the highest heaven of the archheretic Basilides.[28] Indeed, at least one sixteenth-century reader described Utopia as being, if not heaven, at least en route to it. Thus, in a letter prefacing *Utopia*, the French humanist Guillaume Bude, borrowing and modifying a word used to denote the New Jerusalem in Revelations, dubbed Utopia Hagnopolis and extolled the "heavenly life" [caelestis vita] that its inhabitants led. Bude went on to locate Utopia between heaven and earth: it is as far above this world [sic supra mundi huius cogniti colluvionem] as it is below the heavens [ut infra caelum].[29] Likewise, Bude suggests that, if we are to believe Raphael (as Richard Sylvester points out, an important qualification), Astraea the goddess of justice has not yet made her way [necdum in caelum pervenisse] to the sky but has instead remained behind on the island of Utopia.[30]

Even this proximity to heaven, however, is not good enough for the

Utopians, who, we are told just before Raphael's peroration, pray to die and thus to "go to God" [ad deum pervadere] sooner rather than later.[31] The treatment of death, nevertheless, in Utopia is generally hard to distinguish from what Bude identified as the tantalizing Utopian prospect of enjoying a "celestial" life on or near to earth. Thus, significantly, the Utopian dead are supposed to return to Utopia to see friends, and they do so, we are told, for reasons of "mutuus amor charitasque" [mutual love and charity].[32] The Utopian belief in this practice and the virtue that motivates it suggest that the Utopians see the boundary between Utopia and heaven as permeable.

Before he wrote *Utopia*, More lectured on Augustine's *City of God* in a London church. Yet the ambiguous situation of Utopia and the angelic namesake and mission of its ambassador, Raphael Hythlodaeus, offered to Bude and perhaps others the possibility, or perhaps the temptation, of at least partially dissolving what for Augustine was an absolute binary between the City of God and that of Man. Indeed, Augustine's own discussion of suicide in the *City of God,* which More would both subtly and explicitly use in *A Dialogue of Comfort against Tribulation,*[33] raises, albeit only to dismiss, the possibility of suicide's providing a shortcut to an unearthly life. Thus, Augustine argues that, if suicide were really permissible, then men would have to be exhorted [hortandi sint homines] to kill themselves immediately after baptism in order to avoid a life full of temptations to sin.[34] Such exhortations would replace the usual postbaptism lectures [exhortationes] on the need to live a good life, but Augustine goes on to argue that this scenario is unspeakable [nefas], much less worthy of enactment.

Raphael's final praise of Utopia, however, does include the implication that Utopia makes possible the life free of sin that Augustine's hypothetical suicides are persuaded to seek. Raphael asserts that in Utopia the roots of pride and ambition have been removed, even as he also laments the stubborn persistence of pride elsewhere. For in other countries pride is so deeply fixed in the human breast that it cannot be easily removed, and this irremediability of pride explains why, despite the authority of Christ, the rest of the world has not adopted Utopian institutions.[35] Raphael may here betray his own failure to understand Utopian society, many of whose institutions seem predicated upon the need to combat pride rather than its absence. Nevertheless, Raphael's peroration presents Utopia as precisely the kind of paradoxical temptation of a sinless life that Augustine warns against in his strictures concerning suicide.

The potentially suicidal character of Raphael Hythlodaeus' logotherapy inevitably highlights issues of secrecy, too. That is, to whom should such a dangerous medicine be administered? More's decision to write *Utopia* in Latin indicates that he did not want Raphael's description of Utopia shouted from the rooftops, but, despite its defense by "More," the court does not figure in *Utopia* as the ideal forum for humanist radicalism either. Instead, an Erasmian community of friends, Giles, Raphael, and "More," provides such a forum, and this community mediates between the openness of the rooftops and the intense secrecy of court deliberations that Raphael derides in book 1. More and Giles act as a kind of filter, approving some and yet rejecting much of what Raphael says.

More and Giles, however, do give Raphael the kind of hearing that he would not get at court, and their willingness to take his ideas seriously marks them as belonging to a more open-minded group than, for instance, Cardinal Morton's retinue. Nevertheless, the garden where the three men talk in Latin is necessarily a sequestered environment, too. With the interesting exception of More's pupil, John Clement, the garden contains only grown men. More reaches the garden after leaving behind his family for a time just as Raphael inaugurates his own travels by renouncing his patrimony and thereby permanently relieving himself of further familial obligations. To get into the garden one also has to have contacts. Thus, Raphael does not simply tell his story to More, but rather he is first introduced to More by Giles.

In the form of its translation in Caxton's *The Golden Legend* (1483), the Book of Tobit was itself widely available in the vernacular, and a passage from this translation provides a model for the problem of secrecy as it affects Raphael Hythlodaeus:

> Then said he [i.e., Raphael] to them privily: To hide the sacrament of a king it is good but for to show the works of God and acknowledge them it is worshipful. Oration and prayer it is good . . . and more than to set up treasures of gold. . . . I show to you therefore the truth, and I shall not hide from you the secret word.[36]

This passage contains the germ of what we have seen to be Raphael Hythlodaeus' rejection of the councils of kings as a place for his brand of religion and philosophy in book 1 of *Utopia*. The courts of kings in both *Utopia* and Tobit are places of secrecy whereas the word of God demands disclosure. The word of God may also demand disobedience to the king. Thus, in Tobit the monarch figures are those of the Assyrian captors of the Jews, whose commands Tobit, "more dreading God than the king," ignores in order to bury the Jewish dead. Similarly, Raphael's comparison of overly pliable courtiers to bad preachers suggests that, if revealed at court, the word of God might amount to an act of defiance.

Like the angel Raphael, Raphael Hythlodaeus offers a discourse that purports both to be a revelation and to be distinct from the affairs of monarchs. Indeed, the "sermo" of Raphael Hythlodaeus concerns a polity that for Raphael is only nominally monarchical.[37] Yet both the "sermo" of Raphael Hythlodaeus and the secret "sermo" or "word" of the angel Raphael hover between divulgation and secrecy. Thus, just as Raphael Hythlodaeus offers his own "sermo" to the select and circumscribed audience of More and Giles, so the angel Raphael reveals the "secret word" of God "privily" to Tobias and Tobit. The disclosure of this "secret word" to an audience of two is not the same thing as its dissemination.

Published in book form, however, Raphael Hythlodaeus' discourse could not remain so sequestered, and this lack of sequestration figures in More's prefatory letter to Giles as the risk of making Utopia known, or "vulgata":

By making know the commonwealth of Utopia [Utopiensium per me *vulgata* republica], I should certainly dislike to forestall him [i.e. Raphael] and to rob his narrative of the flower and charm of novelty.

Nevertheless, to tell the truth, I myself have not yet made up my mind whether I shall publish it at all [an sim omnino aediturus]. So varied are the tastes of mortals, so peevish the characters of some, so ungrateful their dispositions . . . [my emphasis][38]

A catalog of such ungrateful and hypercritical readers, a hydralike multitude, follows and reaches its nadir with those who "sit in taverns, and over their cups criticize the talents of authors" and do so "just as they please" [utcumque lubitum est].[39] Most irritatingly, these readers, even as they exploit the vulnerability of the author, make their remarks "out of shot," a reference to an Erasmian adage.[40] Nevertheless, "More" does order his book to provide such a diverse group of readers with a "feast" at their own "expense" [tuis impensis epulum]—a kind of indiscriminate conviviality that recalls the *agapai*. Yet, as described by More, this indiscriminate conviviality also bears a resemblance to the drunken uproariousness into which the early *agapai* had, according to Erasmus' Paul, degenerated.

More's fantasy of the tavern reader may be an exaggeration of his vulnerability in 1516. But Tyndale's own description, in his preface to his translation of the five books of Moses (1530), of his attempt to find a "place" and patron for his project of translating the New Testament into English does provide a demonstration of the Reformation vulnerability of Tunstal, Erasmus, and More to being rewritten in ways that they might not have appreciated. This description also indicates one manner in which a Lutheran reformer, whether wittingly or not, might reenact the uncompromising stance of Raphael Hythlodaeus:

As I this thought, the bishop of London came to my remembrance, whom Erasmus (whose tongue maketh of little gnats great elephants, and lifteth up above the stars whosoever giveth him a little exhibition) praiseth exceedingly, among other, in his Annotations on the New Testament, for his great learning. Then thought I, if I might come to this man's service, I were happy. [Tyndale goes on to describe the presentation of a translation of Isocrates to Tunstal.]

Whereupon my lord [Tunstal] answered me, his house was full; he had more than he could well find; and advised me to seek in London, where I could not lack a service. And so in London I abode almost a year . . . and beheld the pomp of our prelates . . . and understood at the last not only that there was no room in my lord of London's palace to translate the new Testament, but also that there was no place to do it in all England.[41]

In other words, before leaving England for Germany (as well as, later, the Netherlands) and offering his English New Testament to the swarm of German printers that Erasmus castigated in the 1526 "Festina lente" and *De Lingua,* Tyndale approached Tunstal as a possible patron of his translation. Tyndale did so because he connected Tunstal to Erasmian humanism and, in particular, the application of this humanism to scriptural exegesis. David Daniell points out that Erasmus does not actually praise Tunstal in the *Annotationes,* even though Tunstal did assist Erasmus in his New Testament scholarship.[42] But *Utopia,* which does contain a brief encomium of Tunstal, linked Tunstal to Erasmian humanism.[43]

By selecting Tunstal as a possible patron, Tyndale demonstrated his own faith in the printed word and the associations that it could create between people. Tyndale, however, demonstrated this faith even as he was in 1530 using print for a somewhat different purpose, that of publicly disassociating himself from Tunstal, the "pomp" of English prelates, and (as Tyndale saw it) an overly servile Erasmian humanism, able to flatter gnats into thinking they possessed the weight and importance of elephants.[44] Thus, on the one hand, Tyndale assumed that if Tunstal was praised in a text such as the *Annotationes* or *Utopia,* Tunstal would necessarily support a project whose goal was to carry the work of the *Annotationes* even further. From this perspective, then, Tyndale's description of his bid for Tunstal's patronage is really an account of Tyndale's failure to become a part of a particular humanist network. By Tyndale in 1530, at least, is also able to invert this failure and turn it into evidence of his superiority. Not possessing Erasmus' craven and duplicitous eloquence, Tyndale describes himself as being unable to gain what is anyway a dubious benefit, the patronage of an English bishop.

Tyndale's rejection of Erasmian humanism, however, disguises his indebtedness to it. For disavowing Tunstal and Erasmus, he also recalls the unwillingness of Raphael Hythlodaeus to serve the powerful in *Utopia*. As we have seen, Raphael's own experience at the table of the English prelate, Cardinal Morton, helps to convince him that there is no "locus philosophiae" [no place for philosophy] among rulers, and thus Raphael must find a "nowhere" for philosophy in the New World. Likewise, Tyndale, after beholding the pomp of English prelates, casts himself in the mold of the fictional Raphael and concludes that there is "no room" for his New Testament in Tunstal's palace and "no place" for it in all of England. But this conclusion leads Tyndale to the nearby tumult of Germany and its printers rather than to the remoteness of the New World, and, more generally, it causes Tyndale to break with the Erasmian humanism that gave him his initial impetus. Nevertheless, Tyndale's uncompromising stance echoes a humanist literary source even as he breaks with this humanism.

Tyndale, however, was not the only Protestant reformer to repeat the unwillingness to compromise of More's Raphael. Luther, too, was quite capable of such inflexibility. Indeed, parts of Luther's debate with Erasmus resemble the disagreement between "More" and Raphael in *Utopia*. But neither Erasmus nor Luther had to be consciously imitating *Utopia* for this resemblance to occur. More likely, both the disagreement between "More" and Raphael as well as the Erasmus-Luther debate owed much of their substance to similar contradictions within Erasmian humanism.

Responding to Erasmus during their debate on the will, Luther used much the same language as Raphael Hythlodaeus, but he used this language to argue in favor of divulging Christian doctrine, as Raphael had only done implicitly. Truth and doctrine [veritas et doctrina], according to Luther, must always be preached [praedicanda] and never slanted [obliquanda]. For this doctrine is a "virga rectitudinis" [a straight branch, i.e., the opposite to the Lesbian rule], and thus it is meant to be divulgated and reign [vulgari et regnare]. Indeed, Luther also notes that Paul, too, did not want difficult aspects of Christian doctrine to be preached "in angulum," and he uses terms such as "invulgari" and "in publicum" to describe the alternative to "in angulum."[45]

In the "Preface to the Reader" at the outset of his *The Obedience of a Christian Man* (1528), Tyndale makes a similar argument in favor of reading the scripture in English:

Nay, say they, scripture is so hard, that thou couldst never understand it but by the doctors. That is, I must measure the meteyard by the cloth. Here be twenty cloths of divers lengths and divers breadths: how shall I be sure of the length of the meteyard by them? I suppose rather, I must be first sure of the length of the meteyard, and thereby measure and judge of the cloths.[46]

"Meteyard" is Tyndale's version of Luther's "virga rectitudinis" and the notion of Christian doctrine that Raphael Hythlodaeus opposes to the flexibility of the Lesbian rule in *Utopia*. Tyndale, however, here divulges the measure to its farthest extreme. Not only does the preacher shout Christian doctrine from the rooftops and thereby rigidly apply Christian doctrine to the human institutions, but each reader of scripture has the means to judge the authority of doctors. In Tyndale's formulation, the measure has become a truly universal one.[47]

THE HUNT FOR HERESY

Defending the execution of Charles I against what was supposed to be a book written by the dead king, John Milton described what he saw as the disadvantages of trying to confute monarchs in print:

Kings have gain'd glorious titles from their Favourers by writing against private men, as Henry the 8th did against Luther, but no man ever gain'd much honour by writing against a king, as not usually meeting with that force of Argument in such Courtly antagonists, which to convince might add to his reputation.[48]

Milton, however, made an international reputation for himself as a defender of regicide, and Luther, too, gained notoriety, if not glory, from his willingness to attack a king in *Contra Henricum* (1522). In effect, Luther used the printed page as a kind of pulpit from which to assault publicly both the pope and Henry, and in so doing he made Raphael's shouting from the rooftops a louder and more indecorous activity than ever before. Luther's willingness to employ his vituperative skills against secular and religious authority also offered a vivid demonstration of what Erasmus and More had long seen as the difficulty, if not impossibility, of keeping attacks on church and state separate.

Luther was never the advocate of lawlessness and disobedience that More made him seem in the *Responsio*. Both before and after the Peasants' Revolt Luther emphasized obedience to secular authority. Yet we have seen that even in a work such as "On Temporal Authority" Luther could combine exhortations to obedience with rather inflammatory denunciations of secular princes. With similar ambiguity, Tyndale's *The Obedience of a Christian Man* (1528), which More termed Tyndale's "holy boke of dysobedience," advised obedience to a king "though he be the greatest tyrant in the world."[49] Moreover, Luther had demonstrated the ability of the vituperative language of printed polemics to level, to some degree, differences of status between disputants, who became equally vulnerable to insult.[50] Indeed, Luther amusingly began his *Contra Henricum* with the observation that Henry proved the truth of the Erasmian adage that one ought to be born either a king or a fool [aut regem aut fatuum nasci opportuit],[51] and he then went on to claim that his purpose in *Contra Henricum* was to smear the majesty of the English king with dung.[52]

The *Responsio,* which was published pseudonymously, defends Henry against such vilification, and it shows that, *pace* John Milton, a "courtly antagonist," or at least a courtier, could be a formidable opponent. Most flagrantly, the *Responsio* hurls some excremental language of its own at Luther, but it is also artfully arranged in a manner that should be familiar to readers of *Utopia.* Thus, the *Responsio* begins with a letter from the pseudonymous William Ross to the equally pseudonymous John Carcellius. This letter tells of Ross' decision to enter the lists of print on behalf of his king. Ross claims to have believed initially that Luther's works speak for themselves; they are so full of "scurrilous railing and heresies abhorrent to the ears of all good men" that they should be read everywhere rather than forbidden. No one will, upon comparing Luther's *Contra Henricum* to the king's *Assertio,* think that Luther is anything but a madman.[53]

Ross' interlocutor, however, replies more pessimistically:

"I grant you," my dear Ross, he said, "that the work does not require an answer if one considers both sides of the question [in utranque partem intendat oculos]. But how many persons do you think will be so diligent in reading the work of Luther that they will detect his trickery by examining the book of the prince as well and comparing the actual words of each writer [collatis utrinque verbis ipsis]?"[54]

In other words, ordinary readers cannot be trusted to perform the *in utramque partem* deliberations required to separate the king's argument from Luther's misinterpretation of it. Thus, Ross must create an orchestrated *collatio* of passages [collatis utrinque verbis ipsis], one, however, that does not really leave room for readers to exercise their own prudence either. Part of the interest of Ross' letter lies in its deployment of a recognizably humanist vocabulary of deliberation on both sides of the question and textual collation in a work of outright Henrician propaganda. The letter is itself an example of the kind of elaborate framing device used to introduce humanist texts that were more open to the ambiguities of rhetoric *in utramque partem* than the *Responsio.*

When the *Responsio* goes beyond an orchestrated *collatio* of texts and engages in open vituperation, the trope of the book as feast reappears—but with Luther as the main entertainment:

But lest the venerable father be irritated by the name of fool [nomen stulti] . . . let another be fashioned not clearly a fool, but nearly a fool, . . . and finally a clout-pate, who in some hinterland of Bohemia coming in on a feast of rustics [rusti-corum convivium], . . . begins to imitate an idiot [imitari morionem], and in order to present a prime example of folly [stultitiae specimen] he comes out naked into the company covered only with a net, as if someone persuaded him that such a spell has been cast over him that he can be perceived by no one . . . while he alone who seeks the laugh is laughing—just as a dog when provoked usually laughs—and the rest indignant, finally tear off the net . . .

This buffoon [scurra], I know, would not displease Luther. . . . For the naked-ness of the fellow is no more conspicuous than that of Luther, whose obscenities the king's book uncovers and unveils so thoroughly that his own book with which he pretends to be covered covers him no more than the net covers that other buffoon, nor is that fellow's nakedness more shameful nor more shameless than that of this scoundrel of ours who, . . . so simulates a simpleton [stultum], and under the mask of a simpleton [persona stulti], not at a rustic feast [in rusticorum convivio] but in the theater of the whole world [in totius orbis theatro], not in a trifling matter but in a matter of religion and of faith, so shamelessly abuses the license of playing the wicked buffoon [scurrandi licentia].[55]

Here, More seems to be using two feigners of folly to describe Luther's public and published antics. On the one hand, Luther, like Erasmus before him, makes the "persona stulti" serve as a mask to hide the part that he is really playing. On the other hand, Luther also recalls the "scurra" from book 1 of *Utopia*—one of the banqueters at Cardinal Morton's table. For that "scurra," too, was said to be playing the fool [imitari morionem] by mocking friars,[56] and such mockery might have seemed in retrospect to have adumbrated some of the characteristics of Lutheranism. Indeed, the "scurra" of *Utopia* could have been meant as a cautionary figure even in 1516: playing the fool in public—as Erasmus of course had done so brilliantly—is not to be taken so far that it turns into scurrility. Thus, in book 1 of *Utopia* the "scurra" plays his part so well that he is said to have come too close to the real thing.

The "scurra" of *Utopia,* however, performs his antics within the confines of Cardinal Morton's house and table whereas Luther is likened to a buf-foon at a rustic "convivium"—a significant change of locales. For the fear that Lutheranism increasingly aroused was that of inciting tumult and sedition, and thus the question of what words are appropriate to say to a king gives way, in the description of Luther as "scurra," to the issue of maintaining or failing to maintain decorum at a feast of rustics. But this carnivalesque feast is representative of the still larger problem posed by publication. To publish a book is to appear in the theater of the world. Thus a writer had better beware of what masks he dons for such a performance. Again, More's point may be directed at Erasmus as well as Luther. For despite the excuses More made for Erasmus in their final letters, Erasmus never distinguished his own positions from Lutheranism to the satisfaction of More.[57]

Ultimately, More's depiction of Luther's shamelessness has the same rhetorical basis as that underlying the critique of Raphael in *Utopia.* Thus, Luther appears in the *Responsio* as an obstreperous representative of the Cynicism that Erasmus muted in the Diogenes of the "Sileni." By contrast, Luther "blathers" [eblaterat] without any regard for person, time, or place [quid, apud quos, in quos, ubi], and in the "manner of the Cynics" [more Cynicorum], hurls abuse at anyone [in quemvis]. More's ascription of a Cynical lack of decorum to Luther is all the more interesting because one of More's first forays into Lucianic satire had been his Latin translation (1506) of Lucian's *Cynicus,* a dialogue that, in his prefatory letter to Thomas Ruthall, More had tried to reconcile with "Christian simplicity" and the "strait and narrow path which leads to Life eternal."[58] But, in contrast to this kind of reconciliation, More described Luther's purpose in 1523 as that of infecting the "Christianum vulgus" with poisons [venena], that is, his books.[59]

The Peasants' Revolt demonstrated to More that his warnings had been apt. Thus, in a 1526 letter (not published until 1568) to the Lutheran John Bugenhagen, More described how "rustici," seduced and goaded by Luther's doctrine, had looted monasteries [religiosorum coenobia] and then had undergone the punishment of God, massacre and enslavement. Luther, according to More, then betrayed to the nobility the peasants that he had encouraged. The very writings [scripta] that had served to flatter the peasants with doctrines such as the Christian liberty now sounded their death knell. So, too, in the *Confutation of Tyndale's Answer* More castigated the "venemous words and malicious ways" that led to "debate, dissensions, schysmes, strife, and sedycion" in Germany.[60]

But at least some of the "venemous words" of the Lutherans were not as far apart from the healing *sermo* of Raphael as More would have wished. For instance, Tyndale's rejection of the "pomp of prelates" and his realization that there was "no place" for his translation in England was itself an oblique reference to a central Lutheran doctrine, that of the invisible church, as was More's assertion of Tyndale's ability to be both nowhere and everywhere at the same time. For this church, as originally defined by Luther in works such as his *Ad Librum eximii Magistri Nostri Magistri Ambrosii Catharini, Defensoris Silvestri Prieratis acerrimi, responsio* (1521) and *Contra Henricum* (1522) was something of a "nowhere" institution. It was both an alternative to prelacy and a church that was not tied to any particular place. As such, it constituted a complete rejection of the authority of the Roman church.

In his *Ad Librum Catharini* Luther used the corruption of the papal church and Christ's dictum that the gates of hell must not prevail against the church to argue that the Roman church was not the church of Christ. Rather, the church of Christ is both nowhere in particular yet everywhere: "omnis locus Christiano quadrat et nullus locus Christiano necessarius est" [everyplace suits the Christian and no place is necessary for the Christian]. The real church of Christ is necessarily a hidden one, and indeed Paul has removed all respect of place [locus] and persons [persona] from it. Hence, the true catholic church never and nowhere appears [nusquam numquam apparere].[61]

Luther's English opponents followed the trail of Luther's nowhere church, and it led them to Utopia. Thus, as quoted by More in the *Responsio,* the king in the *Assertio* had argued that a church without the sacrament of orders or the pope would either have to exist "nusquam" or else be reduced to "two or three heretics buzzing in a corner about Christ" [de Christo susurrantes in angulo]. The king is responding here to both *The Babylonian Captivity of the Church* as well as Luther's *Ad Librum Catharini,* and in doing so he makes the interesting point that even if "some obscure corner" [obscurus aliquis angulus] existed in which the sacrament of orders was not known it would not be comparable to the church of Christ, which is not only under Christ but the pope as well. Indeed, whatever peoples obey the pope—that is, the known world—would have to be segregated from this invisible church.[62]

In the *Responsio,* this quotation from the king's *Assertio* receives the following marginal annotation: "Eam [i.e., this invisible church or *ecclesia*] fortasse vidit in Utopia" [perhaps he has seen it in Utopia].[63] More or the printer of the *Responsio,* Richard Pynson, inserted this note, but either way it raises and rather nervously dismisses a proto-Luthern reading of Utopian Christianity. This nervousness also finds expression in the letter to Bugenhagen, wherein More mockingly asks for the location of the Lutheran invisible church and finally concludes that neither any people [nullus umquam populus] nor any individual [nec ullus usquam homo] ever believed the Lutheran heresy. Here again the language punningly recalls the originally Latin title of *Utopia* "Nusquama," even as it applies the paradox of Utopia to Lutheranism: that is, the only existence of the invisible church would be nonexistence.[64]

The Utopians could have, in retrospect, appeared to adumbrate Luther's paradox of a church that is everywhere and nowhere. For they are a people that negate, as much as they can, distinctions of "place." Thus, we learn that all Utopian cities are alike as far as the "loci natura" permits.[65] Likewise, their habit of uprooting entire forests and moving them also suggests an indifference to their original location.[66] What we have seen to be Raphael's own favorite motto—"From all places it is the same distance to heaven"—gives such indifference to place an explicitly religious cast, and, in retrospect, this motto too could have seemed a critique of the Roman church, tied as it was to a specific place and the forms of worship and religiosity that issued from that place.

Utopia, moreover, anticipates the specifics of Henry's own "nowhere" church, whose Christianity is neither dependent upon the pope nor the sacrament of priestly orders. For at the end of book 2, Utopian Christianity has yet to acquire crucial features of the Roman church such as an ordained priesthood. Thus, after spreading Christianity among the Utopians, Raphael grieves that neither he nor any of his four remaining European companions was a priest. Because of this absence of a priest, the Utopians lack the sacraments, all but baptism, that only a priest can perform.[67] Indeed, Raphael leaves the Utopians on the verge of deciding whether "without the dispatch of a Christian bishop" [since Christiani pontificis missu] they could elect and consecrate their own. Such an election would diverge radically from the sacrament of ordination, but it would be in accordance with already existing Utopian practices. For before the arrival of Christianity, the Utopians' priests were elected "a populo."[68]

The willingness of the Utopians to decide for themselves whether to accept the hierarchy of European Christianity is startling, and it is a telling sign of the unique and decidedly lay character of the Christianity that Raphael has imparted to them. We should be wary of assuming, however, that even persona "More" is unsympathetic to Utopian self-determination. Thus, in the letter of More to Giles, the character "More" describes the "holy suit" of a certain "theologian," who wants the pope to make him a bishop so that he can continue the missionary work of Raphael among the Utopians and extend the domain of what "More" terms "religio nostra." This theologian is awaiting orders from the pope [ut mittatur a pontifice], and the echoing of this phrase in the phrase, "Christiani pontificis missu," indicates that he is the solution to the Utopian problem of acquiring a properly ordained sacerdocy. Yet "More" presents himself as unable (perhaps, conveniently so) to specify the geographical coordinates of "nowhere," and thus the arrival of the Roman church in Utopia is indefinitely postponed.[69]

Measured against sixteenth-century Europe, the Utopians are late converts to Christianity, but, paradoxically, they offer Europe the prospect of a

Christianity that is closer to the apostolic model than the Roman church. A priesthood whose authority derives from the people rather than the church hierarchy has a scriptural basis, too, and it is one that Protestant reformers, taking further Erasmus' own scriptural philology, would exploit in the 1520s and 1530s. Most importantly for English readers, Tyndale had gone back to the original New Testament Greek and argued that the designation for the church leadership in Acts and the Pauline epistles, *presbuteroi,* had no sacerdotal meaning but simply denoted "seniors" or (as it became in 1534) "elders."[70] Furthermore, as Luther pointed out, Acts does show that some church leaders, the "diakonoi" or deacons, were elected by the early church rather than appointed. Tyndale's translation of *presbuteros* as "senior" did not necessarily mean that Christian priests should be elected by their congregations, but the antisacerdotal character of Tyndale's translation opened the door to this possibility by lessening the gap between clergy and laity.[71]

In *A Dialogue Concerning Heresies,* More made the point that, since the English "senior" denoted age but not the office of priesthood, Tyndale's real purpose was to undermine the sacramental character of the Christian priesthood and show that "a preste is nothyng els but a man chosen amonge the people to preche." Nevertheless, More's efforts to find a scriptural basis for the *presbuteros* as "priest" are strained since, as Tyndale pointed out, neither the Vulgate nor Erasmus ever translated *presbuteros* as *sacerdos,* the Latin for "priest." Thus, ultimately in *The Confutacion* More cites Jewish precedent for such priestly ceremonies as anointing and shaving and thereby demonstrates that the Old Testament could at times provide a better model than the New Testament for the priestly prerogatives with which More was not entirely willing to dispense.[72]

But Tyndale was aware that in *Utopia* More had permitted Raphael to articulate a much more ambiguous position concerning the status of the priesthood than More would allow Tyndale. Tyndale makes this awareness clear in an allusion to a crucial problem that afflicts the Utopians after their conversion to Christianity—their own lack of a priest and consequent inability to have certain sacraments that only a priest was entitled to perform. Tyndale makes the issue of women priests the vehicle of his allusion:

If a woman, learned in Christ, were driven unto an isle, where Christ was never preached, might she not there preach and teach to minister the sacraments, and make officers? . . . Nay, she may not consecrate. Why? If the Pope loved us as well as Christ, he would find no fault therewith, though a woman at need ministered the sacrament, if it be so necessary as ye make it.[73]

The situation that Tyndale describes here is reminiscent of the island Utopia, which accepts Christianity but is left without a priest to perform the sacraments that only a priest could perform. In Utopia, however, women are eligible to become priests, and, as the Yale *Utopia* notes, the qualifications of women priests resemble those required for the women who held positions of authority in the early church.[74] Tyndale is thus indicating another ambiguity left unresolved when Raphael leaves Utopia. That is, will the Utopians still allow women to be priests and thus perhaps approximate the apostolic church to a greater degree than European Christianity or will their priesthood be assimilated to the European model? Much depends upon whether the Utopians decide to await the emissary of the pope or not.

But if it did not fully anticipate the attacks of Protestant reformers on the sacramental priesthood, the popular election of priests in Utopia served even in 1516 as a powerful critique of the pomp and rigid hierarchy of European Christianity. The corollary of such popular elections is the Utopian *pontifex,* a high priest (but with papal and episcopal overtones, too), whose one distinguishing mark is a "wax candle borne before him" [praelatus cereus].[75] Here, we have a "prelacy" based upon illumination instead of "sacred ambition." Similarly, the pacific mediations of the Utopian priests during wars offer a striking contrast to their European counterparts and in particular to the war-mongering Pope Julius II. Thus, a marginal note exclaims, "O priests far more holy [sanctiores] than ours!"[76] The Utopian sacerdocy constitutes a kind of unbending rule, or, as Tyndale would later put it, "meteyard" against which to measure the lapses of European religious leaders.

The connection between Utopia and the controversial aspects of Erasmian humanism extended beyond, even as it included, scriptural interpretation. Raphael's conversion of the Utopians to Christianity, in particular, problematizes the meaning of what "More" in his letter to Giles terms "our religion":

But after they had heard from us the name of Christ, His teaching [doctrina], his character [mores], His miracles, and the no less wonderful constancy of the many martyrs whose blood freely shed had drawn so many nations far and wide into their fellowship [secta], you would not believe how readily disposed they, too, were to join it, whether through the rather mysterious inspiration of God or because they thought it nearest to the belief [haeresis] which has the widest prevalence among them. But I think that this factor, too, was of no small weight, that they had heard that His disciple's common way of life [communism suorum victus] had been pleasing to Christ and that it is still in use among the truest societies of Christians [apud germanissimos Christianorum conventus].[77]

The Christianity to which the Utopians convert is not that of the theologian who wants to be bishop of Utopia. Rather, this Christianity recalls what Raphael described in book 1 as a form of preaching that is faithful to what Christ taught [Christus docuit]. Although the "doctrina" of Christ in this passage could refer to the teachings of the church, nevertheless, little is said about the church as an institution that had undergone considerable evolution since the time of Christ and the apostles. Rather, the emphasis is here primarily moral—Christ's own "mores," or character, and the communism of the early church.

Only a marginal note seems to direct the reader's attention to the contemporary church by identifying "coenobia," or monasticism, with the Christians recognized by the Utopians as the truest societies, or, "germanissimi conventus," of Christians. Yet, if More's 1520 Letter to a Monk is any indication, More was scarcely blind to the distance between sixteenth-century monastic orders and the "common way of life" that drew the Utopians to Christianity. For there he described communism as a teaching of Christ, who tried to "recall mortals again to what is common from what is private" [in commune conatus est rursus a privato revocare mortales].[78] But More accused monastic orders of being divided into "sectae" and of being attached to private ceremonies in contrast to the more "communal" virtues of faith, hope, and charity. In book 1 of *Utopia*, the "coenobia" of the Benedictines is even the suggested repository for beggars and other idle loafers.[79]

Rather than identifying Utopian communism with monasticism, the marginal reference to "coenobia" may be a precedent for what we have seen to be Taverner's attempt to wrest this term from "monkery" in his translation of the Erasmian adage, "Common are the things of friends." Indeed, Erasmus' *Paraclesis*—his exhortation to read the Bible—also provides a clue to the interpretation of the "germanissimi" Christians in *Utopia*.[80] For in the *Paraclesis*, Erasmus argues that a true "Theologus" or "doctor" does not rely upon contorted logical devises but rather uses his or her life and "mores" to teach certain truths such as the contempt of wealth, the cherishing of others as members of the same body, and finally death as the passage to immortality. Erasmus further claims that these precepts, however bereft of the subtleties of professional theologians [idiotica], are the source of true Christians, "tot germane Christiani."[81]

The Utopians, who practice communism and defecate on gold, provide a good example of contempt for wealth. But, in addition to such contempt, a technological development, the arrival of the printing press in Utopia, links the Utopians to Erasmian humanism and its manifold uses of the technology of print. Indeed, the Utopians are already a community of readers, and the arrival of the printing press in Utopia only underscores the already important place of books and "litterae" in Utopian society. The Utopians even begin each meal with a reading conducive to morality [quae ad mores faciat].[82] Most important, those who devote their life to letters are exempted from work, and only literati are eligible for most Utopian offices, including those of priest and prince.[83] Utopian attitudes toward the integration of humanist letters in virtually every aspect of their life contrasts strikingly with the diminished importance of "litterae" on More's tombstone.

Despite its own communitarian ethos, however, we have seen that Erasmian humanism was not without the potential to provoke hostility and divisiveness. Thus, Raphael's Christianity significantly comes to Utopia as a "secta," one that is said to be close to the chief Utopian "haeresis." Likewise, the Utopian "religiosi," their counterpart to European religious orders, are said to be divided into two "haereses."[84] *Secta* is in fact the Latin translation of the Greek *haeresis,* and neither word necessarily has a pejorative meaning. Thus, in the New Testament the Christians themselves begin as merely another sect, and accordingly in Acts 24:5 the Jewish highpriest identifies Paul as the leader of the Nazarene "heresy." Yet it is hard to believe that More used these words to denote Utopian Christianity and religion without intending to evoke their more controversial significance as well.

Erasmus, too, noted the equivalence of "haeresis" and "secta" in his *Annotationes in Novum Testamentum* (1516). "Haeresis," according to Erasmus in his commentary on Acts 24, was not in the New Testament the odious name that it later became. Rather, "haeresis" denoted a "secta," and it is because of the supposed concord of Christians that a name indicating "division" [divisonem sonans] has acquired such pejorative connotations. Yet Erasmus was also aware that the very absence of concord among Christians was responsible for the shift in the meaning of heresy that his philology had detected. Thus, in "Sileni Alcibiades" Erasmus suggested that the pejorative use of the word "heresy" was a sign of the divisiveness of sixteenth-century Christianity and its distance from the Christianity of the Gospels. "Masters of theology" use the stigma of heresy to criticize ways of life and teachings that are nearer to Christ's message than their own.[85]

In addition to criticizing the division of monastic orders into rival "sects," More also noted the tendency of conservative theologians to brand their opponents and, in particular, Erasmian reformers as "heretics." Thus, defending a humanist curriculum at Oxford in 1519, More wrote that the opponents of Greek studies dub "heretics" all those who desire to learn Greek "literae" and apply them to, among other things, the reading and interpretation of the New Testament.[86] Raphael is the emissary of both Christianity and Greek "literae" to the Utopians, and this combination may help to explain Christianity's manifestation as a "haeresis" in Utopia. Endowed with the knowledge of Greek, a printing press, and a version of Christianity that is *germanus,* the Utopians would seem to have all the tools they needed to become "heretics" of an Erasmian stamp.

Or rather they have all the tools but one. For as Richard Marius has argued, although Raphael carries a rather impressive cargo of Greek books to Utopia, he does not bring either a Greek or Latin New Testament.[87] This omission reinforces the undecided future of Utopian Christianity at the time of Raphael's departure.[88] The distance of Utopian Christianity from the Roman church and its apparent proximity to Erasmian human-ism are offset by the absence of the primary text of this humanism. Will the Bible ever arrive in Utopia and become a part of the readings condu-cive to morality that accompany Utopian meals? This question belongs in the same category as that of the eventual conversion of the Utopians to the Roman church. In the end, we do not know whether the Utopians will receive either a properly ordained priesthood or the book that would allow them to challenge convincingly the authority of that priesthood.

Despite this ultimate ambiguity, the chief emissary of Christianity to Utopia is a literalist as far as scriptural exegesis goes. To be sure, Raphael brings no Bible with him to Cardinal Morton's court. But in his argument against punishing thieves with death, Raphael proves a strict interpreter of both the Old Testament commandments, in particular, "Thou shall not kill," and what he terms the "new law of mercy" [nova lex clementiae]. His argument is that to interpret one part of the Bible in a flexible manner is to expose the entire scripture to dangerous compromise. By contrast, Raphael is an equitable interpreter of human laws [humana iura],[89] and he argues that such laws, based as they were on "consensus," should always yield to the Bible when the two conflict.

Raphael's scriptural legalism notwithstanding, Utopian Christianity remains an open question, and this lack of closure may have been part of what allowed More to revise his understanding of Utopian society in later works. Such revisions show More experimenting with different endings to his book in the light of subsequent historical events. Thus, in the *Responsio* More uses *Utopia* to dispute Luther's claim that the "lex evangelica" super-sedes "leges humanae":

But he thought he had brilliantly handled this very silly opinion when he replied at Worms that the law of the gospel [lex evangelica] alone would ultimately be sufficient and human laws [leges humanae] useless if magistrates were good and the faith truly preached. As if even the best magistrates could manage either that the whole Christian people would want to live in common or that the wicked would not steal or that any preaching of the faith could procure that no one anywhere [nulli usquam] would be wicked. If the law of the gospel does not permit stealing, surely the human law which punishes stealing is not useless; and the human law which alone apportions ownership of goods binds Christians; if this ownership is done away with, there cannot indeed be stealing. But if he should say that from this premise the argument is drawn that we would do better to be without that law from which the ownership of goods arises and would do better to live in a certain natural community with the occasion of stealing eliminated, it does not help his case even if we should grant him this argument. For even if we could live in common with far fewer laws, we still could not live altogether without laws. For the obligation to work would have to be prescribed for certain classes, and laws would be needed to restrain crimes which would run riot even in that kind of life.[90]

A Utopia-like communism, where the number of laws has been reduced and the crime of stealing is meaningless, functions here as More's *a fortiori* example of the impossibility of human laws ever becoming obsolete.[91] If a "natural" social order based on communism cannot eliminate the need for laws, how could the evangelical law do so? Indeed, More here sounds like the "More" of book 1 of *Utopia,* who wonders how a society that holds goods in common can get its people to work. Treating communism in the *Responsio,* moreover, More defines "public" law as "consensus," whether established in usage or writing, and he upholds the very standard whose authority Raphael questioned at Cardinal Morton's table.[92] Not only do the law of the Gospel and human law not conflict, but they are even mutually reinforcing. The law of the Gospel prohibits stealing, and it depends upon human law for its enactment.

In the *Responsio* More notes that human law alone, without the support of evangelical law, provides a basis for private property, but he does not state that evangelical law enjoins communism either. Rather, communism belongs to a "natural" form of community, one that does not necessarily possess any divine sanction. This shift may reflect More's growing sense of caution in the 1520s as he changed from someone charged with defending the "heretical" Erasmus to a defender of orthodoxy against new forms of heresy. In the *Dialogue Concerning Heresies,* it is the Lutheran Messenger who argues that the "name" of "heretic" is a false one.[93] Yet, even in a Tower work such as *A Dialogue of Comfort against Tribulation,* More never entirely relinquished communism as a specifically Christian desideratum. For in an exchange concerning damnation, Vincent proposes that the rich should not keep their wealth while the poor are in need of relief. Anthony's response does not immediately dismiss this point but rather emphasizes the need of attending to "circumstaunces." Anthony makes the allusion to the healing *sermo* of Raphael all the clearer by using the analogy of a physician dispensing medicines to illustrate what he means by "circumstaunces." Taken at the wrong time, a medicine might become a poison and do "no good but harm."[94]

Nor did More ever completely lose sight of the possibility of communistically distributing interpretive property, although he was careful to qualify this possibility in the antiheretical works. Thus, in *A Dialogue Concerning Heresies,* a work that recalls the *Phaedrus* by being set in the suburban retreat of More's Chelsea house, the persona of "More" even declares himself a supporter in principle of an English Bible. More makes use of Erasmus' distinction in "Festina lente" between "communes literae" and hieroglyphics to note that the Bible was itself written in "common letters" rather than in "secret cypher." A product of the "vulgar tongue" of its own day, the Bible should not be kept from English readers.[95]

In *A Dialogue Concerning Heresies,* however, More also describes the Bible as a kind of drug, a "medicine for him that is sicke and fode for him that is hole." Thus, it is the responsibility of a "physycion," that is, bishop, to "discerne betweene the hole and the sick and bytwene dysease and dysease" and to distribute this medicine in different doses to different readers.[96] Such prudent distribution of medicine qualifies the commonness of the letters in which an English Bible, at least, should be written, and it partakes of the same caution as the hedged allusion to Utopian communism in *A Dialogue of Comfort.* In response the Messenger critiques the plan of "More" by asserting that people will prefer to buy a Bible from the "printer than have it of the bysshop free."[97]

Utopian society itself anticipates such selective divulgation. For despite their practice of religious toleration, the Utopians are unwilling to allow the dissemination of any religious idea. The diversity of Utopian religious beliefs cannot all be expressed publicly. Thus, for instance, Utopians who do not believe in the afterlife cannot articulate those opinions "apud vulgus."[98] Rather, such opinions must be confined to an audience composed primarily of an elected and lettered sacerdocy.[99] Nevertheless, the rationale for such censorship is social rather than religious. A nonbeliever in the rewards and punishments of the afterlife would lack sufficient incentive to obey the law in this life.

Albeit an alternative to the European sacerdocy, Utopian priests also represent the other side of what we have seen to be the antipriestly elements of Erasmian humanism. That is, Utopian priests, selected for their devotion to "letters," are humanists elevated to the position of a priestly order, one that dislodges, only to replace, the clerisy of the Church. More's own "cursus honorum" would exemplify this kind of appropriation of a priestly office when he became the first lay chancellor of England. But not even More's reading was free of clerical mediation. Thus, Cuthbert Tunstal may have been a character in *Utopia* and a contributor to Erasmus' scriptural labors, but, when he gave More a license to read heretical books in the vernacular, he was acting in the capacity of Bishop of London. As a reader of heretical works, More was himself the patient in need of a physician's prescription.

The Messenger's opposition, however, between a printed Bible and one received from the bishop leaves the Utopians once again precariously poised in the middle, for they possess a printing press but neither a Bible nor a bishop. Yet this opposition also provides further evidence of how Utopia's controversial neutrality helped to script More's later career as a polemicist on behalf of orthodoxy. Indeed, such scripting was not confined to More alone. Rather, it extended to later generations of English humanists, who also found themselves acting, on a somewhat different stage, the roles for humanism that *Utopia* did so much to define. These roles, however, proved particularly difficult to manage in the England of the 1530s, which vacillated wildly when it came to identifying the meanings of heresy and orthodoxy.

THREE

"To Devulgate or Sette Fourth":

Humanist Talent and Reformation Politics in Sir Thomas Elyot's Popularizations

Thomas Elyot's ambition to "devulgate or sette fourth some part" of his "studie" in *The Boke Named the Governour* (1531) marks one of the first significant attempts by English humanists to make their learning accessible to a vernacular reading public. It is also, to use terms that Mary Crane has highlighted, a dazzling "gathering" and "framing" of a wealth of humanist erudition. But Elyot's loss of high government office in 1530 does not necessarily make his use of such wealth a "defensive posture against failure," as Crane, developing the argument of Alistair Fox, has termed Elyot's other literary productions of the 1530s.[1] Rather, discharged from his clerkship to the King's Council, Elyot made a virtue of necessity. *The Governour* inaugurated Elyot's second career, ending with *A Preservative Agaynst Deth* (1545), as a popularizer of humanism in addition to other kinds of lore, including medical knowledge and the first Latin-English *Dictionary* (1538).[2] A failure in one sense, Elyot was remarkably successful in another: he negotiated English humanism's passage from Latin to the vernacular, not as a response to the threat of heresy, but rather as a way of broadening the audience for "litterae." Yet Elyot could not avoid questions of religious beliefs and political loyalties either. Rather, his role as popularizer forced him to engage these questions as he decided what parts of humanism to divulge to an English readership and what to leave encoded in Latin.

More's depiction of a "vulgata" Utopia, in particular, is an important subtext to Elyot's *The Governour,* which takes the vulgarization of ideal republics further by offering the "fourme of a just publike weale" in the "vulgar tunge," not Latin. Even more than More's *Utopia,* Elyot's *The Governour* and his other vernacular works were exposed to the unsettling variety of readers that More's Letter to Giles had mockingly located "out of shot" in a tavern. Yet, at the same time as he was popularizing humanist studies, including elements of *Utopia* itself, Elyot stood between his readership and aspects of humanism as effectively as the Utopian sacerdocy of "letters" shields the Utopian people from dangerous religious beliefs in *Utopia*. Thus, *The Governour* significantly divulges only "some part" of Elyot's studies. Yet Elyot's priestly mediations will prove to be a function of his recognition that, as a popularizer, he was playing the part of an antipriest, too. That is, his popularizations had an important religious analogue in the efforts of figures such as Erasmus, Luther, and Tyndale to disseminate religious texts.

THE TALENT OF A POPULARIZER

Elyot's assumption of the roles of both priest and antipriest occurred during a decade when England radically redefined the power and authority of its clergy and church. The executions of More and John Fisher (1535), the submission of the clergy (1532), the dissolution of the monasteries (1536–40), preachers who railed against what they saw as religious superstitions, the Great Bible (1539), and instances of Catholic backlash such as the Pilgrimage of Grace (1536) all helped to make the 1530s a decade of unprecedented transformation and upheaval. At the same time, Henrician policy included its own backlash against reform. Thus, the decade ended with the reactionary Act of Six Articles (1539) and the execution of Cromwell (1540), events that set limits to England's willingness to follow Continental religious models.

One consequence of drastic change combined with sudden reversals of policy was the need to be alert to all signs of discontent. For instance, in Cambridgeshire, Elyot's home during the 1530s, even tavern talk could lead to trouble, nor were its practitioners necessarily "out of shot." Eamon Duffy describes the case of the vicar of St. Clemens, Cambridge who, speaking confidentially to a tavern companion in 1535, was denounced to Cromwell for calling the king a "despoiler" of the church.[3] On the other hand, a 1538 royal proclamation, directed primarily at Anabaptists, vehemently castigated those who were wont to "argue and dispute in open places, taverns and alehouses, not only upon the holy sacrament of baptism, but also upon the blessed sacrament of the altar."[4] Here, the tavern figures as the site of discontent from yet another quarter, that of Continental heresies.

As a recently dismissed civil servant, Elyot would not have been above the suspicion of harboring some discontent toward the Tudor regime. For whatever reason Elyot lost his government position, its circumstances introduced Elyot to the sometimes illusory character of benefits bestowed from above.[5] After several years of service as Clerk to the Council, Elyot was "dischargid withoute any recompence, rewardid onely with the order of knighthode honorable and onerouse."[6] In other words, Elyot was fobbed off with a title that he viewed as more of a burden than a benefit. This dismissal occurred while More was chancellor, and thus we must wonder how firm the supposed friendship of More and Elyot ever was.[7]

Elyot's intriguing combination of a knighthood and downward mobility, in turn, makes his social standing difficult to pinpoint. Even apart from this downward mobility, however, Elyot's standing and attitude toward hierarchy have received contradictory readings from biographers and critics, who have identified him both as a member of the landed gentry and what has been termed the "new Tudor aristocracy," a parvenu elite that included figures such as Wolsey, More, and Thomas Cromwell. A graduate of the Middle Temple, Elyot had risen to the clerkship after holding a series of lesser posts. In the The Governour Elyot described the law as that "honorable studie wherby my father was advaunced to a juge, and also I my selfe have attayned no lytle commoditie."[8] Albeit landed, Elyot and his father demonstrated the same kinds of ambition as the urban More and his father, both of whom had also gained no small commodity from the law. Yet, unlike More, who in 1521 acquired his knighthood as a sign of his rise in the Tudor bureaucracy, the discharged and newly titled Elyot of 1530 might have had difficulty identifying himself as either a new or old Tudor aristocrat.[9]

Likewise, Elyot's religious politics have proven elusive or, as Stephen Foley puts it, "circuitous."[10] In 1537 Elyot was accused of being a papist,[11] and Constance Jordan has even argued that Elyot was a party to a Catholic conspiracy to depose Henry and place Catherine on the throne.[12] But, after the publication of The Governour, Henry did entrust, albeit briefly, an important diplomatic mission to Elyot.[13] Elyot represented the king at the court of Charles V, and his assignments while abroad included furthering the cause of the king's divorce and apprehending William Tyndale. Moreover, during the 1530s Elyot frequently corresponded with Thomas Cromwell and attempted to assuage Cromwell's anxieties concerning Elyot's religious beliefs and loyalties. In 1539 Elyot even reaped some of the fruits of the dissolution of the monasteries.

Elyot's project of popularizing learning, moreover, was itself an outgrowth of printing and the Reformation. To be sure, the ability of the printing press to serve the religious needs of lay people was not the exclusive discovery of Protestantism. Nevertheless, Elyot's success as a popularizer owed much to what Elizabeth Eisenstein has identified as the tendency of the Protestant elevation of vernacular translations of scripture to lead to the proliferation of other kinds of vernacular translations.[14] Thus, Tyndale may have been Elyot's quarry in 1531, but his activities as a translator of the Bible helped to make possible Elyot's literary endeavors. As Ted Brown has shown, works such as Elyot's *Castle of Health* were part of an outpouring of vernacular medical treatises that received a good deal of its momentum from the Reformation. Thomas Gale, a translator of Galen, wrote in 1586 that his translation was for "prentises and young men, which have not been trained up in schooles, neither yet can understand the Greeke and Latin tongue, and yet can understand and reade English."[15] Although acquiring access to medical rather than religious texts, this audience is not too far from the one that Erasmus had celebrated in the *Paraclesis* as scripture's ideal readership and that Tyndale's translations had helped to make a reality for England.

Elyot's popularizations, however, also have a royal context. The king's printer, Berthelet, published all of Elyot's books, including the anonymous and caustic *Pasquil the Playne* (1533). *The Governour*, too, is dedicated to Henry VIII. Yet Elyot was not directly hired to write propaganda for the government, and even *The Governour* cannot be described as "official" to the same degree that works such as Richard Morison's *A Remedy for Sedition* (1536) were.[16] Indeed, the praise of monarchy is brief in *The Governour*, and Elyot soon turns to the topics that are his real focus— education, nobility, benevolence, and justice.[17] These topics are, in turn, meant to engage a broader readership than Henry alone, and the printing history of *The Governour* bears out the existence of such a readership. Reprinted six times between 1531 and 1565, *The Book Named the Governour* was, if not a runaway bestseller, at least a successful book.

Yet Elyot's own success as a popularizer was probably not financial. In the *Image of Governance* (1541), a life of Alexander Severus and supposedly a sequel to the *Governour*, Elyot quotes his detractors as "dispraysinge my studies as vayne and unprofitable, sayinge . . . I have nothing wonne therby, but the name only of a maker of bokes, and that I sette the trees, but the printer eateth the fruites."[18] Elyot does not deny that his books have not done much for his "private commodity." Indeed, given the lack of an authorial copyright in England, this failure to harvest any of the monetary fruits of his books is not surprising. Nevertheless, Elyot's claim in the same preface that his books served "others necessity" as opposed to his own is somewhat disingenuous.[19] For they were also profitable to him, if only in the form of an enhanced reputation.

Elyot's interest in the enhancement of his reputation is evident from his favorite metaphor for intellectual wealth, talent. Thus, looking back in the preface to the *Image of Governance,* Elyot defends his use of his talent:

But to excuse me of foly, I will professe without arrogaunce, that whan I con-sydered, . . . the terrible checke that the good maister in the gospell gave to his ydel servaunte, for hiding his money in a clowte, and not disposinge it for his maisters advantage, those two words so sterid my spirites, that it caused me to take more regarde to my last rekning, than to any riches or worldly promotion. And all thoughe I do neither dyspute nor expounde holy scripture, yet . . . my poor talent shall be, God willinge, in such wise bestowed, that no mannes con-science shalbe therwith offended, my boke called the Governour, instructinge men in suche vertues as shalbe expedient for them, which shal have authority in a wele publike. . . . The Doctrinal of princis . . . The Education of children, . . . The little Pasquill, although he be merry and playne, teching as well servantes how to be faythfull unto their maisters, as also masters how to be circumspect in espying of flaterars . . . The Castle of Helth . . . My Dictionary.

Although professing not to expound scripture (and thereby usurp the office of a preacher), Elyot does offer a reading of the parable of the talents (Matthew 25:14–21) here. Indeed, Elyot's description of his books gives them a homiletic character. But the parable itself offers Elyot a way of casting writing and the publication of his writings as the fulfillment of a divine command, one that prohibits the sequestration of God-given abilities. To not "bestow" this talent on the printed page would constitute self-burial. Yet, however abject and humble he pretends to be (his talent is a "poor" one), Elyot is nevertheless still displaying his "talent." According to Elyot, his *Governour* performs the function of "instructinge men in such vertues as shal be expedient for them, which shal have authority in a wele publike." But Elyot's reference to his talent is a way of demonstrating his own authority, the abilities that give him the right to instruct the future governors.

The parable of the talents, unlike more egalitarian parables such as that of the laborers in the vineyard, celebrates the inequality of spiritual gifts and rewards. Talent was, as Max Weber has shown in *The Protestant Ethic,* easily assimilated to a later Protestant emphasis on prosperity, or what Elyot disparagingly terms "worldly riches and promotion."[20] But Elyot's highlighting of his talent represents the beginning of a distinctly human-ist way of articulating the possession and disbursement of a more intangi-ble wealth. "Talent" authorizes Elyot to perform an implicitly homiletic role on the printed page, and it enables him to negotiate between tradi-tionally aristocratic values and the exigencies of social mobility and pro-motion. "Talent" is an endowment from above: therefore, one cannot quarrel with the amount one receives. Yet investment and initiative do yield a reward. Even the servant alloted only one talent has the opportunity to acquire more.

The Image of Governance was published near the close of Elyot's career as a popularizer, but the topos of the talent, a frequent one in Elyot's works, marks his project of divulgating learning as described in the proem to *The Governour:*

> more over, thaccompt that I have to rendre for that one little talent delivered to me to employe (as I suppose) to the increase of virtue, I am (as god juge me) violently stered to devulgate or sette fourth some part of my studie, trustynge therby tacquite me of my dueties to god, your hyghnesse, and this my contray. Wherefore takinge comfort and boldeness, partly of your graces moste benev-olent inclination toward the universal weale of your subjectes, partly inflamed with zele, I have nowe enterprised to describe in our vulgare tunge the fourme of a iuste publike weale: whiche mater I have gathered as well of the sayenges of most noble autours . . . as by myne owne experience, I being continually trayned in some dayly affaires of the publike weale of this your moste noble realme all mooste from my chyldehode.[21]

Here, Elyot's talent is said to be "little," and his masters seem to be many, God, the king, and England itself. Nevertheless, Elyot's description of the sources of his book, that is, reading and experience, also implies that the talent belongs to him and that it is a potentially rich one. Elyot may have gained his experience while working for the Henrician regime, but the ex-perience is now a kind of capital that he can invest as he pleases. Indeed, Elyot's decision to describe in the "vulgare tunge the fourme of a just pub-like weale" is not necessarily an investment calculated to reassure Elyot's putative master, Henry. For the relationship of a "just publike weale" to the "publike weale" of Henry's "noble realme" remains to be seen. Elyot could here be establishing the basis of an unflattering comparison.

In addition to Henry's realm, Elyot's authors are also "noble," and *The Governour* arguably evinces Elyot's own desire to join their company. That is, as an author, Elyot hoped to become a part of an aristocracy of books and letters, one whose titles had the potential to mean more than Elyot's onerous knighthood. Moreover, Elyot's investment of his talent in the proem to *The Governour* does yield a distinctly aristocratic return, an "in-crease of virtue." At the outset of book 2 of *The Governour,* which mostly concerns the qualities that constitute "very nobility," Elyot writes that the "most sure fundation of noble renome is a man to be of such vertues and qualities as he desireth to be openly publisshed."[22] The ability of publishing to convert virtue into noble renown recalls the "noble" authors of the proem, and such publishing suggests that, as interest earned on a talent, an "increase of virtue" may constitute a real profit.[23]

Such nobility has a religious basis, too, that of charity.[24] Indeed, Elyot's charity is reminiscent of the ways in which Erasmus cast himself as an unappreciated and Herculean laborer on behalf of the public good. For both Erasmus and Elyot, the use of the press to disseminate learning in a responsible manner became a display of religious virtue. It was also a good defensive tactic. For opponents of such "charity" necessarily defined themselves as mean-spirited churls.

Charity, however, was a problematic virtue for Tyndale and other reformers since it suggested that human endeavors might contribute to salvation. Indeed, this virtue highlights a vulnerability of Protestant *sola fide*—the apparent lack of incentive for doing good works. Tyndale's *The Parable of the Wicked Mammon* (1528), an assault upon a works- or charity-based understanding of Christianity, cites only defensively the parable of the talents, as a way of countering the charge that the priority of faith and grace to charity means an end to good deeds. Thus, Tyndale writes that "God giveth no man his grace, that he should let it lie still . . . but that he should increase it and multiply it with lending it to other, and with open declaring of it."[25] A marginal gloss identifies the allusion to the parable of the talents, yet this parable is itself marginal to *The Parable of the Wicked Mammon,* whose focus is still faith.

Elyot's charitable use of his talent, however, is central to his popularizations. As part of his attention to the necessary qualities of "gentilness" and "benevolence" in book 2 of *The Governour,* Elyot writes that "[b]enevolence, if it do extende to a hole contraye or citie, it is proprely called charitie, and some tyme zele."[26] In the proem to *The Governour,* on the other hand, after identifying his talent, Elyot had described himself as "inflamed with zele" and moved to divulgate by his recognition of Henry's "benevolence" to his subjects.[27] In *The Governour* both Elyot and Henry exercise charity from above. Indeed, the title page of the 1539 Great Bible, which shows the king handing the Bible, via the clergy, to the laity, demonstrates that, in the end, Henry was not averse to extending Elyot's kind of popularizing zeal or benevolence to the Bible itself.

Moses, however, is the chief biblical example of benevolence in *The Governour,* and he exercises charity apart from a court. Thus, Elyot, relying upon Josephus as well as Exodus, writes of how Moses was the favorite of Pharaoh and might have lived "in moche honour and welth" if he had not felt the need to liberate the Israelites:

But he inflamed with fervent benevolence or zele, towarde them, to redeme them out of their miserable bondage, chase rather to be in the daungerous indignation of Pharao, to committe his persone to the chaungeable myndes of a multitutde, and they most unstable, . . . than to be in the palice of Pharao where he shulde have bene satisfied with honour, richesse, and ease. . . . Who that redeth the boke of Exodi shall finde the charitie of this man wonderfull.[28]

As a model for Elyot, the figure of Moses might seem a bit grand. Indeed, the implied comparison of Elyot and Moses obscures an important differ-ence: Elyot did not abandon the palace of his Pharaoh but was dismissed. Nevertheless, like Moses, Elyot did leave the court and had to entrust himself to the vicissitudes of a multitude. But, as Elyot casts it, he and Moses are both inflamed with zeal, or charity, and this quality makes the multitude his concern. This quality also makes Elyot a leader of sorts and a potential rival of the authority of the English Pharaoh, whose "dangerous indignation" he may incur.

The leadership that Elyot is trying to exercise in print could threaten other potentates besides the king. Thus, in his preface to the 1541 edition of *The Castle of Health,* Elyot alludes to Erasmus' "Festina lente" to justify the charitable distribution of medical knowledge in a manner threatening to the authority of the medical profession:

But if phisitions be angry, that I hav wryten phisike in englyshe, let theym remembre, that the grekes wrate in greke, the Romanes in latyne, Avicena and the other in Arabike, whiche were their own propre and maternal tonges. And if they had bene as moche attached with envy and covaytise, as some nowe seeme to be, they wolde have devysed somme particuler language, with a strange syphre or fourme of lettres, wherein they wold have writen their science, which language or lettres no man shoulde have knowen that hadde not professyd and practised phisycke: but those, although . . . painimes and Jewes, in this parte of charity they farre surmountid us Christianes.[29]

Here, "strange syphre or fourme of lettres," a "particuler language," is reminiscent of the mysterious writing of the Egyptian priesthood against which, as we have seen, Erasmus had defined the "communes literae" of "Festina lente."[30] Elyot gives this opposition a distinctly Christian cast by invoking charity as the virtue prohibiting the use of a secret code to communicate medical knowledge. Albeit not challenging religious au-thorities here, Elyot is acting the part of a religiously motivated antipriest, dispossessing a quasi-sacerdotal elite (the medical profession) of the exclu-sive ownership of their texts and knowledge. Moreover, Elyot is taking further Erasmus' own self-construction as someone who labors tirelessly for the common good as opposed to narrow interests representing only "envy" and "coveytise." Yet Elyot is laboring on behalf of the common good in a language, the vernacular, that he defines as both less "particuler" and more "propre and maternal" than Erasmus' Latin.[31] Elyot nationalizes the "common letters" of "Festina lente" and makes them "propre," and, in so doing, he shows the degree to which he is "studiouse about the weale of his countray" as opposed to an international, Latinate republic of letters.[32]

The preface to Elyot's last published work, *A Preservative Agaynst Deth* (1545), on the other hand, uses the trope of the talents to articulate what has been implicit in Elyot's earlier works—his sense of having usurped some of the function of another elite, that is, the priesthood:

Truely I confesse, that priestes ought to preache, and that it is their propre office. And yet no christen man is excluded to gyve good counsaile in that whiche pertayneth to the lawes and commandementes of almighty god. And he that can do it, and will not (though he be no priest) I dout not but he shall make a straite reknynge for hydynge his talent. A knyght hath received that honour not onely to defende with the swerde Christis faithe and his propre countrey . . . but also, and that most chiefly, by the meane of his dignitie . . . he shuld more effectually with his learnyng and witte assayle vice and errour, most pernicious ennemies to christen men, having therunto for his sworde and speare his tunge and his penne. And where for the more reverence due to the order of priesthode, it is most congruent and fittyng, that preaching in commune assembles, be reserved onely to that ministracion, yet where a knight or other man . . . being zealous of virtue and moved only by charitie, wolde fayne have other men to remembre their state and condicion, and according to their dueties . . . to love god, . . . whatlawe or raison should lette hym . . . to set furth in writing or print, that which shalbe commodious to many men?[33]

The significance of this apologia extends beyond the *Preservative* to include Elyot's entire career. Elyot emerges as someone who, "being zealous of virtue and moved only by charitie," repeatedly set forth in writing numerous works meant to be "commodious to many men." But Elyot goes beyond invoking the theological virtue that presented such a problem to *sola fide* Protestantism. For Elyot explicitly shows how his writings were attempts to redefine the role of knighthood in England and make the knight as writer the equivalent to a lay preacher. Thus, Elyot's knight, whose tongue and pen constitute his sword and spear, effectively does in print what priests are supposed to do in common assemblies: that is, he reminds his listeners of their "condicion" and "dueties." Despite Elyot's protestations that he is not trying to perform the office of priest, Elyot's preaching, although confined to the printed page, is a usurpation of one of the crucial functions of the priesthood as defined by Protestants. Indeed, during the 1530s, preachers supported by Cromwell, for instance, Hugh Latimer, John Bale, and William Jerome, had made sermons an important instrument of religious reform as well as a source of bitter controversy in England.[34]

Elyot, however, was aware of the dangers of usurping the authority of established elites. As one sign of this awareness, he is careful in *The Governour* to distinguish between Moses' guidance of the multitude committed to him and a seditious and reckless demagoguery. Thus, before adducing Moses' "charity" in his discussion of "benevolence" in *The Governour*, Elyot warns that "benevolence" does not preclude sharp punishment of those who break the laws. For among other things, such punishment is meant to "preserve a multitude from domage, by puttynge men in feare." Moses himself provides an example of the need for such punishment. For when "Chore, Dathamn, and Abiron moved a sedition agayne Moses, he praied god that the erth mought open and swalowe them, consideryng that the furie of the people moughte nat be by any other meanes asswaged."[35] Although a rebel against the Pharaoh, Moses immediately suppresses sedition in his own camp.

Elyot, however, recognized that he was himself capable of misleading his followers. Thus, in the English preface to his 1538 Latin-English *Dictionary* (Elyot introduced the word "dictionary" into English), Elyot describes himself as having popularized medical knowledge in the form of "proper terms" belonging to "physik, the names of divers herbes known among us." But Elyot's Latin preface to the 1538 *Dictionary* indicates the hazards besetting those who dispense drugs, particularly in the form of words. For there Elyot admitted that, following the advice of unscrupulous "pharmacopoli," he originally inserted these drugs into his *Dictionary* under false names. Thus, he had to add an appendix to the *Dictionary* in order to remove his readers [lectores] from peril [periculum].[36] Elyot sees the danger of this mistake as being proportional to the potential usefulness of the drugs. Just as nothing is more helpful [conducibilius] to human health [humana salus] than the "res herbaria," so nothing is more harmful [noxium] or damaging to the reader [lector] than a poor understanding of this *res*.

Elyot's Latin preface to his *Dictionary* includes the claim that, if it had not been for the king's intervention, he would have consigned his *Dictionary* to the flames [flammis consumpsissem]—an assertion that recalls More's proposed burnings of his works. Elyot's reference to burning, however, is no idle allusion. For Elyot's English preface to the *Dictionary* describes King Henry's interrogation of the Anabaptist heretic John Lambert, who, although Elyot does not discuss this, was burned in 1538.

According to Elyot, Lambert's mistake was one of trusting the "writings" and "interpretations" of his heretical "masters" instead of the "playne context of holy scripture" and the "determinate sentence of holy and great learned doctours."[37] Elyot, on the other hand, presents himself in the *Dictionary* as one who, without the warrant of the king, does not even trust his own writings.

Elyot's "study," however, was at times a discontented one, and he often used the power of the press as a means of advancing ideas that, although not flagrantly heretical like those of Lambert, had the potential to provoke some dangerous indignation on the part of the king. One telling expression of Elyot's discontent is the frequency with which Cynic figures appear in his books. For instance, in *The Governour* Demetrius, a representative of the "cinici" or "doggishe" philosophers, is taught the importance of dancing in an adaptation of Lucian's *The Dance*. Elyot's Cynics generally represent the threat of shame and exposure, and Demetrius, who learns the efficacy of dancing is no exception. For the dance that he witnesses is that of the entrapment of Venus and Mars in a net by Vulcan. This dance, whose subject is adulterous love, was probably in 1531 an allusion to the married Henry's infatuation with Anne Boleyn.[38] Yet, as we have seen from More's castigation of Luther's naked frolics in a net, this image could be used to evoke a wide range of public and published indiscretions.

Scholars have long suspected Elyot of having made the first translation of More's *Cynicus* into English (1530). But even if Elyot was not this anonymous translator, the suspicion that he was certainly has some basis in the works that he is known to have written.[39] At the very least, the Cynic of More's Latin dialogue, whose "pallium" is full of filth and whose language is blunt and unsparing, anticipates the Italian figure that Elyot Englished in his 1533 *Pasquil the Playne*.[40] This Pasquil, a statue who comes to life and espouses a "currishe philosophie," opposes Gnatho, a courtier who "savorith somewhat of rhetorike," and Harpocrates, an Egyptian "prelate," whose "image is made holdinge his finger at his mouthe betokeninge silence."[41]

As a successful, albeit unsavory, courtier, Gnatho is an exaggerated version of the character "More" in *Utopia*.[42] Thus, interpreting a sentence of Aeschylus', Gnatho offers Pasquil a sure way of getting ahead at court: "holdyng thy tonge wher it behoveth the" and "spekyng in tyme that whiche is convenient."[43] As Gnatho sees it, this strategy means that "[i]t behoveth a man to holde his tunge, when he aforeseeth by any experience, that the thinge which he wolde purpose or speke of to his superiour, shall neyther be pleasantly herde nor thankefully taken."[44] In other words, Gnatho forestalls all possibility of the humanist adviser offering any real criticism to the prince. While not denying the importance of time and opportunity, Pasquil, nevertheless, asserts that "opportunitie and time for a counsayllor to speke do not depend of the affection and appetite of hym that is counsayled."[45] In Pasquil's formulation bluntness and a certain amount of rhetorical astuteness are compatible, but, as a consequence of this belief, Pasquil has not been, in the words of Harpocrates, "called to counsayll" at court.[46]

In *Pasquil,* however, Elyot recasts the opposition between rhetorical prudence, as displayed by "More" in the Dialogue of Counsel, and what we have seen to be the apparent willingness of Raphael Hythlodaeus to articulate his Bible-based criticisms of human institutions without sufficient regard for time and circumstances.[47] For Gnatho, the rhetorician who conspicuously carries around a New Testament and quotes from it with abandon, is the clearly Protestant character, and Pasquil, the railer, is the exponent of what Gnatho somewhat disparagingly terms the "lesson of gentiles, called humanitie" as well as the importance of this lesson to a correct understanding of the New Testament. Thus, Pasquil complains that "[s]om wil be in the bowels of divinitie er they know what longeth to good humanitie."[48] As far as the willingness to speak goes, then, humanists and Protestants have traded places in *Pasquil,* where Harpocrates the silent prelate becomes the ally of a Protestant courtier and the target of a distinctly humanist antipriest.

The topicality of Elyot's *Pasquil* is hard to miss. In 1533 Harpocrates, the silent and acquiescent prelate, might well have reminded readers of the recent submission of the clergy to Henry, which placed English prelates in a position resembling that of Harpocrates. Pasquil's origin is also suggestive: he is an "image of stone sitting in the citie of Rome openly: on whom ones in the yere it is leful to every man, to set in verse or prose any taunte . . . agayne whom he list, howe great an astate so ever he be."[49] Protestants had of course cast Rome as the great oppressor, but the Roman character is the source of open criticisms of wrongs in *Pasquil.*[50]

The topicality of the opposition between Pasquil and Gnatho extended to the ambiguous loyalties of Elyot himself. In a 1536 letter to Thomas Cromwell, Elyot wrote, "I perceyve that ye suspect that I savor not truely holy Scriptur."[51] Elyot goes on to assure Cromwell that, "the ordre of Charity savid," he detests what were the standard Protestant charges against the church and pope, charges of adhering to "vayne supersticions" and "superfluouse Ceremonyes." By casting charity as the reservation that keeps him from completely embracing religious reformation, Elyot indicated his awareness of the associations of this theological virtue with salvation through good deeds and merit rather than faith and grace.

The Governour, however, shows Elyot in agreement with Pasquil on the need to understand the lessons of "humanity" before grappling with those of "divinity." For there Elyot's own commitment to the former lessons informs his approach to scriptural interpretation. "I suppose no man thinketh that Esope wrate gospelles, yet who doughteth but that in his fables the fox, the hare, and the wolf, though they never spake, do teach many good wysedoms," argues Elyot in *The Governour* when defending the value of pagan history and poetry.[52] But the comparison, although par-tially asserting the difference between the Word of God and human words, also implies that the efficacy of the Gospels and Aesop are to some extent based upon the same principle, the ability to teach wisdom. Indeed, *The Governour* dubs virtually all kinds of writings "history," and it places the apocryphal and canonical books of the Bible as well as Homer and Aris-totle under this rubric.[53]

"[I]n some places men saye, faythe is tourned to herisye," claimed Elyot's Pasquil in 1533, and the figure of the Bible-spouting courtier, Gnatho, represents Elyot's worst fears of this kind of transformation. If countenanced by the powerful, professions of heresy might become a cre-dential essential to advancement at court as well as the only way to ensure survival anywhere. On the other hand, Gnatho terms Pasquil's railing an "indiscrete libertie in speche," whereby he uses "unprofitable tauntes and rebukes," ones that, if Gnatho were willing to be a "reporter," would cause Pasquil "no littel displeasure."[54] As we have seen, such reporting by infor-mants could even extend to the alehouse. Thus, the anonymous publica-tion of *Pasquil* itself is not hard to understand.

Pasquil does, however, eventually provide a counterargument to Gna-tho's assertion that Pasquil's castigations are "unprofitable" since the ob-jects of Pasquil's blame are not "one iote amended" and Pasquil loses "therby preferment," which his "excellent wit doth require."[55] For re-sponding to Harpocrates' similar accusation that Pasquil and his attacks "profitest so lyttel," Pasquil claims that he causes men to "perceive, that theyr vices, whiche they thinke to be wonderfull secrete be knowen to all men." Furthermore, "whan they see the thing not succede to theyr purpose they wyl be ashamed."[56] This threat recalls the shaming of Venus and Mars in *The Governour,* but it also is the obverse of what we have seen to be Elyot's definition of true nobility in *The Governour*—that is, to be a person of such "vertues and qualities as he desireth to be openly publisshed." The other side of the ability to promulgate virtue is that of revealing hidden vices.

Like Moses in *The Governour,* Pasquil exercises his own virtues outside the confines of court or palace. But this locale does not necessarily render Pasquil base or in any way inferior to those who have been "called to counsayll" at court.[57] On the contrary, a kind of nobility does adhere to Pasquil. Thus, Elyot describes Pasquil as an "olde Romane" who "by longe sittinge in the strete, and heringe market men chat" is "become rude and homely."[58] Although situated on the street, Pasquil articulates a distinctly "olde," or, conservative and aristocratic, opposition to the social climbing of new men such as Gnatho. But Pasquil has also departed from the practice of an entrenched aristocracy by using the market to call attention to himself. For, as even Gnatho admits, by means of his "longe railinge" Pasquil's "wyt is well knowen."[59] That is, while exposing the blemishes of others, Pasquil has managed to publicize his own virtues.

As a writer whose criticisms of the powerful were published, Elyot cast himself as something of a Pasquil figure. In the preface to *Of the Knowledge Which Maketh a Wise Man* (1533), a dialogue between Plato and Aristippus over the proper way of making rulers aware of their faults, Elyot described Henry VIII as having recognized that Elyot "spared none astate in the rebukynge of vice" in the *Governour*. Elyot went on to liken himself to a "playne and rude persone" of the city of Rome who "alwaye spake in the rebuke of all men." To be sure, in the same preface Elyot also reports that Henry took the rebuking qualities of the *Governour* "in the better part," and the point of the comparison of Elyot to the plainspoken Roman proves to be the tolerance and encouragement of such plainspokenness by the Roman emperor. Nevertheless, Elyot also accuses some of his readers of hoping to bring both his "warkes" and himself "into the indignation of some man in auctorytie."[60]

Henry's own policy shifts made this kind of indignation particularly hard to avoid. Thus, the private correspondence between Elyot and Cromwell reveals the degree to which sudden governmental changes of course could turn Gnathos into Pasquils and vice versa. These letters generally show Elyot trying to prove his loyalty to the Henrician regime, but they also reveal the obstacles that made Elyot's loyalty less than certain. Thus, for instance, in 1536, a year after More's execution, Elyot adapted an Erasmian adage to assure Cromwell that his "amity" with More was but *"usque ad aras"* and thus no obstacle to Elyot's "truthe and fidelity" toward Henry.[61] Whatever the relationship between Elyot and More, the ambiguities of Elyot's renunciation of this friendship (which "altars" define its limits for Elyot?) indicate the difficulty of demonstrating loyalty to a regime bent on redefining its own religious allegiances.

Elyot's qualification of his friendship with More in 1536 needs to be compared to another letter that Elyot wrote to Cromwell in the same year. For this letter also concerns the subject of friendship and Elyot's attempt to clear himself of the suspicion of supporting opponents of the Henrician

Reformation. To be sure, the focus of this letter is more Elyot's own reading than his loyalty to particular individuals known to be on the side of Rome. Yet Elyot also recognizes the degree to which his books define his friendships and allegiances, and thus, describing his reading to Cromwell, he represents himself as being part of a tangled multiplicity of alliances, both intellectual and personal.

Elyot's letter to Cromwell was a response to what Elyot termed a royal "proclamation concerning sediciouse bookes."[62] This proclamation (January 1536) ordered the surrender to Cromwell or the chancellor of "one book imprinted comprising a sermon made by John Fisher, late bishop of Rochester" as well as other writings and books slandering the king or "repugnant" to statutes enacting the "abolition of the usurped power of the Bishop of Rome."[63] The recently executed Fisher had openly opposed Henry's divorce in his writings and in person, and his execution had demonstrated the dangers of taking the stance of Pasquil too far. Indeed, the Bishop of Rochester was one of the few English prelates not to act the part of Harpocrates during this period.

Elyot's letter to Cromwell constitutes, in part, an "Usque ad aras" renunciation of Fisher and his ilk. Thus Elyot refers to arguments with "suche persones as ye [i.e., Cromwell] have thowght that I have specially favored, even as ye allso didd, for some laudable qualities which we supposid to be in theim."[64] But the letter also contains a pointed reminder of the rapid obsolescence of political and religious orthodoxy under Henry. For Elyot claims that, "[a]s for the warkes of John fisshar," he has in his possession "one litle sermon, which aboute eight or nyne yeres passid was translatid into latine by Master Pace."[65] The sermon was given in 1521 upon the occasion of the first burning of Luther's books in England as part of the campaign of both Fisher and others, including More, to support and even, to some degree, script the anti-Lutheranism of their sovereign. But in 1536 Elyot must assure Cromwell that he had only bought the sermon for the translation and not for the "author or mater."[66] A sermon that previously enacted government policy has become potentially treasonous.[67]

In this letter, however, books are not necessarily a source of incrimination. They also help to form personal bonds, as Erasmus had recognized when he inaugurated his own massive compilation of learning with the proverb, "common are the things of friends." Thus, Elyot claims that the "similitude" of his and Cromwell's "studies which undoubtidly is the moste perfeict fundacion of amitie" underlies their friendship.[68] Elyot goes on to detail his own studies: "I have ben ever desyrouse to reade many bookes, specially concerning humanitie and morall Philosophy, and there[for] of suche studies I have a competent number." Here, again, is "humanitie, the lesson of the gentiles," albeit less stridently expounded than in *Pasquil*. Indeed, this "humanitie" does not necessarily remove Elyot from the court as it does Pasquil, but it supposedly links him to Cromwell, who, we are to infer, shares Elyot's passion for books of moral philosophy.

Yet the similitude of studies between Elyot and Cromwell has its limits. Thus, on the one hand, Elyot disclaims any interest in scriptural interpretation: "But concerning holy scripture I have very fewe [i.e., books], for in questionistes I never delyted: unsavery gloses and comentes I ever abhorred: the bostars and advauntars of the pompouse authoritie of the Busshop of Rome I never esteemyd."[69] Elyot also asserts that "moche and seriouse reading" has made him aware of the need for the "reformation" of the church. Nevertheless, in addition to Fisher's sermon, Elyot also admits to having in his possession other "bookes as be now prohibited contayning the busshop of Romes authoritie . . . joyned with diverse other warkes in one grete volume or two at the moste." Elyot claims, somewhat implausibly, never to have read these prohibited books, and he promises to send them to Cromwell. But his possession of contraband religious polemic is suspicious.[70]

In his discussion of friendship in *The Governour,* Elyot makes the point that a "similitude of studies or lerninge" is a great enhancement of friendship, but, if such studies are "to serious or full of contention," friendship is "oftentimes assaulted, whereby it is often in parile."[71] Elyot's 1536 letters to Cromwell suggest that their similitude of studies, too, depended upon the decision to overlook or eliminate matter of contention and was only valid "Usque ad aras." Books as well as putative personal attachments obstructed the possibility of a complete reconciliation of Elyot and the Henrician government during the 1530s. Indeed, some of these books may have been ones written by Elyot. Thus, Elyot's nervousness concerning his studies in 1536 raises the possibility that what he had described in 1533 as the attempts of detractors to bring his works into the "indignation" of "some man in auctoritye" were beginning to take effect.

Elyot's works and studies, however, were vulnerable to another charge besides that of seeming to favor the seditious ideas and books of the Catholic martyrs, More and Fisher. For *The Governour* owed much to an earlier yet still problematic More, the author of *Utopia*. In *The Governour* Elyot tries to define carefully the nature of this debt, which was not restricted to the Dialogue of Counsel as is the case with *Pasquil*. In particular, *The Governour* engages the communism of Utopia, as it tries to define its own best form of a republic and republic of letters. In so doing, *The Governour* demonstrates that even in 1531, when More was chancellor, Elyot's attachment to More—or at least his writings—could only go so far.

ELYOT AND UTOPIAN COMMUNISM

The Governour has been dubbed both "Utopian" and an "anti-*Utopia*,"[72] appellations that do not exclusively concern the issue of communism. But I want to focus on this issue since Elyot so clearly raises it when he claims to be describing in the "vulgare tunge the fourme of a juste publike weale." For this claim does more than alert readers to the possibility of a gap between a just "publike weale" and the one presided over by Henry. Elyot's readers might also have wondered here whether Elyot's form of a just republic was a Utopian one. At the end of *Utopia,* Raphael Hythlodaeus had advanced the argument that, as a communist society, Utopia was not only the best form of a *respublica* but the only one that had the right to call itself a *respublica.* For, according to Raphael, the denizens of other republics might speak of the public good [de publico loquentes ubique commodo], but their real interest had to be their own welfare [privatum curant]. Indeed, in other republics "justitia" could not be anything else but an empty name.[73] Raphael's definition of a *respublica* was not, of course, the only one available to Elyot, but it was a crucial one, as far as Elyot's need to delimit his own politics and those of English humanism was concerned.

At the outset of *The Governour,* however, Elyot provides his own translation of *respublica,* and this translation is meant to dispel the notion that *The Governour* will be an English *Utopia:*

> wherfore hit semeth that men have ben longe abused in calling *Rempublicam* a commune weale. And they which do suppose it so to be called for that, that every thinge shulde be to all men in commune, without discrepance of any astate or condicion, be thereto moved more by sensualite than by any good reason or inclination to humanite.[74]

This tendentious translation of *respublica* provides the most explicit basis for reading *The Governour* as an "anti-*Utopia*," and it seems clearly directed at the peroration of Raphael Hythlodaeus. Yet Elyot's claim that advocates of communism are moved by sensuality rather than an "inclination to humanite" is an intriguing one. For his usage of "humanity," an important word for Elyot, raises the question of why anyone would think that the source of a belief in communism is "humanite." For when Gnatho censured the "humanitie" of Pasquil, he was castigating Pasquil's devotion to the learning of the gentiles, the *studia humanitatis.* But this learning does not include an exposition of the virtues of universal communism that is comparable to the argument of Raphael Hythlodaeus in *Utopia.*

But, as Elyot knew, "humanite" had another meaning besides the learning of the gentiles, and this second meaning gives it Christian resonances. Thus, Elyot defines "humanitie" as follows in book 2 of *The Governour:*

> The nature and condition of man, wherein he is lasse than god almightie, and excellinge nat withstanding all other creatures in erthe, is called humanitie; which is a generall name to those vertues in whome semeth to be a mutuall concorde and love . . . benevolence, beneficence, and liberalitie, which maketh up the said principall vertue called benignitie or gentilnes.[75]

Comprising "mutuall concorde and love, . . . benevolence . . . and liberalitie," "humanity" is analogous to the theological virtue, charity, that Elyot claims to be displaying in most of his published works. "Benevolence" for Elyot can even entail an undifferentiated distribution of goods. Thus, just before his account of Moses' charity, Elyot writes that he is describing "that benevolence onely whiche is moste universall, wherein is equalitie without singuler affection or acceptaunce of personagis."[76] Such benevolence, however, resembles the communism that Elyot condemns at the outset of *The Governour* in as much as it necessitates "equalitie" and does not seem to have any more regard for one person than another.

Elyot's version of "humanitie" recasts Aulus Gellius' twofold definition of "humanitas" in *Noctes Atticae.*[77] Thus, on the one hand, Gellius argues that those who have used the word "humanitas" correctly have made it a translation of the Greek *paideia,* which Gellius explains as "eruditio institutioque in bonas artes," that is, the liberal arts. The humanity of Pasquil comes from this *humanitas* as *paideia.* On the other hand, Gellius also notes that the "vulgar" [quod vulgus existimat] usage of the word "humanitas" makes it synonymous with "philanthropy," which Gellius defines as a "dexteritatem quandam benevolentiamque erga omnes homines promiscuam," that is, a promiscuous benevolence toward all men. Elyot's definition of "humanity" in *The Governour* is a translation of what Gellius sees as the vulgar sense of the *humanitas,* and Elyot's emphasis on the "equality" inherent in benevolence reflects the "promiscuous" character of Gellius' *humanitas.*

Both meanings of *humanitas* are relevant to *The Governour.* As an educational treatise, book 1 of *The Governour* is an attempt to inculcate an English version of *paideia.* Yet, even so, Elyot describes the intended audience of *The Governour* as consisting of "reders . . . who perchance for the more part have nat ben trayned in lerninge contayninge semblable matter."

Thus, he has to "compile one definition out of many, in as compendious fourme" as he can in order to arrive at his translation of *respublica* (and presumably other virtues, too). This description of his audience and method suggests that Elyot's own display of humanity in *The Governour* combines both paideia and philanthropy.[78] That is, Elyot is trying to make the liberal arts, if not available to everyone, at least accessible to a broader readership. Elyot did not view the republic of letters as a utopian commonwealth, but, by addressing himself to untrained readers, he was trying to level some of the differences within this republic.

Parts of *The Governour* seem aimed exclusively at the gentry and nobility, yet Elyot was aware that the readership of *The Governour* had the potential to be a socially promiscuous one. To be sure, any attempt to implement fully Elyot's educational program for future governors would require money and land since this program involves, among other things, hiring tutors and hunting. Nevertheless, at times Elyot also implies that *The Governour* and books like it could serve as substitutes for the very educational program that *The Governour* advocates. Elyot's interest in abbreviating the learning process is initially evident from the methodology that he delineates when defining *respublica*—that of compiling a terse unity out of multiplicity. But throughout *The Governour*, even as Elyot describes the multitude of books that future magistrates should read, he also provides or alerts his readers to the existence of shortcuts to the contents of these books.[79]

If the educational program of book 1 is slanted toward the landed aristocracy, Elyot's most detailed summary of the plan of *The Governour* suggests the possibility of books 2 and 3, at least, having a broader audience and purpose:

I wyll ordinately treate of the two partes of a publike weale, wherof the one shall be named Due Administration, the other Necessary Occupation, whiche shall be devided in to two volumes. In the fyrste shall be comprehended the best fourme of education . . . of noble children. . . .

The seconde volume . . . shall conteine all the reminant . . . apt to the perfection of a iuste publike weale: in the whiche I shall so endeavor my selfe, that al men, of what astate or condition so ever they be, shall finde therin occasion to be alway vertuously occupied; and not without pleasure, if they be nat of the scholes of Aristippus or Apicius . . . from whose sharpe talons . . . I beseche all gentill reders, to defende these warkes.[80]

This passage distinguishes between the "administration" of a "publike weale" and "necessary occupation" within it. The former is the province of "noble children" whereas the latter is open to "al men, of what astate or condition so ever they be." Yet, in typical fashion, Elyot's language also muddies the difference between the two groups and their activities. If virtue is the surname of nobility, then to be "vertuously occupied" in Elyot's public weal is to attain a nobility of a kind. Such virtuous occupation might even encompass administration. Indeed, "all gentill reders" are a nebulous group, with the potential to extend beyond a nobility of birth.

Later in *The Governour,* Elyot echoes this passage in an apparent effort to discourage the poor from trying to educate themselves, but even there his language is slippery and suggestive of the superiority of talent to birth:

Also suche men [i.e., the landed gentry], havyng substaunce in goodes by certeyne and stable possessions, . . . may, (if nature repugn not) cause them [i.e., their children] to be so instructed and furnisshed toward the administration of a publike weale, that a poure mannes sonne, onely by his naturall witte, without other adminiculation or aide, never or seldome may atteyne to the semblable. Towarde the whiche instruction I have . . . prepared this warke . . . only to declare the fervent zele that I have to my countrey and that I desyre only to employ the poure learning, that I have gotten . . . to the benefite thereof, and to the recreation of all the reders that be of any noble or gentill courage, gyvynge them occasion to eschewe idelnes, beynge occupied in redynge this warke.[81]

Again, Elyot addresses the occupation of his readers, and he claims that his own employment of his "poure learning" (a phrase that reappears in the *Image of Governance* as "poor talent") provides them with a way of eschewing "idleness." The eschewal of idleness is also one of the morals that Elyot drew from the parable of the talents, and Elyot here applies this moral to his readers as well as himself. By investing his own small intellectual wealth, Elyot is exercising the talents of his readers in addition to his own. Such self-deprecation is partly ironic, but it also makes the point that a little learning can go a long way. For by Elyot's own admission, *The Governour* is an abbreviation of riches more abundantly available elsewhere. Nevertheless, its abbreviated character does not prevent *The Governour* from helping to maintain full employment in the economy of learning.

Elyot's readers are of "noble or gentill courage," but this phrase conveniently begs the question of their social status. Thus, on the one hand, Elyot claims that the poor do not have the resources to educate their children, and these children, in turn, cannot learn by their own "naturall witte, without other adminiculation or aide." But, as we have seen, the compendious or "poor" learning of *The Governour* provides a relatively cheap version of such assistance. Moreover, even the children of the wealthy are dependent upon natural wit: they can only learn if "nature repugn not." To put it another way, they must possess at least some talent.[82] If reading Elyot's book is an occupation that leads to administration, others besides those having "certeyne and stable possessions" could conceivably become administrators.

We do not know whether the books of *The Governour* as we have them represent the fulfillment of Elyot's initial division of *The Governour* into sections treating necessary occupation and due administration. Nevertheless, Elyot's understanding of the relationship of certain kinds of occupation to administration is intriguing because, among other things, Elyot's proposed second volume on the perfection of a "juste publike weale" sounds Utopian. Thus, the citizens of his just republic will conjoin virtue and pleasure as the Utopians try to do, and, like the Utopians, they will adhere to a rather strict work ethic. Moreover, the threat posed by the school of Aristippus takes even further the affiliation of *The Governour* and its author with ideal republics and their creators. For this threat implies that Elyot is an English Plato, and it anticipates the debate between Plato and Aristippus *Of the Knowledge Which Maketh a Wise Man.*

Humanity is itself a Utopian virtue. Thus, Utopus, the founder of the kind of society that Elyot professes to abhor, is said in *Utopia* to have led a formerly rustic people to a point of "cultus, humanitatisque" [culture and humanity] that surpasses the rest of the world.[83] Since the Utopians are prone to learning and they distribute benefits relatively evenly among themselves, both meanings of "humanitas" are probably pertinent here. Utopian society offers a vision of unprecedented access to knowledge and the necessities of life. Indeed, Utopian society suggests that true paideia and philanthropy flourish best together.

In *The Governour,* however, Elyot seems to want to treat the divulgation of knowledge and the distribution of material goods as separate issues. Nevertheless, in his works of lexicography, this separation does not hold. Elyot's definitions of the Latin *divulgo,* the root of his own "devulgate," apply the language of communism to the meaning of this word. For according to the *Bibliotheca Eliotae* (1542), a revised edition of the 1538 *Dictionary, divulgo* means "to publish abroad, to set a thing in such a condition as every man may use it at his pleasure, to make a thing common." Likewise, the Latin noun, *divulgatio,* is the "publication or making a thing common to all men." Both these definitions seem to be referring to the distribution of a *res,* the making common of a formerly private property.

Elyot's usage of *divulgate* in the preface to *Bibliotheca Eliota,* however, addresses the dangers of making certain kinds of intellectual property "common to all men." Thus, it is

necessary to enterlace the detestable heretykes, with their sundry heresyes, concernynge the substance of our catholyke faythe, justly condemned by the hole
consent of all true chrysten men, to the intente that those heresyes beinge in this
wise *divulgate,* may be the sooner espyed and abhorred in suche bokes, where they
be craftily enterlaced with holsome doctrine. (my emphasis)[84]

Elyot sounds reasonably convinced that by including entries on the meaning of heresies and thereby divulgating the knowledge of those heresies to
his readers he is combatting rather than augmenting the problem. As
Elyot continues to explain and defend his inclusion of heretics, he makes
the communistic impetus of his project clear by defining his goal as that of
making heresies "commune knowledge" in order to alert readers to their
dangers.[85] The phrase "commune knowledge" both makes explicit the
notion of interpretive property latent in "divulgate" and recalls Erasmus'
"literae communes." Yet, in the *Bibliotheca,* Elyot does not make heresies common in such a way that "every man may use them at his pleasure." Rather, each entry concerning a heresy comes with its own sig-
nals that direct the reader's use of an entry to a particular end—usually
condemnation.[86]

As with his dictionary definition of *divulgo,* Elyot's "to devulgate or
sette fourth" refers to more than the vulgarity of the vernacular (the "vulgar tonge"). Rather, it also includes the sense of writing for a not entirely
circumscribed audience. In *The Governour* as a whole Elyot's understanding
of vulgarity has a broad range. Thus, at times Elyot uses "vulgar" to brand
those whom he regards as his social inferiors, and he even makes vulgar a
synonym for "plebeian" or "common."[87] On the other hand, when writing
that nobility is not "after the vulgare opinion of men, but is only the
prayse and surname of vertue," Elyot is using "vulgar" to indicate what he
sees as a lack of understanding or education common to a number of social
classes. Given the shifts of meaning of "vulgar" in *The Governour,* Elyot's
professed purpose of divulgation would seem to be a potentially indiscriminate one.

Again, however, Elyot only claims to have divulgated "some part" of his
studies in *The Governour.* Accordingly, the key classical example of divulgation given in *The Governour* involves holding back knowledge. Such
secrecy is primarily the work of Aristides, an Athenian leader who, according to Plutarch, favored Lycurgus' aristocratic form of government and
was ostracized by the Athenian democracy.[88] Thus, borrowing a story that
appears in Cicero's *De Officiis,* Plutarch's *Life of Themistoceles* and his *Life of
Aristides,* and Erasmus' *De Lingua,* Elyot describes the choice of Aristides—
"for his vertue surnamed rightwise"[89]—who must decide whether to re-

veal to the Athenian people a plan whereby they might treacherously burn the ships of their enemy, Sparta. The plan of burning the Spartan ships is imparted to Aristides by his archrival, Themistocles, who declares that the plan "aught nat to be divulgate or publisshed," and thus he secretly discloses it to Aristides.[90] Aristides, in turn, offers a highly censored account of the plan to the Athenian people, who, not fully knowing what they are choosing, opt for virtue rather than expediency.[91]

Aristides, who has acquired his surname "for his vertue," is by Elyot's own definition a true noble, and one demonstration of his nobility proves to be his skillful manipulation of a multitude. Guiding the Athenian democracy toward virtue, Aristides is also something of a pagan Moses. As such he helps Elyot to elucidate further the kind of leadership that he views himself as exercising in print when confronting the democracy of learning. Such leadership entails mediated divulgation, the making of some but not all knowledge common, and the mediator is necessarily an ambiguous figure. For, depending upon the perspective from which they are viewed, both Elyot and Aristides could seem supporters and opponents of the deliberative power of the *demos*. They appeal to this power at the same time as they try to circumscribe it.[92] Indeed, despite his oligarchic sympathies and ostracism, Aristides was also at times a popular leader, and he was responsible for measures increasing the democratic character of Athens.[93]

The need for mediation informs Elyot's attitudes toward the distribution of other *res* besides knowledge in *The Governour*. Indeed, when Elyot finally comes to examine justice in book 3 of *The Governour*, the justice that concerns Elyot represents yet another qualification of the indiscriminate equality of benevolence. Thus, Elyot makes use of book 5 of Aristotle's *Ethics* to distinguish between "justice distributive" and "justice commutative." Justice distributive involves the "distribution of honour, money, benefite, or other thinge semblable." Given its purpose, justice distributive must have regard to the "persone" to whom these commodities are to be dispensed. Justice commutative, on the other hand, is "corrective" and has no "regarde to the persone, but onely considerynge the inequalitie wherby the one thynge excedeth the other, indeavoureth to brynge them bothe to an equalitie."[94] Justice commutative pertains to activities such as buying and selling, and its goal of equality therefore should not be applied to questions of distributive justice.

Elyot, however, gives his most sustained depiction of distributive justice before he actually defines this term, and this depiction proves to be, yet again, an application of the parable of the talents to social hierarchy:

And therfor hit appereth that god gyveth nat to every man like gyftes of grace, or of nature, but to some more, some lesse, as it liketh his divine maiestie.

Ne they be nat in commune, (as fantastical foles wolde have all thyngs), nor one man hath nat al vertues and good qualities. Nat withstandyng for as moche as understandyng is the most excellent gyfte that man can receive in his creation, wherby he doth approche most nyghe unto the similitude of god, which understandynge is the principall parte of the soule: it is therfore congruent . . . that as one excelleth an other in that influence, . . . so shulde the astate of his persone be avanced in degree or place where understandynge may profite. . . . And unto men of such vertue by very equitie appertaineth honour, as theyr juste rewarde and duetie. . . . For as moche as the saide persones, excelling in knowledge wherby other be governed, be ministers for only profite and commoditie of them which have nat equall understandyng: . . . Wherfore it can none other wyse stande with reason, but that the astate of the persone in preeminence of lyvvynge shulde be estemed with his understandyng, labour, and policie: where unto muste be added an augmentation of honour and substance.[95]

Here, Elyot expresses an opposition to both communism and the prerogatives of birth. In place of these two alternatives, he proposes a society governed by a class of "persones" who, in the manner of Aristides, mediate between complete democracy and a too entrenched oligarchy. The gifts of understanding are not common, and therefore rewards should not be evenly distributed either. Nor, we are to infer, should the less able, however high their social standing, receive an unfair share of privileges. We are left then with an aristocracy of talent. But this aristocracy is also one of benevolence. Thus, by virtue of "equitie," the talented should have their substance augmented because they are "ministers for only profite and commoditie of them which have nat equall understandynge." Paradoxically, a willingness to bestow one's gifts in a way that corrects or at least alleviates inequality becomes the basis of a system of social differences.

"Equity" is the key alternative to equality here, and it is a word that also appears as part of Elyot's definition of a *respublica*. Thus, before castigating the translation of *respublica* as "commonwealth," Elyot defines it as follows: "A publike weale is a body lyvyng, compact or made of sondry astates and degrees of men, which is disposed by the ordre of equitie and governed by the rule and moderation of reason."[96] Elyot's argument that rewards in a republic should be distributed according to gifts of understanding serves, then, to amplify what Elyot means by "equitie" in his initial definition of *respublica*. For equity, as Elyot uses it in this amplification, is the underlying principle of distributive justice, a regard for differences of persons rather than mere equality.

Elyot's equity has a rhetorical analogue, that is, decorum, or the kind of considerations of person, time, and place that Erasmus had tried to impress upon Luther and that are a central issue of fictional dialogues such as *Utopia* and *Pasquil the Playne*. Indeed, Pasquil's claim to rail at all estates constitutes a disregard for differences of person, and it represents an explicitly antirhetorical equality. Everyone, no matter how high or low their position is, becomes equally subject to Pasquil's rebuke. *The Governour*, too, despite its insistence that future governors learn rhetoric, contains a rather lengthy castigation of empty rhetorical knowledge. Elyot even borrows a word from the *Phaedrus, logodaedali,* to censure the teachers of a vain rhetoric.[97] Yet as an exemplary figure, Aristides suggests that considerations of decorum and prudence kept Elyot from entirely commiting himself to the stance of Pasquil—at least, in *The Governour*.

Raphael Hythlodaeus' most radically egalitarian successors, however, were not Luther and Tyndale but the Anabaptists, who had begun to infiltrate England in the late 1520s. In 1535 a royal proclamation had ordered those who had "of their own presumption and authority lately rebaptized themselves" to leave England at once.[98] A 1538 proclamation, too, inveighed against the "false opinion of the Anabaptists and Sacramentaries ben lately come into this realm, where they lurk secretly in divers corners and places."[99] These proclamations do not mention the issue of communism, but, as we have seen, the 1538 proclamation does castigate an excessive liberty of speech and the discussion of important doctrinal issues in taverns as one of the consequences of Anabaptist infiltration.

In *The Governour*, Elyot expands upon an Erasmian adage, "Nosce te ipsum," to criticize what he sees as the leveling tendencies of Anabaptism and to define the boundaries of charity. Thus, the self-knowledge of an "inferior persone or subjecte" consists of accepting the necessity of inequality:

howe farre out of reason shall we iudge them to be that wolde exterminate all superioritie, extincte alle governaunce and lawes, and under the coloure of holy scripture, whiche they do violently wraste to their purpose, do endeavor them selfes to bryng the life of man in to a confusion inevitable. . . . Sens without governaunce and lawes the persones moste stronge in body shulde by violence constraigne them that be of lasse strength. . . . Than were all our equalitie dasshed, and finally as bestes savage the one shall desire to slee another . . . except these evangelicall persones coulde perswade god or compelle him to chaunge men in to aungels, makinge them all one disposition and confirminge them all in one fourme of charitie. And as concerning all men in a generalitie, this sentence, knowe thy selfe, . . . induceth men sufficiently to the knowlege of iustyce.[100]

Here, Elyot refutes an explicitly Christian defense of equality, one promulgated "under the coloure of holy scripture," and supposed to confirm men in a single form of charity. The "evangelicall persones" that Elyot is overtly rebuking here are the Anabaptists, who were also known for their refusal to accept the need for government at all. But the confirmation of men in one disposition and form of charity is suggestive of Utopian society, too, which conjoins charity and conformity. Moreover, the situation of Utopian society between heaven and earth reappears here as the attempt to transform men into angels. Indeed, what Elyot sees as the mistakes of overly fervent evangelists could apply to Raphael Hythlodaeus, too. For Raphael wrests the Bible to his purposes and has a first name suggestive of an overlap between angelic and human nature.

The charity, however, against which Elyot rails here was an important part of his own self-definition as a popularizer. Thus his attack upon Anabaptists also indicates the limits to which Elyot's credo of charity and benevolence can be taken. Elyot's association of a misuse of charity and Utopian ideas with the Reformation receives further confirmation from a letter that Elyot wrote to the Duke of Norfolk during his 1531 diplomatic mission for Henry VIII. The letter concerns Elyot's travels through Germany, and it contains an explicitly licentious version of communal property:

The City of Spire as I here say keepeth yet their faith well, except some say there be many do err in taking too largely this article *sanctorum commnionem* which hath induced more charity than may stand with honesty.
[Elyot proceeds to describe the public displays of "lovers" and their "paramours" in the city.]
[T]he woman sate with their heddes discovirid. . . . I suppose it was the tryumphe of Venus or of the devil or of bothe.

Elyot goes on to describe a vernacular mass in Nuremberg:

In the meantime the subdeacon goeth into the pulpit and readeth to the people the Epistle in their vulgare. After they peruse other things as our priests do, then the priest readeth softly the gospell in Latin. In the mean space the deacon goeth into the pulpit and readeth aloud the gospel in the Almaign tongue . . . afterward the priest and the choir do sing the Credo as we do. The secrets and the preface they omit. . . . And after the Leviaton the deacon turneth to the people, telling to them in Almaign tongue a long process how they should prepare themselves to the communion of the flesh and blood of Christ; and then may every man come that listeth without going to any Confession. But I lest I should be a partner of their communion departed then. . . . One thing liked me well . . . all the priests

had wives, and they were the fairest women of the town . . . which caused all
the people in the church to wonder at us as though we had been greater heretics
than they.[101]

Elyot is witnessing a transitional mass here, and, as K. J. Wilson notes, the
provenance of the reference to the priests having the fairest wives in the
town is *Utopia*. The Utopian elements of Elyot's description also extend to
the word "communion,"[102] but in Spire "communion" has become the
common possession of women, while in Nuremberg it turns heretical. As
we have seen, in Plato's *Republic* the adage "Common are the things of
friends" denoted sexual communism, and in Utopia, too, some rather
peculiar rites attend marriage. Elyot draws on the tradition of a link
between imaginary republics and bizarre sexual mores to suggest that in
Spire a "Utopian" vision of religion and religious community has led to
anarchy, which takes the form of unbridled carnal appetite, or, as he
termed it in *The Governour*, "sensuality."

Charity, too, has gone awry at Spire, and it even becomes associated
with the triumphs of Venus when Elyot castigates the lovers and their
paramours for displaying "more charity than may stand with honesty."
Indeed, Elyot's description of the open flaunting of paramours in the city
recalls the exposure of Venus in *The Governour* and its effect upon the Cynic
Demetrius. Yet here Venus is not ashamed but exultant. The women sit
with their "heddes discovirid," and they thus, like Demetrius himself,
seem to have abandoned all shame in their words or deeds.

Such shamelessness also extends to the priests choosing the fairest
women of the city as wives. Elyot's reference to priestly marriage is again
an attempt to use sexual license to connote a breakdown of traditional
social structures. Here, however, the reference to *Utopia* may not only be to
communism but also to the popular election of Utopian priests and the
way in which this practice anticipated Reformation efforts, aided by Erasmus' own philology, to redefine the priesthood. Indeed, earlier in the same
letter, Elyot gives a mocking *ad fontes* philological interpretation of the
Greek word for "bishop," *episcopus*, and the point of such philology is to
ridicule the ineffectuality of the Bishop of Wormes, a city that, in Elyot's
view, has been lost to Jews and Lutherans.[103]

But, for Elyot, the stigma of being a "partner" of the communion at
Nuremberg is not escaped so easily. For the leaders of the service, who
continually shift between Latin and the "vulgare," have more in common
with Elyot than he is willing to admit. Or rather he was not willing to
admit such a partnership in 1531. For as we have seen, in the preface to
Elyot's last work, *A Preservative Agaynst Deth*, Elyot would claim the role

of a lay preacher, one who usurped some of the function of the priesthood and reminded a vernacular readership of their "condition." But in 1531, despite his evident fascination with the linguistic exchanges taking place during the service at Nuremberg, Elyot leaves abruptly, and he thus both separates himself from this service and calls attention to his need to do so.

Elyot's letter to Norfolk depicts the Reformation as a potential source of the chaos that occasions such fear and trembling in *The Governour.* But the arguments of *The Governour* in favor of a certain kind of hierarchy would prove most useful to the Henrician government when combating an insurrection that was a reaction to the Reformation. In 1536, the Pilgrimage of Grace put the Tudor government in the somewhat difficult position of, as Arthur Ferguson puts it, having "to justify the promotion of men like Cromwell on the ground of careers open to talent" but also having "like any other government of the period when faced with rebellion, to preach the generally accepted doctrine of obedience within a society of order and degree."[104] The Pilgrimage of Grace was a heterogeneous uprising, combining the outrage of Northern nobles against social climbers such as Cromwell, anti-Reformation religious sentiments, and some popular anger at economic and social injustices. Thus, the Tudor government had to adopt a somewhat contradictory position in order to counter such eclectic grievances.

Richard Morison's *A Remedy for Sedition,* published in 1536 by the king's printer and Elyot's publisher, Berthelet, is an officially sanctioned equation of nobility with virtue, not inherited position. Morison, himself a humanist of low birth, makes considerable use of Elyot and the metaphor of the talent that pervades *The Governour* to keep this meritocracy from dissolving into a Utopian commonwealth. Thus, Morison first castigates the rebels because they "imagine . . . a commonwealth" where the poor appropriate the belongings of the rich:

we [i.e. the rebels whom Morison is impersonating here] imagine a certain commonwealth in word and outward appearance which, if we baptize right and not nickname it, we must needs call a common woe. We think it is very evil that so many of us be poor; we think it were a good world if we were all rich. We think it is very evil that so many of us be poor; we think it were a good world if we were all rich. We think it is very evil that so many of us be poor; we think it were a good world if we were all rich. I pray you for a season let it be as we desire; let us imagine we be all rich, doth it not straight follow: I as good as he, why goeth he before, I behind? I as rich as he, what needeth me to labor? The maid as proud as her dame, who milketh the cow? The farmer having no more cause to toil than he that looketh for the rents, who shall till the ground? . . . What were more to be

103

wailed than such wealth that should bring either every man or the most part of men to extreme confusion?[105]

Here, Morison echoes standard anti-Utopian arguments, as expressed by the character "More" in *Utopia* and Elyot in *The Governour*. More specifically, Morison's equation of a communistic commonwealth with "confusion" recalls Elyot's discussion of the "confusion inevitable" of Anabaptism in *The Governour*. Indeed, Morison's reference to the need to "baptize right and not nickname" an egalitarian "commonwealth" anything but a "common woe" is suggestive of Anabaptism as well as reminiscent of Elyot's charged translation of *respublica* as "publike weal." Here, the Tudor government's fear of the kind of popular Utopianism represented by the Protestant Anabaptists even extends to uprisings with Catholic sympathies.

Although he makes the point that everyone cannot be rich, nevertheless, Morison also wants to argue that everyone has the opportunity to become rich. Hence he castigates the rebels for denying themselves the possibility of social mobility:

They be angry that virtue should be rewarded when she cometh to men that had no lords to their fathers. They will that none rule but noblemen born. Let them have that they require; who toucheth this so sore as themselves and all their posterity? What do they leave unto theirs, when they take away the possibility of better fortune?[106]

That is, here Morison accuses the rebels of being too committed to the existing distribution of wealth and title and thus being insufficiently Utopian. But what prevents everyone from asserting their virtue and thus demanding a redistribution of wealth that might approximate Utopian "confusion"? The answer is the inequality with which "gifts of the mind" have been distributed, an inequality, however, that still presents a challenge to the status quo:

Now, as there is a difference in these things, so must we put also a difference in men that are endued with them. They must be best esteemed that have most gifts of the mind, that is, they that do excel in wisdom, justice, temperancy, and such other virtues. They next that have most gifts of the body as health, strength, quickness, beauty. They thirdly that have riches and possessions, the laws notwithstanding, having evermore their strength; that is, no man presuming (of what qualities soever he be) to prefer himself to any office or lands, but as the governors or laws shall call him to.[107]

This passage recalls Elyot's discussion of the decidedly noncommunistic distribution of the "most excellent gift" of "understanding" in *The Gover-*

nour. Morison remakes Elyot's point that the "gifts of the mind" "be not in common." But, faced with an actual rebellion, Morison goes on to stipulate that the attempt to translate talent into material wealth must proceed lawfully rather than by means of insurrection. Yet, in Morison's formulation, the government and the law are all that stand between wealthy landowners and attacks upon their property. No natural superiority or strength protects these landowners. Here, Morison's reaffirmation of the status quo of the propertied classes actually represents the triumph of talent over them.

But, if propagandists such as Morison found Elyot useful, so would writers whose connection to the government was as ambiguous as Elyot's. In particular, another disgruntled civil servant, Ralph Robinson would again deploy Elyot's trope of the talent to introduce his translation of *Utopia* into English, and he would do so at a time when landowners felt threatened by assault from below and the apparently sympathetic government response to this assault. Ralph Robinson will demonstrate that the range of responses to the politics of English humanism was as wide as Elyot (and, for that matter, More) feared it would be. Elyot conspicuously holds in check the possibility that the exercise of talent in print might be tantamount to trying to incite a multitude to attack their social superiors. But Robinson, as we shall see, was far less careful, and he made *Utopia* the vehicle of his willingness to take risks eschewed by Elyot.

FOUR

Topical Utopias

Ralph Robinson's *Utopia* and
Thomas Chaloner's *The Praise of Folie*

R alph Robinson's *Utopia* (1551) and Thomas Chaloner's *The Praise of Folie* (1549) were published during one of England's most Protestant periods—the brief kingship of the boy-ruler, Edward VI (1547–53). Indeed, Edward acceded to the throne only twelve years after More's own execution marked the ineluctable progress of the Reformation in England. Both translations were also published at a time when religious change, political dissent, and popular uprising had once again become linked.[1] But the connection that More in 1532 had implied between vernacular translations of humanist texts and of the Bible also proved prophetic. For Robinson's *Utopia* and Chaloner's *Praise of Folie* derived some of their impetus from a decidedly Reformation zeal for the vernacular. In addition to receiving part of its own inspiration from texts such as Erasmus' *Paraclesis* and *Paraphrases,* however, this zeal also extended to what we have seen to be the more apocryphal works of Erasmian humanism.

Elyot's Gnatho, a caricature of *sola scriptura* courtliness, was somewhat premature in 1533. Indeed, despite the licensing of the Matthew Bible of 1537 and Henry's transmission to the laity of the Great Bible in 1539, the Henrician regime was never entirely at ease with a widely available vernacular Bible. The 1543 Act for the Advancement of True Religion forbade Bible reading to the very readership that Erasmus had celebrated in his *Paraclesis.* On the other hand, Edward's reign saw a royal injunction (1547) that licensed Bible reading for all as well as related developments such as the first vernacular liturgies—that is, the 1549 as well as the 1552 Book of Common Prayer—and the provisioning of Nicholas Udall's translation (1548) of Erasmus's *Paraphrases* in every parish church. In addition, long-standing heresy statutes and the specifically Henrician prepublication censorship of religious opinion were revoked. It was a period of greater freedom of the press than any England would enjoy until the 1640s.[2]

The Edwardian government's sponsorship of translations of religious texts overlapped with its sponsorship of vernacular versions of less explicitly religious works. Thus, Robinson's dedication of his *Utopia* to William Cecil—the future Lord Burleigh but then "one of the two principal secretaries to the king"—is telling.[3] For Cecil was an important patron of Protestant printers and writers during the Edwardian period. John King has rightly argued that Robinson's dedication of *Utopia* to Cecil can be viewed as a complicated request for patronage, which Cecil did finally grant Robinson, although not to Robinson's complete satisfaction. Thus, in his 1551 letter to Cecil, which accompanies an English translation of More's prefatory letter to Giles, Robinson, like Elyot in the *Image of Governance,* alluded to his own "poore talente."[4] Moreover, Robinson signed a letter to Cecil written sometime after 1572 "Rodolphus Robynson. For some place to relieve his povery."[5] Nevertheless, from Cecil's perspective such poverty might have seemed deserved. For, as we shall see, in 1551 *Utopia* was perhaps the last text that Cecil would have wanted publicly dedicated to himself.

The title page of the 1551 *Utopia,* however, further complicates Robinson's social position and that of his intended readers. For this title page labels Robinson a "citizen and Goldsmythe of London," and it ascribes Robinson's translation to "the procurement and earnest request of George Tadlowe Citizen and haberdasher of the same citie."[6] This conspicuous identification of Robinson as a London citizen suggests that such citizens might have been another targeted audience of the translation. Indeed, despite the social position of Cecil (he was recently knighted) and his importance to the king, Robinson's prefatory letter to Cecil also stresses Robinson's friendship with George Tadlowe "an honest citizein of London, and in the same citie well accepted and of good reputation." Among other things, Robinson argues that Tadlowe, as the "chief persuadour" of the publication of Robinson's translation, must "take upon him the daunger, whyche upon this bolde and rashe enterpriyse shall ensue."[7] Robinson, however, does not make the nature of this danger entirely clear in his letter to Cecil.[8]

Robinson published another edition of his translation in 1556, and the textual apparatus to this later edition highlights by contrast the character of the 1551 preface. In 1556 Robinson eliminated his letter to Cecil (no longer a powerful figure during the Marian period), but he kept his translation of More's letter to Giles. The 1556 edition also included a new letter of Robinson's own, entitled "The Translator to the gentle reader." This letter to the "gentle reader" apologizes for mistakes in the 1551 edition, and it blames such mistakes on "a frende" (probably Tadlowe), whose "meanesse" of "learninge" forced Robinson to "submit" and "attemper" his "stile."[9] The title page of the 1556 edition significantly dubs Robinson a "sometime fellowe of Corpus Christi College in Oxford," not a goldsmith and citizen of London. The publication of William Rastell's edition of More's English *Workes* in 1557 would demonstrate that the Marian period was a good time for the reception of books by England's most accomplished writer against heresy, but Robinson's 1556 revision of his 1551 translation mentions neither More's martyrdom nor his religious polemics.[10] Rather, the evident function of the textual apparatus to the 1556 edition is to cut Robinson's citizen ties. The reader of Robinson's translation is now identified as a "gentle" one, and Robinson figures as a university graduate who is embarrassed to have subjected his style to the "meanesse" of a London citizen.

Goldsmiths and, more generally, London citizens were not necessarily poor, as *Utopia* itself reveals,[11] but Robinson's shifts between gentility and meanness do give at least some indication of an unstable social position. Unlike Robinson, however, Chaloner was the picture of a humanist who acquired solid and relatively secure benefits through a lifetime of state service, and, in the *Praise of Folie,* he generally articulates the stance of, if he does not explicitly address, the gentle reader. Between 1546 and his death in 1565, Chaloner was knighted, acquired substantial properties, and undertook numerous diplomatic missions for both Mary and Elizabeth. The title page of *Praise of Folie,* in turn, reports that the work was "Englished by sir Thomas Chaloner knight." Cecil was described as the "chief mourner" at Chaloner's funeral.[12]

Chaloner, however, also knew that the medium of the popularization was not one that could be restricted to the interests or readership of the gentry. Thus, in his preface, Chaloner describes himself as having "bestowed an englisshe liverey upon this latine boke."[13] This metaphor is not only a suggestive way of describing the relationship of Latin and the vernacular, but it also positions Chaloner's translation in a wonderfully ambiguous social space. Both the retainers of the nobility and the members of London companies such as that of the goldsmiths wore liveries, and thus Chaloner's bestowal of an "englisshe liverey" affiliates his translations with an urban corporate ethos and one of feudal service. As we shall see, Chaloner uses Folie to reinforce the necessity of hierarchy, but the ambiguity of "livery" suggests an awareness that popularizations, whatever their immediate political goals might be, have the effect of helping to create a socially mixed readership.

Chaloner's populism is largely stylistic, but more than style is at stake in both the 1551 and 1556 editions of *Utopia*. For some of Robinson's changes in 1556 represent a modification of the politics of the 1551 edition—the "daunger" mentioned in the letter to Cecil. This danger, however, does not appear to have been that of More's Catholicism. To be sure, Robinson prefaces his 1551 translation of *Utopia* by lamenting More's refusal to see "the shining light of Godes holy truthe in certein principal pointes of Christian religion." Nevertheless, this refusal does not seem to vitiate the value of *Utopia* for Robinson or his readers. "But letting this matter [of More's religion] passe, I retourne againe to *Utopia*." Robinson goes on to write, and he thereby renders More's Catholicism and the meaning of *Utopia* separate issues.[14] Moreover, despite More's obstinacy in the service of Catholicism, Robinson goes on to maintain that *Utopia* contains an "aboundaunce" of "good, & holsome lessons." Robinson even claims that attacks upon his *Utopia* will come from those who dislike what is "both frutefull and godly."[15] The possibility of such attacks, still unspecified, nevertheless provides yet another hint of danger.

In his preface, Robinson does not make explicit what he means by "godly," an adjective that More never applies to his *Utopia*. Nevertheless, the religious significance of Robinson's *Utopia* becomes more evident from one of the outright interpolations that he makes in his translation. Thus, the heading to book 2 of the 1551 *Utopia* appears in Robinson's translation as follows:

The Second Boke of the Communication of Raphael Hythlodaye, concernyng the best state of a common wealth: conteynyng the discription of Utopia, with a large declaration of the Godly governement, and of all the good lawes and orders of the same Illande.[16]

On the other hand, in More's Latin we read of the "Sermonis quem Raphael Hythlodaeus de optimo reipublicae statu habuit, Liber Secundus."[17] "Best state of a common wealth" is clearly Robinson's translation of "De optimo reipublicae statu" but nothing in More's Latin here corresponds to "Godly government." "Godly government" would seem to offset the studied ambiguity of More's presentation of Utopia. To be sure, a marginal note in book 2 of the Latin *Utopia* does term Utopia a "sanctam rempublicam & uel Christianis imitandam,"[18] but the marginalia to *Utopia* were supposedly written by Erasmus and Giles, not More. However, even if Erasmus and Giles' marginalia can be said to represent, to some degree,

More's point of view, Robinson, whose 1551 translation contains no marginalia, chooses a much more conspicuous place than is used in the Latin *Utopia* to suggest that Utopian society is perhaps the way in which true Christians are supposed to govern themselves.

Robinson's overt ascription of godliness to the Utopian form of government confuses his own perceptions of Utopia with those of Raphael Hythloday—Robinson's anglicization of Raphael Hythlodaeus. For in Robinson's translation Raphael Hythloday praises Utopian "wyse and godlye ordynaunces," a phrase that renders the "prudentissima et sanctissima instituta" extolled by Raphael Hythlodaeus in More's *Utopia*.[19] The echoing of "wyse and godlye ordynaunces" in "godly governement" and "good lawes and orders" suggests that Robinson is less concerned than More was to distinguish between his own voice and that of Raphael. Indeed, the coincidence of names—Ralph and Raphael—creates a link between translator and eulogizer of Utopia in much the same way that the presence of a skeptical character named "More" in *Utopia* might initially seem to give authorial validation to a skeptical reading of Raphael's laudatory description of Utopia.

Stylistically, too, Ralph Robinson and Raphael Hythloday are difficult to tell apart. As J. H. Lupton puts it, Robinson's English is that of the Book of Common Prayer,[20] and it matches the "homely, plaine, and simple speche" that, in Robinson's translation, the character "More" ascribes to Raphael Hythloday. On the other hand, as Elizabeth McCutcheon has demonstrated most effectively, in the Latin *Utopia* the supposed "neglecta simplicitas" of Raphael Hythlodaeus' "sermo" is itself a mark of rhetorical sophistication.[21] In the Letter to Giles, "More" claims that Raphael's speech is the model for his own writing, but this claim only expands the gap between whatever Raphael said and its patently artful reproduction in the written language of the Latin *Utopia*. In Robinson's *Utopia,* however, the proximity of Robinson's language to the homely speech of Raphael Hythloday is more probable.

Robinson's awareness of the boldness of his interpolation of "godly governement" at the outset of book 2 is evident from the fact that he changed it in 1556 when the "godly governement" of the Utopians significantly became a "politike" one.[22] "Politike," with its root *polis*, invokes pagan philosophers such as Plato and Aristotle and suggests that the Utopian government is an outgrowth of an essentially secular and classical "optimus reipublicae" status tradition. Robinson's shift from "godly" to "politike" thus makes Utopia a less authoritative paradigm. The front page of book 2 no longer announces that Utopia presents a specifically Christian pattern of good government.

In 1551, on the other hand, "godly government" could have been read as an allusion to the mixture of political and religious reform espoused by a group of Protestant preachers and publishers, dubbed both "gospellers" and "commonwealth men" by modern historians.[23] These preachers and publishers overlaid, as Arthur Ferguson has argued, Erasmian humanism with the "apocalyptic theology of an embattled Protestantism," and, in their criticism of social and religious abuses, they at times espoused a radicalism that verged on the incendiary.[24] The "commonwealth men" included Hugh Latimer, the eloquent preacher, John Hales, who headed a commission appointed to investigate enclosures, and Robert Crowley, the editor and publisher of, among other things, the first printed edition of *Piers Plowman* (1550). The commonwealth men are particularly pertinent to Robinson's *Utopia* because, in addition to their opposition to enclosures, they seemed at times in their publications and sermons to be espousing a Christian communitarianism that at its most radical recalled the social organization of the early church.

The radicalism of the commonwealth men, however, was not "subversive" in the now familiar sense of undermining the state or government. Rather, between 1547 and 1549 the reformist zeal of the commonwealth men could even be described as quasi-governmental since they had close ties to the Duke of Somerset, the Protector of England and real power behind Edward's throne. They also had ties to Cecil, the dedicatee of *Utopia.* But in 1551 they were no longer at the peak of their influence. Rather, they were under pressure to disassociate themselves from both their earlier championship of the oppressed and their support of Somerset himself, who lost the protectorate in 1549 and his life in 1552. Cecil had succumbed to this pressure and, after a brief stint in the Tower, had made a deal with Somerset's rival on the Privy Council, John Dudley, who allowed Cecil both to return to power and to acquire a knighthood.[25] The main reasons for this pressure and Somerset's downfall were the outspokenness with which the "commonwealth men" discussed social issues such as enclosures and the tumult to which the government's toleration and encouragement of such outspokenness seemed to have led.

Two mid-sixteenth-century appropriations of Elyot's writings exemplify the connections between the radical and the official during the early Edwardian years. In 1548—two years after Elyot's death—Thomas Cooper, the future Bishop of Winchester and participant in the Martin Marprelate controversy of the 1580s and 1590s, revised Elyot's lexicography and, in conjunction with Elyot's publisher, Berthelet, put forth a new edition of the *Bibliotheca Eliotae,* which was itself an updated version of Elyot's 1538 *Dictionary.* Cooper prefaced his edition of the *Bibliotheca*

Eliotae with a letter, or "Proheme," addressed to Edward VI, whose contents would perhaps have dismayed Elyot. The letter praises Edward's "dear uncle," the "Duke of Somerset," and then it goes on to extol the social and religious agenda of the Somerset protectorate:

> We . . . by your most godly procedynges evidently perceive, how your grace willeth that your dear uncle and other most honorable counsaylors and ministers, shulde endeavor and applye them selfes, first, to set up true religion, . . . than consequently to procede foorth to the advauncement of the commonweale, that is, truely to minister justice, to restreigne extortion and oppression: to set up tillage and good husbandrie, whereby the people maie increase and be mainteined. Your godly herte wolde not have wilde beastes increase and men decaie: grounde so enclosed up that your people shoulde lacke foode and sustinaunce: one man by shuttyng in of fieldes and pastures to be made, and an hundred thereby to be destroid.[26]

This passage does not identify the "advancement of the commonwealth" with the kind of communistic Utopianism abhorred by Elyot, but it does define such an advanced commonwealth as one without oppression or monopolistic enclosures. Indeed, Cooper sounds here a bit like Raphael Hythlodaeus, who castigated enclosures and man-eating sheep in book 1 of *Utopia*. Thus, in Robinson's 1551 translation Raphael laments that "that one covetous and unsatiable cormoraunte and very plage of his natyve countrey may compasse abowte and inclose many thousand acres of grounde . . . the husbandmen be thrust owte of their owne."[27] Godliness and social reform entail one another in Cooper's "proheme" as they do for Raphael in *Utopia*. Of course, the proheme is not innocent of self-interest, and it can be read as a bid for patronage. (Cooper's use of lexicography to attract the attention of a royal patron did not really yield fruit until Elizabeth.) But, although Edward was not the first English monarch to address the problem of enclosures, Cooper's attempt to gain the favor of the powerful indicates the unusual degree to which a commitment to social justice had become an identifying feature of the Edwardian regime.

The preface to a 1549 edition of the sermons that Hugh Latimer preached before Edward VI invoked a different side of Elyot; for it identified Latimer with "such Plain Pasquyls . . . as will keep nothing back."[28] Indeed, like Elyot's Pasquil, Latimer, one of the most zealous and eloquent of the "commonwealth men," was nothing if not outspoken, and he accordingly had a volatile relationship with three English monarchs—Henry, Edward, and Mary. Burned in 1555, Latimer became one of the Marian martyrs, but even before Mary's accession to the throne, he had evinced a good deal of unwillingness to change his opinions to suit those of his superiors. A Cromwell-sponsored preacher during the 1530s, Latimer was in 1535 made Bishop of Worcester, but in 1539 Latimer's opposition to the notorious Act of Six Articles, which asserted the orthodoxy of transubstantiation, forced him to resign his bishopric. When Edward acceded to the throne in 1547, Latimer devoted himself to preaching, or as John Foxe put it in *Acts and Monuments,* "discharging his talent . . . whose sermons be now set forth in print as also at London in the convocation-house; and especially before the king at court."[29] A good deal of Latimer's preaching defended the policies of the Edwardian government, but his sermons also exceeded that function and made trouble for both Latimer and the government.

Although the same preface that dubbed Latimer a "plain Pasquyl" also warned readers against "pernicious Anabaptistical opinions," Latimer's own opinions had a strongly communitarian, if not communistic, element.[30] Thus, in Latimer's famous "Sermon on the Ploughers" (1548) he made an analogy between "two kinds of inclosing," one that hindered the harvesting of physical sustenance and one that obstructed the preaching of God's word:

The bodily ploughing is taken in and inclosed through singular commodity. For what man will let go, or diminish his private commodity for a commonwealth? And who will sustain any damage for the respect of a public commodity? The other plough [that is, preaching] also no man is diligent to set forward, nor no man will hearken to it. But to hinder and let it all men's ears are open . . . I fear me some be rather mock-gospellers, than faithful ploughmen.[31]

Latimer's immediate target here is churchmen who do not preach, but the passage also indicates some of the broader implications of the "commonwealth" as an Edwardian ideal. Like Cooper, Latimer makes his "commonwealth," with its apparent opposition to "private commodity," sound suspiciously Utopian, and certainly his attack upon enclosures also owes something to Raphael Hythlodaeus' anti-enclosure diatribe in book 1 of *Utopia.* Moreover, this attack anticipates the translation of that diatribe in Robinson's *Utopia,* where Raphael Hythloday accuses enclosers of "nothyng profyting, ye, muche noyinge the weale publique."[32] Indeed, Latimer gave his Sermons on the Plough at Paul's Cross in London, and he thus helped to prepare the way for Robinson's attempt to convey a similar message to a London audience.

Albeit a supporter of the Edwardian government, Latimer was sufficiently true to the role of Pasquil to assert the importance of criticizing monarchs and their ministers. Thus, preaching before Edward in March 1549, Latimer argued that "the preacher cannot correct the king if he be a transgressor of God's word, with the temporal sword; but he must correct and reprove him with the spiritual sword; fearing no man; setting God only before his eyes, under whom he is a minister, to supplant and root up all vice and mischief by God's word."[33] Latimer's language here is decidedly inflammatory. Furthermore, since Latimer's sermons were generally printed soon after delivery, he was not merely making such inflammatory statements before a courtly audience. He was effectively shouting them from the rooftops.

In so far as Latimer fulfilled the role of government spokesman, he did so dangerously. In another sermon given before Edward in March 1549, Latimer claimed that he had "evermore been burdened with the word of sedition,"[34] and events were about to increase this burden. For in the spring and summer of 1549, the outspokenness of Latimer and others seemed to have borne an unsettling fruit as England experienced a series of rebellions that included instances of class strife in Cornwall and, most explicitly, Norfolk. Modern historians disagree over the precise degree to which different instances of social unrest in 1549 had religious or economic motivations, but anti-enclosure and anti-gentry rioting seems to have been common to both the Catholic-inspired uprising in Cornwall as well as the rebels in Norfolk, who, although loyal Protestants, were disturbed with economic conditions. Most terrifyingly, the Norfolk rebellion, although led by a relatively prosperous tanner and landholder, Robert Kett, nevertheless involved the appropriation of the property of wealthy landowners and the establishment of a rudimentary and short-lived form of lower-class rule in and about Norwich before the rebels were defeated by an army under the leadership of Somerset's political opponent, John Dudley.[35]

Sixteenth-century historiography of Kett's rebellion is replete with references to social conflict. Thus, for instance, Alexander Neville's *De Furoribus Norfolciensium, Ketto Duce, Liber Unus* (1575) refers to the army of John Dudley as an army composed of "nobiles," and it makes reference to the ambush and murder of "gentiles" by the distinctly plebeian rebels.[36] Both Neville's *De Furoribus Norfolciensium* and a manuscript account of the uprising in English, Nicholas Southerton's "The Commoyson in Norfolk 1549," locate the source of the uprising in anti-enclosure riots that the government's own opposition to enclosures had instigated. Thus, according to Sotherton, the "occasion" of the revolt was the "commandment" of the prince "upon complaint made for enclosing of divers common grounds."[37] The reference here is to the efforts of the enclosure commission, headed by John Hales, to limit the ability of the gentry to expropriate land traditionally held in common.

Sixteenth-century accounts of and responses to Kett's rebellion indicate that the rebels were trying to exploit the official radicalism that the Somserset government had encouraged. Thus, seated under a "tree of reformation," Kett and his fellow leaders, claimed to be acting in the king's name, and they even went so far as to forge this name in writing. In his "The Hurt of Sedition: Howe Grevous it is to a Communewealth" (1549), Sir John Cheke accused the rebels of having "sent out in the kinges name, against the kinges wil, preceptes of al kindes, and without commaundment commanded his subjectes, and unrulily . . . ruled."[38] Likewise, the account of the rebellion in Hollinshed's *Chronicles* (1587) includes a rebel proclamation from the "king's friends and deputies" granting "license" to "all men" to bring into the rebel camp "all manner of cattle and provision of victuals" without any "violence or injury" being done to any "honest or poor man."[39] Neville, on the other hand, claims that the rebels seized certain royal "diplomata" whose purpose was to confer power upon particular members of the nobility. The rebels then deleted the names of the nobles and substituted their own.[40]

Another name that the rebels were supposed to have abused was that of the "commonwealth" or "republic." Thus, Cheke attacks the rebels as follows:

Ye pretende a commonwealth. Now a mende ye it, by killinge of gentilmen by spoilinge of gentilmenne, by emprisoninge of gentylmen. A marvelous tanned commonwealth. Whi shuld ye thus hate them, for their riches or for their rule? . . . If ye felte the paine that is joined with governaunce, as ye se and like the honoure, ye woulde not hurte otheirs to rule them, but rather take great paine to be ruled of them.

Cheke also makes arguments against the rebels that recall the distrust of communism evinced by the character "More" in *Utopia:*

Would ye have all alyke rich? That is the overthrow of laboure, and utter decaye of work in the realme. For who will laboure more, if when he hath gotten more, the idle shall by luste without righte, take what hym lust from hym, under pretence of equalitie with him. This is the bringing in of idleness which destroyeth the commune wealth, and not the amendment of labour, that mayntaineth the communewealth.[41]

Cheke's rhetoric not only recalls the reservations of the character "More" in More's *Utopia,* but it also owes something to the anti-Utopianism of Elyot and Morison. Cheke's attack on the rebel "commonwealth" thus includes an argument that "More" only implicitly makes in *Utopia*. That is, Cheke goes on to claim that an egalitarian commonwealth would eliminate the possibility of social mobility: "If there should be such equalitie, then ye take all hope away from yours to come to better estate, than you now leave them." Cheke's anti-Utopianism reflects the problem that occupied Elyot and Morison in the 1530s—that is, the discovery of arguments and topoi that could both justify and limit social mobility. This problem was pertinent to Cheke himself, who, like Morison, did not come from a particularly illustrious social background.[42]

But Cheke was also a member of Somerset's circle, and the supposed sympathies of this circle may have made the necessity of disavowing Utopian commonwealths more pronounced. Thus, for instance, A Discourse of the Commonweal of this Realm of England (1549), written by the disaffected Sir Thomas Smith, a former adherent of Somerset who had lost the favor of the Protector, contains numerous references to the problems of insurrection, disorder, and the seditious "diversity of opinions" sown by ministers. Yet, despite the literary debt that Smith's Discourse owes to More's Utopia, the possibility of a Utopian solution to England's economic and social woes suffers rejection in favor of an apparently more realistic economic policy: Utopia, claims Dr. Pandotheus (his name even sounds like Hythlodaeus), the main speaker of the Discourse, "had no traffic with any other outward country" and thus cannot serve as a model for England. "What harm is it, though we imagined here a whole Commonweal among ourselves, so it be not set forth as though we would needs have it after our devise?" another character asks nervously. "It is dangerous to meddle in the King's matters," Dr. Pandotheus replies, and indeed the Discourse circulated in manuscript but was not itself "set forth" in print until after Smith's death.[43]

Given Pandotheus' and Smith's caution, the publication of a text that designated Utopian society as a "Godly government" in 1551 could not have been more inopportune or (depending upon one's perspective) apt. The same can be said of its dedication to Cecil, only recently released from the Tower. After 1549 censorship once again tightened in England as the gentry realized that the freedom of the press permitted by Somerset had helped to create a climate of rebellion. Robinson's suggestion that a communistic society is "Godly" thus recalls the "commonwealth" reformers of the late 1540s, but it does so prudently—under the guise of translation rather than originality. As Annabel Patterson has argued, during the Renaissance "[c]ensorship encouraged the use of historical or other uninvented texts, such as translations from the classics." Translation in Patterson's view both allowed an author to "limit his responsibility" for a text and "provided an interpretive mechanism" whereby the reader was "invited to consider the timeliness of the retelling of another man's story."[44]

Indeed, Robinson employs the technique of "retelling another man's story" to preface his *Utopia* with an allusion to recent events. The story that he retells is from Lucian's *How to Write History*—that of Diogenes and his tub. The French humanists, Guillaume Bude and François Rabelais, had already used this story as a somewhat ironic prefatory topos in *Annotationes in Pandectas* (1508) and the *Tiers Livre* (1546). But Robinson's version of Diogenes and his tub quite topically emphasizes the "vocation" of writers laboring on behalf of a commonwealth that may be under attack:

Upon a tyme when tidynges came to the citie of Corinthe that Kyng Philippe . . . was comming thetherwarde with an armie royall to lay siege the city; the Corinthians, being forth with stricken with greate feare, beganne busilie and earnestly to looke aboute them and to falle to worke of all handes. . . . The which busie labour and toile of theires when Diogenes the philosopher saw, having no profitable business wherupon to set himself on worke . . . immediately girded about him his philosophicall cloak, and began to roll and tumble up and down hether and thether upon the hill syde, that lieth adjoyninge to the citie his great barrel or tunne, wherein he dwelled, for other dwellynge place would he have none. . . .

This seing one of his frendes, . . . came to hym: . . . whie does thou thus, or what meanest thou hereby? . . . I am tumblyng my tubbe . . . (quod he) bycause it were no reason I only should be ydell, where so many be working. In semblable manner, right honorable sir [i.e., Cecil], though I be, as I am in dede, of muche lesse habilitie than Diogenes was, to do any thinge that shall or may be for the adavncement . . . of the publique wealth of my native countrey; yet I, seeing, every sort and kynde of people in theire vocation and degree busilie occupied about the common wealthes affaires, and especially learned men daily putting forth in writing newe inventions and devises to the furtheraunce of the same, thought it my bounden duetie to my God and my countrey so to tumble my tub [i.e., translate *Utopia*].[45]

Robinson's Diogenes still possesses some attributes of aloofness and detachment as in Lucian and Rabelais. Indeed, the "philosophicall cloak" that Robinson's Diogenes dons here reappears in book 1 of Robinson's *Utopia* as the "philosophers apparrell" that the character "More" accuses Raphael Hythloday of wearing when Hythloday defends his own detachment from politics by demonstrating the "no place" for the philosopher at court.[46] In book 1 Raphael speaks despairingly of books, too: philosophers have "put forth" books of advice for kings, but these monarchs are not willing to "folowe good counsell."[47] Yet, unlike Lucian, Rabelais, or Raphael Hythloday in book 1, Robinson's preface includes a more encouraging allusion to "learned men daily putting forth in writing newe inventions and devices to the furtheraunce" of the "commonwealth's affairs" in conjunction with those who are contributing to the cause of such affairs through other forms of labor. In Robinson's version of the story, the "vocation" of learning is already a politically engaged one, and thus Robinson's preface both articulates and undermines the philosophical isolation of Diogenes and, by implication, of *Utopia* itself. Learned men are already creating a place for philosophy in England, and one obvious referrent for those learned men in 1551 would have been figures such as Latimer and Crowley.[48]

These learned men, however, owed something to Elyot, even though Elyot would have abhorred the suggestion that his writings had helped to give birth to a vernacular *Utopia*. Yet Robinson's Diogenes recalls the Cynic personae that populate so many of Elyot's works. By identifying himself with Diogenes, Robinson is signifying his own willingness to use a voice—that of the railer—that Elyot had done so much to develop in the 1530s. The story that Robinson tells about Diogenes reinforces his status as an oppositional figure. For, to the extent that the conflict engages him, Robinson's Diogenes is joining forces with a city against a royal army. So Robinson may be doing the same when he and other learned men write in support of the commonwealth. Indeed, the 1549 revolts had subjected a number of English cities to siege by both royal and rebel forces, and they had made places such as Norwich and Exeter foci of national attention.

The tale of Diogenes and his tub is, however, particularly interesting because it features a display of shame by the usually brazen philosopher. Diogenes is ashamed to be idle where everyone else is working, and this shame extends to Robinson's portrayal of learned men in England. In Utopia the *literati* are exempt from labor and their studies are considered a form of earned leisure. In Robinson's translation, the Utopian learned enjoy a "perpetual license from labour to learnyng."[49] Robinson's preface, on the other hand, shows the influence of what Max Weber has identified as the Protestant valuation of work in the world as a "calling," and consequently his learned men have a "vocation" that keeps them as "busily occupied" as anyone else.[50] In his Sermon on the Ploughers, Latimer had made a similar point about spiritual leadership: "right prelating is busy labouring, and not lording," and one purpose of the sermon was to represent preaching as being akin to the hard physical toil of ploughing rather than the pastimes of "gallant gentlemen."[51]

Even in *The Governour* intellectual studies are not a form of leisure that prepare future governors for leadership as they are in *Utopia*. Rather, studies constitute a form of "necessary occupation," perhaps the most necessary one, and this occupation, in turn, leads to "due administration." Indeed, Robinson's depiction of Corinth and the fervor of those of his countrymen who are laboring on behalf of commonwealth affairs recalls what we have seen to be Elyot's own intermittently Utopian vision of a just public weal in *The Governour.* For one of the defining characteristics of this public weal is full employment, whether in the form of studies or other labor.

The emphasis on labor and military conflict that inaugurates Robinson's *Utopia* recurs in other parts of Robinson's translation, too. The 1551 edition of Robinson's translation contains no marginalia, and thus Raphael's claim that the Utopians take to Christianity because the "rightest Christian companies,"[52] a rendering of "germanissimi Christianorum conventus," practice this kind of "communitie" remains a wonderfully open one. Who are these "rightest Christian companies" in Robinson's England? They are certainly no longer monasteries, if they ever really were in More's Latin. "Companies" is suggestive of guilds such as the goldsmiths company to which Robinson belonged. But there are other possibilities, too, including military "companies," a meaning difficult to overlook in the aftermath of armed rebellion and the assaults upon private property that were one of its most notable features. The question remained undecided until 1556 when Robinson reinserted marginalia and identified these companies as "religious houses."

But perhaps the most startling feature of Robinson's translation that the story of Diogenes anticipates is Raphael's sympathetic portrayal of a vanquished rebellion—that of Cornwall in 1497. This portrayal, which occurs during Raphael's account in book 1 of his stay at Cardinal Morton's table, might easily have reminded readers in 1551 of the more recent rebellion in Cornwall as well as the one in Norfolk. Indeed, Raphael's first reference to the 1497 rebellion is unspecific and could easily double as an allusion to more recent events:

Many times have I chaunced upon suche prowde, lewde, overthwarte, and waywarde judgments, yea, and ones in England.

I praye yow syre, (quoth I) [i.e., More], have yow bene in owr contrey?

Yea forsothe, (quoth he) [i.e., Hythloday], and thir I tarried for the space of iiii or v monythes together, not longe after the insurreccion, that the westerne English men made agaynst their kinge, which by their owne miserable and pitefull slaughter was suppressed and ended.[53]

This sympathy with the rebels is present in More's Latin, but expressing such sympathy in the vernacular just after the vanquishing of another insurrection of Western Englishmen is quite remarkable. The next reference to this rebellion is historically specific, but this specificity demonstrates Robinson's awareness of the possibility of ambiguity:

Nay, quod I [i.e., Hythloday], you shall not skape so: for, fyrste of all, I will speake nothynge of them that come home owte of the warre maymede and lame, as not

longe ago owte of Black heath field [Cornubiensi praelio] and a lityll before that
owt of the warres in Fravnce; such (I say) as put their lives in jeopardy for the weal
publiques or the kinges sake [qui vel Reipublicae impendunt membra, vel regi].[54]

The insertion of "Blackheath field"—the deciding battle in 1497—
militates against temporal ambiguity here. Nevertheless, Robinson's evident nervousness, like Taverner's additions to Erasmus' first adage, also
serves to underscore the pertinence of the very interpretation that he is
trying to forestall. Furthermore, such anxiety highlights the potential
topicality of Raphael's allusion to the danger of class warfare in book 1 of
the 1551 *Utopia*. For, criticizing the notion that the retainers of the nobility make good warriors, Raphael argues that "those same handy craft
men of yours in cities, nor yet the rude and uplandishe ploughmen of the
contrey, are not supposed to be greatly affraid of your gentilmens ydil
serving men."[55] Attacks on enclosures and the gentry in both Cornwall
and Norfolk had demonstrated this point only too vividly in 1549, and,
albeit defeated in the end, the rebels had shown that they could constitute
a military threat to their social superiors.

In contrast to Robinson's willingness to take risks in the vernacular, the
commonwealth men were, for the most part, attempting to curtail their
more radical pronouncements after Kett's rebellion. As Penry Williams
notes, "the spokesmen for the oppressed—men like Latimer, Hales, and
Crowley—were careful after 1549 to express their abhorrence of revolt."[56]
That is, these "spokesmen for the oppressed," were also trying, not always
successfully, to distinguish their own opposition to enclosures and other
social injustices as well as their, at times, communist-sounding rhetoric
from Anabaptism and the kind of social strife that had erupted at Norfolk.
The writings of Crowley and Latimer reveal a good deal of defensiveness
concerning their own role, however unintended, as fomenters of disobedience and violence.

The commonwealth men had reason to be on the defensive. Robert
Crowley in his pre-Norfolk *An Information and Petition against the Oppressors
of the Poor Commons of the Realm* (1548) sounds like Raphael describing
Utopian communism:

But as for the oppression of the poore . . . I canne scarsely truste that any
reformacion canne bee had; unlesse God do nowe worke in the hertes of the
possessioners of thys realme, as he dyd in the primitive church, when the possessioners wer contented and very wyllynge to sell theyr possessions and geve the
price therof to be commune to all the faithful belevers.[57]

To be sure, Crowley does add that he does not want "men to make all
things common," but he nevertheless comes dangerously close to advocat-

ing communism organized according to the model of the primitive church as the only just society. Thus, in his 1550 *The Way to Wealth, wherein is Plainly Taught a Most Present Remedy for Sedition* Crowley is careful to advocate passivity on the part of England's oppressed and to eschew the desirability of communism. Yet, when he summarizes the complaints of the landowners against the rebellious peasants, Crowley reveals his own defensive position:

Nowe if I should demaund of the gredie cormerauntes what thei think shuld be the cause of Sedition. they would saie:—"The paisant knaves to be welthy, provender priketh them! They knowe not themselves, . . . they regard no lawes, they would have no gentlemen, thei wold have al men like themselves, *they would have all things commune!* They would not have us maisters of that which is our owne! (my emphases)[58]

Note here that the accusation of the gentry is not only one of communism but also includes a lack of self-knowledge: "they knowe not themselves." The passage thus shows how the events of 1549 revived Elyot's anti-Anabaptist rhetoric of the 1530s. For, as we have seen, Elyot had used a discussion of the Erasmian adage "Nosce te ipsum" to launch his attack upon the Anabaptists. But even more importantly the accusation, "they would have all things commune," would also seem to include Crowley himself since he had expressed this same wish in his *An Information* (1548). Hence, Crowley dismisses this accusation as part of the attempt of the gentry to justify its position. Yet, while distancing himself and the peasants from such communism, Crowley is not particularly kind to the gentry class either in *The Way to Wealth.* Thus, the gentry figure here as greedy cormorants as they would a year later in Robinson's *Utopia.*[59]

Given the pressures that Crowley clearly felt in 1550, his edition of *Piers Plowman,* the first printed one, offers a fascinating comparison to Robinson's *Utopia. Piers Plowman* constituted the literary legacy of another period in English history—that is, the late fourteenth century—when religious reform and social turmoil accompanied one another, and it was thus an apt choice for Crowley in 1550. In Crowley's edition of *Piers Plowman* Envy teaches friars to prove by Plato and Seneca that "all thinges under heaven ought to be in commune," but this ascription of communism to Envy rather than to a nobler passion is denigrating.[60] Nevertheless, Crowley's "The Printer to the Reader" does provide some indication of the charge that Langland's text might have possessed for a Protestant audience in 1550:

In whose time [i.e., the reign of Edward III] it pleased God to open the eyes of many to se his truth, geving them boldness of herte to open their mouthes and crye out againste the worckes of darkness, as did John Wiclilefe [Wycliff], who also in those dayes translated the holye Bible into the English tonge, and this writer who . . . doeth most Christianlye instruct the weake. . . . There is no manner of vice, that reigneth in any estate of men, which this writer hath not Godly, learnedlye, and wittily rebuked.

Printing *Piers* enables a much broader audience to hears its own cry against the "worckes of darkness," and thus Crowley's editing and printing of *Piers* is analogous to Robinson's translation of *Utopia*. Both *Piers* and *Utopia* became more accessible and less sequestered texts in the aftermath of Kett's rebellion, and, despite the historical divide that initially separated them, both works converged in the mid-sixteenth century to respond in different ways to the problem of maintaining the possibility of radical religious critique of social structures without necessarily countenancing rebellion.

In Crowley's "Brief Summe of the Principall Pointes that be Spoken of in this Boke," he notes that *Piers* rebuketh "the folye of the commune people that cluster togythers in conspiracies against such as God hath called to office under their prince," but he also observes that *Piers* "secretly in Latin verses rebuketh their [i.e., kings' and princes'] cruelnes and tyranny." This notion of Latin as a language in which political criticisms can be made "secretly" may owe something to More and Erasmus as well as Langland. That is, Crowley's point may be to emphasize what we have seen to be the humanist interest in prudence and discretion. For writing in Latin may or may not elude censorship imposed from above. But such secret writing surely keeps certain kinds of social criticism out of the ken of the "common people," and it thus prevents these criticisms from being appropriated on behalf of "conspiracies against such as God hath called to office."

But *Piers Plowman* was only one possible source of the more cautious religious politics of the commonwealth men. For, in the last sermon that he preached before Edward VI, Latimer the arch-Protestant was not above quoting from More's antiheresy tracts to alleviate the "burden of sedition" that he clearly felt:

But here is now an argument to prove the matter against the preachers. Here was preaching against covetousness all last year in Lent, and the next summer followed rebellion: ergo, preaching against covetousness was the cause of rebellion. . . . Here now I remember an argument of Master More's, which he bringeth in a book that he made against Bilney [i.e., Tyndale]: and here by the way I will tell you a merry toy: Master More was once sent into commission into Kent to help to try out . . . what was the cause of . . . the shelf that stopped up Sandwich Haven. . . . "Forsooth," quoth he [More's somewhat dense interlocutor], ". . . And before the Tenterton steeple was in building, there was no manner of speaking of any flats or sands that stopped the haven; and therefore I think that Tenterton steeple is the cause of the destroying of Sandwich haven." And even so to my purpose is preaching of God's word the cause of rebellion, as Tenterton steeple was the cause of Sandwich haven is decayed.[61]

Latimer's illustration of the *post hoc, ergo propter hoc* fallacy comes from More's *A Dialogue Concerning Heresies,* where it refers to the supposed decay of Christendom since Christians began fighting the Turks and persecuting heretics. In *A Dialogue* the character More caricatures the Lutheran opposition to such Christian militancy as the mistaking of sequentiality for causality. More, on the other hand, ascribes the decay of Christendom to the Lutheran "sowing of schisms and sedycions among Christian people."[62] Indeed, according to More's argument, figures such as Latimer would be responsible for this decay, too.

Both More and Latimer, however, are using the anecdote of Tenterton steeple and Sandwich haven to address the broader issue of the character of the visible church and its ability either to facilitate or "stop" a "haven"—that is, the possibility of salvation. On the one hand, More opposes the authority of the institutional church—the steeple—to the sowing of schisms and seditions—that is, the preaching of God's word that Lutheranism emphasized. In a post-Reformation version of the same allegory, however, Latimer virtually identifies Tenterton steeple with "preaching against covetousness," and he tries to exculpate this preaching from the charge of fomenting sedition. Nevertheless, despite such differences, Latimer's appropriation of this anecdote betokens a desire to affiliate more closely his own preaching with the ecclesiastical establishment from which he had so often distanced himself in the past. That is, Latimer wants to show that the sowing of the word and Tenterton steeple are not contraries but rather complement one another. Albeit in a distinctly Protestant way, Latimer, like More before him, is seeking refuge from the storms of sedition and radicalism within the solid edifice of the visible church.

Robinson's translation of *Utopia* also recalls More's anti-heresy writings:

Yea, they reason and dispute the matter earnestly amonge themselves, whether without the sendying of a christian bishoppe, one chosen out of theire owne people may receave the ordre of priesthode. And truly they were minded to chuse one: but at my departure from them they hadd chosen none.[63]

Whether wittingly or not, Robinson's translation echoes More's complaint in the *Dialogue* against reformers who would turn a priest into a "man chosen amonge the people to preach." Indeed, Robinson's translation later goes on to specify that the office of priests is "to gyve good exhortations and cownsell." This passage shows that the same man who figures in Robinson's letter to Cecil as a stubborn opponent of Protestantism entertained the possibility of one of the most radical of Reformation ideas. The effect of Robinson's translation here is to demonstrate that More was not always the paragon of Catholic orthodoxy who stubbornly refused to see the shining light of God's truth. At the same time as Latimer was using the antiheretical More to protect himself from the charge of seditiousness and, implicitly, to provide a model for his own changing allegiances, Robinson's *Utopia* presented the contradictions of More's religious beliefs and public career. From the perspective of figures such as Latimer and even Cecil, this presentation would have been a disquieting one, for it demonstrated the inevitability of a discarded radicalism returning to haunt its former adherents.

The man who preaches Christianity to the Utopians too fervently, however, is called a "sedytious person" and "raiser up of dissension" in Robinson's *Utopia*.[64] In 1551 the Utopian punishment of this preacher could seem to have prefigured More, the hunter and confuter of supposedly seditious heretics, and also to have served as a rebuke directed against the pre-Norfolk Latimer. Nevertheless, the point of punishing this seditious preacher—tolerance, or the right of everyone not to be "blamed for reasonynge in the mayntenauce of his owne religion"[65]—was also topical in 1551. In 1516 the Utopians are merely, like Utopus himself, skeptics. In 1551, on the other hand, the Utopian punishment of an intolerant preacher presents a striking contrast to the antiheretical More and those of his ilk, for whom the punishment of seditious preachers was meant to promote orthodoxy rather than tolerance. Moreover, the Somerset protectorate had made a limited tolerance of religious differences an issue in England. For an immediate consequence of this protectorate was the repeal of heresy laws originally enacted to combat Lollardy, and this repeal meant a brief absence of executions for religious reasons. Thus, the Anabaptist Joan Bocher was tried by ecclesiastical courts while Somerset was in power, but he never ordered her execution. Rather, she was burned in 1550 after Somerset's fall.

The Christianity that the Robinson's Utopians learn of is a "sect"—that is, the translation of the original meaning of *haeresis*—among other sects rather than an institution with a hierarchical and potentially repressive structure.[66] On the other hand, Robinson's Utopians are strikingly tolerant of "heresy," a word that Robinson uses not to translate the original meaning of *haeresis* but rather to signify an unorthodox religious opinion. Thus, in More's Latin the Utopians are said to distinguish between the errors of those who do not believe in the immortality of the soul and those who, because of a "vitium longe diversum" [far different vice], think that the souls of beasts are immortal. In Robinson's translation, however, "vitium longe diversum" appears as follows: "Their heresye is much contrary to the other."[67] The Utopians allow the latter heretics to "speake their mindes," while they restrict the speech of the former to an audience composed of "pryestes and men of gravity." Either way, however, no one is burned.

The burning of Joan Bocher was an indication of the degree to which the reaction to rebellion entailed not only getting rid of Somerset but some of his policies as well. For after Norfolk the English government continued in the path of religious reform even as it sought to purge itself of what it perceived to be extremism. The king himself, as he put it in a letter to Archbishop Cranmer, wanted to continue religious reform "grounded upon Holy Scripture, agreeable to the order of the primitive church."[68] But it was a selectively defined "primitive church." Anthony Aucher notwithstanding, the king did not will the "decay of gentelmen." Nor was such religious reform meant to evoke the social leveling practiced at Kett's tree of reformation.

However, the language of religious change could evoke the more radical and hence Utopian-like elements of Christianity. Thus, for instance, the Anglican ritual of "communion"—a translation of the Greek *koinonia*—had etymological and scriptural ties to the kind of communistic "communion" that Taverner castigated in his translation of the Erasmian adage, *Amicorum Omnia Sunt Communia* as well as the "community" that the Utopians so admired in the early church.[69] Nevertheless, the fellowship of Anglican communion, which did lessen the distance between priests and the laity, was obviously not an attempt to implement a Utopian "commonwealth." On the other hand, the Utopian embrace of early church "community" in Robinson's translation did amount to an egalitarian "commonwealth" and thus demonstrated to a wide audience that certain kinds of social and religious reform were equally rooted in the practices of the early Church, or, to use Utopian terminology, the sect of Christianity. The "Godly government" of the Utopians thus could not but have indicated the limitations of the English government's own commitment to recreating the "primitive church."

Despite Robinson's attempt to affiliate his *Utopia* with the productions of other learned men, in 1551 his translation might have seemed as isolated and vain an act as Diogenes' tub-rolling. For, although Crowley did combine his retractions of sedition with condemnations of the gentry, learning was on the side of the royal army after Norfolk. Chaloner's preface to his *Praise of Folie* clearly reveals that his Folly is meant to allay passions that might lead to rebellion:

And seeing the vices of our daies are suche as can not enough be spoken against, what knowe we, if Erasmus in this booke thought good between game and ernest to rebuke the same? And chiefly to persuade (if it might be) a certaine contentation in everie man, to holde him agreed with suche lotte and state of living as ariseth to him. For whiche purpose was I also soonest moved to englisshe it, to the end that meane men of baser wittes and condicion, might have a maner coumfort and satisfaction in theimselves. In as muche as the hiegh god, who made us all of one earth, hath natheless chosen some to rule, and more to serve. . . . For surely if a man of the poorer sorte, whose eyes is dased in beholding the faire gloss of wealthe and felicitee whiche the state of a great lorde or counsailour in a commen wealth dooeth outwardly represent, did inwardly marke the travailes, cares, and anxietees, whiche suche a one is driven to susteigne (doing as he ought to dooe) in serving his maister and country, whereby he is nothing lesse than his owne man: now I beleve he would not muche envy his state, nor chose to chaunge conditions of life with him.[70]

Like Robinson's use of Diogenes in his preface, this passage offers a reading of the text that it prefaces. Thus, for instance, Chaloner's distinction between what a great lord "dooeth outwardly represent" and the "travailes" that one might "inwardly marke" in such a lord evokes the Silenus image that Erasmus' Stultitia employs to such effect in *Moriae Encomium.* But Chaloner's evocation of the Erasmian Silenus puts this figure to much different use than in the *Moria.* Chaloner suggests that the envious and rebellious poor view the powerful as hard workers rather than, as they are in the *Moria,* fools and beasts on the inside. Once the "glosse of wealthe and felicitee" is removed, Chaloner's Sileni-like great lords present a much different interior than their Erasmian precursors.

Chaloner's preface indicates that his Folly, unlike Erasmus' Stultitia, will be a quietist one, not likely to incite controversies. Indeed, as a figure who tries to keep the "poorer sorte" in line, she has obvious ties to the figure of Menenius Agrippa that she herself extols: "What thing also revoked the comminalitie of Rome, rebellying against the *senate,* to agreement? Was it any philosophical oration? No, forsovth. What then? Even a foolishe Aesopes fable feigned of the bealie."[71] She offers Folly as an antiphilosophical form of placating the masses. Modeled after Menenius Agrippa's use of a "foolishe Aesopes fable," the brand of Nepenthe she dispenses would seem to be a *pharmakon* that eludes the problem of interpretation. That is, the manipulative tale of the belly controls its interpreters rather than becoming subject to their control.

Chaloner's *The Praise of Folie* shows how the populist elements of Erasmus' *Moria* could also lend themselves to anti-egalitarian purposes. Thus, in Erasmus' *Moria,* Stultitia, eschewing more ostensibly abstruse disciplines, identifies herself with "sensum communem, id est, Stultitiam." Chaloner translates this phrase as "common sense and capacitie of all men (that is to saye) to Folie."[72] Given the tenor of Chaloner's preface, however, Chaloner's democratizing translation of "sensus communis"— that is, all men have it—puts the commonness of sense in implicit opposition to that of wealth and power, which all men cannot have. As a further gesture toward the "capacity of all men." Chaloner's Folly uses a plain and homespun manner of speech that anticipates that of Robinson's Raphael Hythloday. Nevertheless, the point of such plainness is to suggest that those who would incite the "poorer sorte" to rebel are the true elitists— that is, the highbrow philosophers.

Chaloner, as Clarence Miller has noted, was not above overtly changing the content of the Erasmian original:

For short conclusion, (I saie) so muche lacketh that any maner friendship, societie of life, or companiying together, maie without mine access be pleasant, . . . as not the people woulde longe beare their ruler, nor a servaunt his maister, a maide her mastres, a scholer his teacher . . . unles by turnes atwixe them selves they shuld sometime err, sometimes flatter, sometimes wincke for the nones, and now and then coumfort their bittreed tast with some hony of foolisshenesse.[73]

Miller points out that Folly here makes the "dissatisfaction come from below" whereas in the original it comes from above. That is, in accordance with his preface, Chaloner's Folly demonstrates that she provides the powerful with a way of making the burden of oppression appear to be lighter than it is. Folly offers herself as a kind of bread-and-circuses approach to government, and thus she effects the ultimate transformation of the Erasmian ideal of a communistic social fabric whose basis was also friendship and the mutual tolerance of faults. The only thing that such friends have in common in Chaloner's account of the social fabric is a shared desire to comfort their "bittered taste" with the "honey of foolishnesse."

But the opposition to philosophers of Chaloner's Folly becomes most interesting and anachronistic when she laughs at Utopia:

Let the Stoikes therfore (if they list) take their wiseman to theim selves, and make muche on him alone, or (if they thinke good) go and dwell with him in Platos citee, or in the land of Fairie, or Utopia.[74]

Neither in 1511 nor 1515 could Erasmus' "Stultitia" have known of Utopia, and indeed the locale that Utopia replaces in Chaloner's translation is the "Gardens of Tantalus." Chaloner's Folly claims that the only places fit for Stoic *apatheia*—that is, lack of passions—are Utopia, Plato's ideal city, and Faerie land, and her reference to Utopia provides a fascinating (mis)reading of More's text. For in *Utopia* the Utopians are said to be more prone to Epicureanism than Stoicism so that Chaloner's Folly is demonstrating here that, like her original, she is capable of cleverly misusing her sources.[75] Indeed, in Chaloner's translation the heaven of the Abraxians—to which haughty theologians and monks are relegated in the original—becomes "Pasquilles heaven," a change that also suggests that the texts of early sixteenth-century English humanism are mediating between Chaloner's Folie and Erasmus' Stultitia.[76] For, by turning the refuge of arrogant "religious men" into Pasquil's heaven, Folie suggests that the figure of the railing satirist is as much of an elitist as the occupants of this heaven.

But Folly's implication that Utopian society would entail the impossible—that is, a complete transformation of human nature—does have some warrant in *Utopia.* For as we have seen, at the end of his description of Utopia, Hythlodaeus suggests that "superbia," or, pride, the leading attribute of fallen human nature, has been uprooted in Utopia. Even before the character "More" expresses his reservations, Hythlodaeus thus provides the basis for a critique of Utopian society as an impossibility. This kind of critique is consonant with Folly's banishment of Stoic man to Utopia in Chaloner's translation. For the point of this banishment is to associate Utopia with a lofty superiority to human nature that is itself an indication of pride. Indeed, in Chaloner's translation pride would seem to link the denizens of Pasquil's heaven and the Stoic Utopians.

But Chaloner's Folly may also owe something to Juan Luis Vives' *De Communione Rerum* (1539)—a Latin tract written to counter Anabaptist communism. For one of Vives' critiques of such communism is that it does not adequately take into account human nature:

Tolle ab hominibus hos animorum motus qui affectus dicuntur, fortasse communionem rerum perfeceris; finge novos quosdam homines et rempublicam Platonis non solum a philosophis derisam, sed a natura ipsa rerum ejectam; nam in his hominibus, et his affectibus, non communionem introductes, sed odia, dissensiones, . . .

[Remove from men these motions of spirit that are called affections, and perhaps you will have created a perfect communism; fashion certain new men and the Platonic republic not only derided by philosophers, but rejected by the nature of things. For in these men, and in these affections, you will not introduce communism, but hatreds, dissensions. . . .][77]

Although Vives does not explicitly mention Utopia anywhere in *De Communione Rerum,* his reference to the Platonic republic does invoke the tradition from which Utopia emerged, and thus Vives helps to prepare the way for Folly's point that the only possible inhabitant of both Plato's republic and Utopia would be a man who did not partake of human nature. Repeatedly in *De Communione Rerum* Vives argues that the communism of the early Church was a special case; the blood of Christ was still "fervens" in the hearts of Christians, and therefore the normal vices of human nature were temporarily suspended. Chaloner's Folly merely extends this kind of argument to the text that Vives undoubtedly also had in mind when criticizing Anabaptism—*Utopia.* Both Chaloner and Vives thus offer revisions of Utopian communism in the light of later events that made the notion of a return to the communism of the early Church a distinctly unsettling prospect.

But the locale that Utopia replaces in Chaloner's translation—the Gardens of Tantalus—is also revealing. For this garden can be found in Erasmus' *Adagia,* where it is said to denote goods that cannot be enjoyed [bonis, quibus tamen frui non liceat], and it of course originates with the story of Tantalus, who is tormented by the sight of fruits that he cannot eat and water that he cannot drink.[78] A reader of Chaloner's translation who was also familiar with the Latin could not miss Chaloner's point: Utopia is itself a kind of tantalizing vision that can only lead to dissatisfaction, frustration, and perhaps, in the case of the English poor, outright insurrection. But Utopia could never work as a solution to England's economic problems, for the constitution of human nature forbids the enjoyment of the goods that it seems to offer. Chaloner's Folly seems to agree here with Smith's Pandotheus, whose observation that Utopia has no "traffic" with any "outward country"—including, presumably, England—also reduces Utopia to an object of unfulfillable desire.

Folly's nervous banishment of the wise to Utopia did, however, prove useful to another Renaissance English writer addressing the problems of rebellion and dissension. As part of his *A Sermon of Christ Crucified* (1570), whose subject is the need for "reconciliation," John Foxe once again associates Utopia with a Stoic refusal to accept human nature as it is:

Such stoicall stomackes and unsociable natures, which neither live here like Angels, nor yet remember themselves to be but men amongst men, are to be sent ad rempublicam Platonis, or to Mr. More's Utopia, either there to live with themselves or else where as none may live to offend them. With what measure ye meete to other, the same shall be mette unto you, sayth the voice of justice. But here speaketh the voice of mercy and desireth you, that as God hath measured unto you, so ye will measure to other.[79]

Here I suspect that Foxe is assimilating Folly's critique of Utopia to a nascent discourse of antipuritanism. Foxe certainly could not have preached the message of reconciliation at a more apposite moment. The recent Catholic-inspired rebellion (1570) of the northern earls and the Duke of Norfolk had been quelled, but the pope had excommunicated Elizabeth and absolved her subjects from the sin of disobedience.[80] Furthermore, events such as the Vestiarian controversy of the 1560s showed that Catholicism was not the only threat to the national church that Foxe's writings would help to establish. The appropriation of Folly's castigation of Utopia in the service of antipuritanism would have been a natural one since the word "puritan" itself entered the English language during the 1560s as a designation for Anabaptists.[81] Foxe merely updates the neglect of human nature that Vives ascribed to Anabaptists and Chaloner's Folly to Utopians so as to make this neglect an attribute of a new form of Protestant radicalism. This passage also represents the ultimate transformation of Erasmus' Stultitia; for, originally a parodic preacher, she becomes part of a genuine sermon.

Such transformations may explain the contrast between the "swim-with-the-stream" Erasmus and the outspoken More in Nashe's *The Unfortunate Traveller. Utopia* and *Praise of Folly* reconverge during the Edwardian years to define two opposed ways of reading humanism in England. One way tries to turn parody, satire, and even a leveling Christian populism into a kind of homily on obedience. The other assimilates humanism to a more threatening version of Protestant homiletic discourse—for instance, the supposedly "seditious" sermons of Hugh Latimer. Even as sixteenth-century humanists asserted the legitimacy of the former way of reading their works, they continued to be haunted by the possibility of more illegitimate readings, which they themselves helped to articulate. Indeed, the proximity of radical and official during the Edwardian period provided a disturbing paradigm for understanding later outbursts of enthusiasm for social leveling.

FIVE

Utopia and Faerie Land

Despite the claim of Chaloner's Folie that Faerie Land, Utopia, and Plato's republic occupy identical nowheres, Spenser does not advertise any such connection. Rather, as expressed in the letter to Raleigh, the poetics of *The Faerie Queene* exclude the goal of forming a "Commun wealth such as it should be," that is, the very goal that served to define the imaginary polities of Plato, More, and their imitators. As a road conspicuously and repeatedly not taken, however, Utopia and the more general threat of a radicalized humanism form an important part of the topography of Faerie Land. This is particularly true of the 1596 *Faerie Queene,* which was published without the letter to Raleigh. (Its rejection, however, of ideal commonwealths sets the pattern for what we will see to be Spenser's other attempts to address this problem.) Books 4–6, moreover, which first appeared in the 1596 *Faerie Queene,* represent a turn from "private" to more public, or, at least, social virtues. This chapter, then, will have as its primary focus those figures from books 4–6—most importantly, Agape, Ate, the egalitarian Giant, and the Blatant Beast—who are meant to raise the specter of a radicalized humanism, but it will also address those places from earlier works that show Spenser's consciousness of this dangerous possibility.

Ate, the Giant, and the Blatant Beast are all divulgators of a sort, and in their negative way they manifest what we have seen to be the keen humanist awareness of the importance of audience and context to the political significance of words. Thus, for instance, the Giant speaks directly to the "vulgar" (5.2.33) and incites them to rebellion. On the other hand, the Beast, likened to the "hell-borne Hydra" (6.12.32), recalls the forces of democratized learning, the nemesis of the published writer in Erasmus' "Herculei Labores," and his "iron teeth" (6.12.26) are suggestive of the metallic type of the hand-operated screw press. Likewise, the Beast's tendency to speak "reproachfully, not caring where nor when" (6.12.27) and his canine features link him to Cynic figures such as Pasquil and Diogenes. The Beast is the ultimate monster of antidecorum, Erasmus' "lingua" taken to its most powerful conclusion.

An associate of Envy, the Beast also threatens hierarchy, and his depredations affect a rather indiscriminate mélange of social and religious orders. Thus, Ben Jonson's comment in his *Conversations with Drummond* that "by the Blating Beast the Puritans were understood"[1] is, in part, a function of the tendency of anti-Puritan rhetoric to absorb and redeploy earlier castigations of social leveling and Anabaptism, castigations that also included Utopian polities.[2] For the Beast is a retrospective as well as contemporary monster in more ways than has generally been realized. We are familiar with the possibility that the Beast's rampage through the monasteries at the end of book 6 may refer to the Henrician dissolution of the monasteries, but this rampage will also show Spenser viewing early-sixteenth-century Erasmian humanism through the rather dark glass of his own time.

The Martin Marprelate controversy of the late 1580s and early 1590s is the crucial contemporary referent for the intertwining of religious and social issues that the Beast exemplifies. These anonymous and illegally printed satires against episcopacy inaugurated, as Peter Lake has argued, the "radical stage" of English Presbyterianism, and Martin's "eerie combination of moral furey and jokey ridicule marked the final abandonment of the claim to inclusion within the magic circle of Protestant respectability."[3] To be sure, Marprelate's chief target was one familiar to Presbyterians—the power of the English bishops and the degree to which the offices of the visible church had come to resemble secular magistracies. But Marprelate often derided particular bishops by name, and, like the Blatant Beast, he aggressively wielded the threat of unlimited public exposure:

And you brethren bishops take this warning from me. If you do not leave your persecuting of godly christians and good subjectes . . . all your dealing shalbe made knowen unto the world.[4]

Here, we are not too far from the Blatant Beast, who breaks into the "sacred Church" and is said to have "all confounded and disordered there" (6.12.25). Thomas Cartwright had argued the Presbyterian case in a staid manner, but Marprelate made use of invective and dramatic vignettes rich in social implications. His *Oh Read over D. John Bridges* (1588), for instance, is replete with incidents of "citizens" and their wives confronting prelates who are little better than thieves.[5]

The immediate occasion of the Marprelate controversy was the publication in 1587 of Bishop John Bridges' *A Defence of the Government Established*

in the Church of England, a massive opus written to counter Presbyterianism. Marprelate's desire, however, to make the "dealing" of bishops
known to the world soon led to an escalation of the controversy. Hack
writers such as Thomas Nashe and John Lily entered the fray on the side of
the bishops, and their responses to Marprelate imitated his style rather
than that of the tedious Bridges. In 1593 Parliament, reacting, in part, to
Marprelate's assaults, passed a bill that made "seditious sectaries" liable to
the same punishments as Catholic recusants. The same year saw the execution of a number of Protestant dissidents, including John Penry, who was
suspected of being Martin Marprelate, as well as the publication of Gabriel
Harvey's *Pierces Supererogation or a New Prayse of the Old Asse,* which contained Harvey's "An Advertisement for Pap-Hatchet, and Martin Marprelate."[6] Harvey, an old school friend and public correspondent of Spenser's, had been tainted with the suspicion of being Martin Marprelate in
John Lily's 1589 *Pap with a Hatchet,* and his "advertisement" to both Pap-
Hatchet and Martin Mar-prelate shows the vulnerability of even the most
pedantic figures of humanist learning to the charge of using the press to
disseminate radical doctrines.

Marprelate, to be sure, was anxious to distinguish between his assaults
upon prelacy and challenges to civil authority. Indeed, an important
premise of Marprelate's argument is that civil government and church
polity are different in kind. Thus, he argued in *Hay Any Worke for Cooper*
(1589) that the realization of "Christs government [of the church] is neither Mar-prince/Mar-state / Mar-law nor Mar-magistrate."[7] Marprelate
also ordered the English bishops to stop slandering "the cause of reformation / or the furtherers therefof / in terming the cause by the name of
Anabaptisterie."[8] Nevertheless, as the 1593 law against seditious sects
would suggest, others were less sure that neither the Marprelate pamphlets nor Presbyterianism in general endangered hierarchies besides that
of the bishops. A secret report (1589) addressed to Cecil, now Lord Burleigh, quoted the Earl of Hertford saying of the Martin Marprelate tracts,
"as they shoot at bishops now, so will they do at the Nobilitie also, if they
be suffred."[9] Here, we see the fear that the collapse of episcopacy would
ruin other parts of the social order, too. Thus, Harvey in his "Advertisement" criticized Marprelate's adherents for attempting to "build a reformation in a monarchy, upon a popular foundation, or a mechanical plot."[10]

Spenser's Blatant Beast and egalitarian Giant are figures of what
the Marprelate controversy had underscored—the potentially dire consequences of words made too public. But, insofar as these monsters wield
language in a public manner, they also exemplify a force that a humanist
poet might hope to harness and control for more salutary and civil ends.

Hence, they invite a reconsideration of what has become a veritable topos of Spenser criticism, Spenser's supposed retreat from the civic and public aspects of the poetic role in books 4–6 and book 6 in particular. For the subject of book 6 is, as James Nohrnberg puts it, the "book-as-subject," and more recently Debra Belt has situated the concerns of book 6 in the context of a vituperative print culture.[11] This subject and such concerns are not, however, easily reconciled to the supposedly "private" and sequestered Spenser who, in the view of numerous critics, increasingly manifests himself in book 6.[12]

In contrast to many of his poetic successors and predecessors, Spenser repeatedly chose print over the manuscript circulation of his poetry, and this choice enabled Spenser to see himself as addressing a potentially broad rather than necessarily circumscribed audience. This lack of circumscription meant that Spenser could not cast the political function of his poetry as merely the verse equivalent of advising or flattering the prince and select members of the nobility. Unlike Donne and Sidney, Spenser was not a "coterie" poet.[13] His poetry did not occupy a protected space between the fire and the press, as Donne's primarily manuscript productions did. Even when Spenser's poetry gestures in the direction of specific audiences or readers, its meaning is not restricted to those audiences. Writing a letter to Raleigh is obviously different from publishing such a letter at the outset of *The Faerie Queene.*

Whatever their own politics may have been, moreover, Spenser and his publishers serviced a reading public whose tastes were not always, from the perspective of the Tudor regime, reassuring. Thus, for instance, unlike the outlaw and fugitive Martin Marprelate, Richard Hooker had trouble finding a publisher for his *Laws of Ecclesiastical Polity* during the 1590s.[14] For in contrast to the comic bite of Martinist tracts, the orthodoxy and moderate tone of Hooker's *Laws* gave it only lukewarm commercial prospects. Hooker, however, was only experiencing a familiar problem that had beset sixteenth-century defenders of orthodoxy since the days of More. That is, heretical and even seditious works could sell better and therefore be more attractive to printers than the books written to counter such works. Mercenary motives as much as ideological factors, then, may help to explain the willingness of printers such as Hugh Singleton, who published *The Shepheardes Calender,* to undertake far riskier books, for instance, John Stubbs' *Discovery of a Gaping Gulf* (1579).

Marprelate's own writings, however, show that populism and learning were not mutually exclusive. Thus, Marprelate justified his efforts to popularize religious controversy by appealing, not only to the desire of attracting readers, but also to the familiar rhetorical principle of decorum:

I sawe the cause of Christs goverment / and of the Bishops Antichristian dealing to be hidden. The most part of men could not be gotten to read any thing / written in the defence of the on and against the other. I bethought mee therefore / of a way whereby men might be drawne to do both / perceiving the humors of men in these times (especially of those that are in any place) to be given to mirth. I tooke that course . . . jesting is lawful by circumstances / even in the greatest matters. The circumstances of time / place and persone urged me thereunto.[15]

Catering to the "humors of men," Marprelate is claiming to be the first rhetorically astute polemicist of the late sixteenth-century quarrels over the future of the English church. The "most part of men" certainly could have found such quarrels dull until the advent of his lively brand of polemic. But, even as they address the "most part of men" and avoid the mistake of being staid, Marprelate's writings also display learning. Thus, Marprelate's apparent populism is rooted in humanism's emphasis upon context, or circumstances. To be sure, arguing the lawfulness of his style from "circumstances of time / place and persone," Marprelate was also distorting this emphasis since its point was generally to restrain rather than excuse the kind of railing that Martin Marprelate exemplified. Nevertheless, the tactic of playfully distorting the doctrines of others was a familiar one to English humanism. Like Erasmus' Folly, Marprelate plunders and perverts the education of an elite even as he makes this education an ingredient of his mass appeal.

Marprelate's combination of regard and neglect for decorum also extended to scriptural exegesis. Like earlier reformers, including Erasmus, Raphael Hythlodaeus, and Tyndale, Marprelate makes the Bible the measure of the need for religious reform, and he appears to regard the "most part of men" as better readers of the Bible than the English bishops are. But, when addressing the application of scripture to church polity, Marprelate also invokes the problem of decorum and its chief measuring rod, the Lesbian rule. Thus, Martin distinguishes between "these questions which are grounded upon the certaine prescript rule of the worde that cannot be chaunged and other questions which . . . depend not uppon any thing prescribed and exactly set downe in the worde / but upon the grounds of . . . the changeable circumstances of time and place." If the issue is an indifferent one, "[c]oncerning which the word hath . . . set downe nothing," then, according to Marprelate, it should be "squared unto the rule / let all things be done honestly by order and edification."[16]

This more flexible rule of honesty and edification is the Lesbian standard as opposed to the rigidly scriptural "rule of the word," and Marprelate might appear willing to temper radicalism with an attention to circumstances of time and place. But this appearance of compromise is deceptive. For Marprelate goes on to apply the Lesbian rule to trivial issues such as whether a pulpit should be made of wood or stone. On the other hand, he wants to use the rule of scripture to adjudicate all the major controversies pertaining to the government of the church. Marprelate proves to be the heir of Raphael's radicalism rather than the timorousness of "More."

Marprelate's use of decorum to justify indecorousness and the Lesbian rule of moderation to countenance a rather sweeping extension of the rule of scripture to church polity make him almost a parody of aspects of English humanism. Yet such parody was also serious, for it indicated the continuing vulnerability of sixteenth-century humanism to reinterpretation, reinvention, and misconstruction. Indeed, Spenser's letter to Raleigh, which appeared in the thick of the Marprelate controversy, presents itself as an effort to avoid "gealous opinions and misconstructions." However, the danger of misinterpretation was not confined to the historical moment when a book first appeared in print, but rather this danger could increase with time. Thus, for instance, *The Shepheardes Calender* may in 1579 have been part of what John King terms a "generalized Protestant satire against Roman Catholic abuses." But, as Spenser claimed in the envoy to the *Calender,* his accomplishment was to have made a "Calendar for every yeare," and this accomplishment necessarily had its perils as well as triumphant aspects. That is, given the four reprintings of *The Shepheardes Calender* between 1581 and 1597,[17] how was such generalized satire read in the 1590s in the wake of Martin Marprelate? Was it susceptible to more particular applications?

One of E.K.'s notes to the May eclogue indicates by its very defensiveness the possibility of such vulnerability even in 1579:

Some gan) Meant of the Pope and his Antichristian prelates, which usurp a tyrannical dominion in the Churche, . . .

Nought here spoken, as of purpose, to deny fatherly rule and godly governaunce (as some malitiously of late have done to the great unrest and hinderaunce of the Churche) but to display the pride and disorder of such, as in steede of feeding their sheepe, indeede feede of their sheepe.

This note is to Piers' description of the corruption of the shepherds of the church from their pristine state of simplicity and humility: "Some gan to gape for greedy governaunce / And match themselfe with mighty potentates, / Lovers of lordship and troublers of states" (121–23). As with Taverner's additions to Erasmus' "Amicorum communia omnia," however, E.K.'s note is testimony to the plausibility of the readings that it prohibits, and it both asserts and undermines a "generalized" interpretation of the satire of the *Calender.* For although E.K.'s caveat protects Spenser, it also suggests that Piers' criticisms of the "greedy governance" of the Church are not entirely distinct from the "hindrance of the church" by a malicious "some." That is, Piers' strictures could apply both to the pope and his "antichristian prelates" as well as to English prelates and what Presbyterians saw as the residue of Catholicism in the English Church.

Piers even suggests the possibility of a restoration of the apostolic church in the May eclogue: "The time was once and may agayn retorne / . . . When shepheards had none inheritaunce, / Ne of land nor fee in sufferaunce" (104–6). Piers' interlocutor, whose name is significantly Palinode, a word that denotes "retraction" in the *Phaedrus,* dubs Piers' speech "fooles talke" (141), but this retraction, like that of E.K., does not eliminate the interpretive problem posed by Piers' utterances. Read in the 1590s, moreover, Piers' nostalgia for the time when the shepherds of the Church fed their sheep rather than lorded over them might well have resonated with Marprelate's strictures against the corruption of Church government since the time of the apostles:

If the Church government be so prescribed in the worde / as it cannot be altered / then either oure government is the same which was therein prescribed, or our Church goverment is a false Church government. If ours be the same which is mentioned in the word: Then Paule and Peter were either no true Church governours or els Paul and Peter and the rest of Church governours in their time were Lordes / for all our Church governours are Lordes. But Paul and Peter were no Lordes.[18]

Marprelate goes on to celebrate a Church government of "Pastors/Doctors/Elders/& Deacons," who, among other things, feed their flock with the "word" of wisdom and knowledge.[19]

Spenser may have introduced Palinode, or the character of "retraction," in *The Shepheardes Calender,* but the perilousness of words made public and the continuing need to qualify or disavow them haunted his later poetic career, too. In the 1591 *Complaints* and in particular the satirical *Mother Hubberds Tale,* whose target rather than dedicatee was Burleigh, Spenser's poetic career would seem to have overlapped with that of his own Detraction, another associate of the Blatant Beast and one who like Spenser, never ceased to "publish . . . to many" (5.13.35) her words. Jean Brink has plausibly argued that the 1591 *Complaints* may have been an unauthorized publication for which the publisher of the 1590 *Faerie Queene,* William Ponsonby, was entirely responsible.[20] If so, this unauthorized publication demonstrated a primary danger of sixteenth-century print culture: publication could ascribe to an author words that he would not have publicly

(or, in some cases, even privately) claimed as his own. Brink's question—
"Who fashioned Edmund Spenser?"—is, then, quite a good one. Self-fashioning was not always an option for a published poet.

Gabriel Harvey went so far as to term Mother Hubberd "canicular,"[21] an epithet that both anticipates the canine Blatant Beast of the 1596 *Faerie Queene* and recalls the Fox or "curdog," who is the one of the two main characters of *Mother Hubberds Tale.*[22] Harvey's remark, which opposes Mother Hubberd to the "sweet" Faery Queene, creates an interesting opposition between Gloriana and the old woman who is the narrator of *Mother Hubberds Tale.* This opposition suggests that Spenser's muse has a double nature. But, by confusing the character of each poem with their two most important female characters, Harvey may also have been trying to lessen Spenser's responsibility for the biting satire of *Mother Hubberds Tale.* Harvey attributes this satire to Mother Hubberd, not Spenser, but this attribution is itself a reminder that others might not be so generous.

Mother Hubberds Tale demonstrated that Spenser was not the only servant of Gloriana who had to contend with the stigma of holding radical beliefs. The supposed targeting of Cecil, now Lord Burleigh, as the fox of *Mother Hubberds Tale* shows that Cecil never entirely escaped his past associations with the "commonwealth" reformers of the 1540s. For the fox of Spenser's *Mother Hubberds Tale* begins his career as an advocate of communism:

> Let us our fathers heritage divide,
> And challenge to our selves our portions due,
> Of all the patrimonie, which a few
> Now hold in hugger mugger in their hand,
> And all the rest doo rob of good and land.
> For now a few have all and all have nought,
> Yet all be brethren ylike dearly bought:
> There is no right in this partition . . .
> That there might be no difference nor strife,
> Nor ought cald mine or thine: thrice happie then
> Was the condition of mortal men.
> That was the golden age of Saturn old. (135–51)

Such is the fox's "counsel" when he and the ape start their journey, and indeed the trajectory of the fox in *Mother Hubberds Tale* from egalitarian communist to the highest and wealthiest counselor of the realm does seem to glance satirically at Cecil's progress from the patron of commonwealth men to Lord Treasurer. Thus, when the fox becomes a counselor to the ape-king, he is criticized not only for making "no count . . . of nobility" (1183), but also for betraying his earlier professions of social justice: "For not so common was his bountie shared; / Let God (said he) if he please care for the manie, / I for my selfe must care before els anie" (1193–96).

The fox uses the "common treasures store" (1170)—that is, the commonwealth—as an excuse for enhancing his own treasure. Burleigh's amassing of riches and his position as Lord Treasurer form the immediate target here, but aspects of the satire are genuinely ambiguous. That is, despite her declaration of concern for the disregarded nobility, Mother Hubberd may also be castigating the fox for not practicing the egalitarian communism that he had preached earlier. The poem gives no indication that Mother Hubberd has any particular interest in the well-being of the nobility. Indeed, Harvey's opposition of Mother Hubberd to the "sweet" Faery Queene suggests the contrary.

Like book 5 of *The Faerie Queene*, *Mother Hubberds Tale* is premised upon Astraea's abandonment of the "sinful world": the tale begins in the month when the "righteous maide," who for "disdaine of sinfull worlds upbraide / Fled back to heaven," receives the sun into her bower. In accordance with this premise, the communistic fox is an advocate of recapturing a lost golden age that also has Christian significance since the fox adduces the "brethren ylike dearly bought" (142) in favor of his arguments. Likewise, the fox's companion, the ape, uses the "iron world" (254) as an excuse for his having to beg. In other words, the fox and ape express a view of the world that is self-serving but not entirely distinct from the satirical perspective of the narrator of the poem. But this view may have proved an embarrassment to Spenser, especially if he did not authorize its publication in 1591.

Harvey's comment, however, that *Mother Hubberds Tale* was "canicular" gains its full force from its satire against the clergy. For this satire, albeit ambiguous in places, could have been read as Martinist. Thus, the fox and ape encounter a priest who tells them of "jollie prelates, worthie rule to beare, / Whoever them envie: yet spite bites near" (423–24). As read in 1591, biting of "spite" could easily have suggested Martinist attacks upon prelacy, but the priest's portrayal of clerical avarice and laziness also carries some bite of its own. By telling the fox and ape how to succeed as clerics, he provides grist for opponents of clerical and episcopal prerogatives. Although the priest defines himself as an opponent of popery, he is not as far from it as he thinks.

But the ambiguities of *Mother Hubberds Tale* become even more perilous in the light of Spenser's own connection to the source—that is, printed letters—of the charges of Martinism that Lily brought against Harvey in *Pap with a Hatchet:*

One we will conjure up, that writing a familiar epistle about the natural causes of an earthquake, fell into the bowels of libelling . . . he is a mad lad, and such a one as cares as little for writing without wit, as Martin doth for writing without honesty, a notable coach companion for Martin, to draw divinitie from the colleges of Oxford and Cambridge, to shoo-makers hall in Saint Martins.[23]

In his "Advertisement to Pap Hatchet and Martin Mar-Prelate," Harvey calls the suspicion of his having been Martin both "unlikely" and "monstrous," but its improbability did not prevent Harvey from including in the "Advertisement" his own defensive retraction of Martinism.[24] Not surprisingly, however, Harvey only succeeded in further provoking his opponents and detractors (this may even have been his purpose). Yet, in his *Have with You to Saffron Walden,* Thomas Nashe, a participant in the public quarrel against Harvey as well as Martin Marprelate, has one of the characters of this vituperative satire declare that "to talk treason he [i.e., Harvey] may be drawn unawares and never have any such intent, for want of discretion how to manage his words."[25] Despite his heaping of considerable abuse on Harvey, Nashe here demonstrates an awareness of the vulnerability that both he and Harvey shared as published writers. This vulnerability appears in Faerie Land as Detraction, who is ever ready to "misconstrue of a mans intent" (5.12.34).

Lyly's own misconstruction, however, of Harvey's intentions had the potential to extend beyond Harvey. For the incriminating "familiar epistle" to which Lily referred was a part of *Three Proper and Wittie, familiar Letters, lately passed between Two Universitie Men: Touching the Earthquake in April last* (1580), a published collection containing the letters of Harvey and a S. Immerito, the pseudonym employed by Spenser a year earlier in *The Shepheardes Calender.* This letter presents an interpretive problem similar to that of *The Shepheardes Calender.* For Harvey's satire here, albeit too early to be Martinist in intent, addresses issues of "Heresy in Divinity" such as the Vestiarian controversy that had anticipated the intensification of religious debate and polemic during the late 1580s.[26] Originally, the accusation of libel seems to have involved a poem that may have been a satire directed at the Earl of Oxford.[27] But his rather broad response to Lyly's accusation in 1593 shows that Harvey, when defending himself, went back to other parts of these letters besides the offensive poem.

As part of his own retraction of Martinist radicalism, Harvey had to engage the specter of Utopian equality, too. Thus, in his 1580 letter Harvey wrote of "Geometrical proportion seldom, or never used, Arithmeticall overmuch abused," and his response to Lyly, "Advertisement for Pap-Hatchet and Martin Mar-prelate" makes the import of this comment clear:

Equality, in things equall, is a just law: but a respective valuation of persons, is the rule of equity: & they little know, into what incongruities, and absurdities they runne headlong, that are weary of Geometricall proportion, or distributive Justice, in the collation of publique functions, offices or promotions, civile or spiritual. God bestoweth his blessings with difference and teacheth . . . the Prince to estimate, and preferre his subjects accordingly. When beter Autors are al-ledged for equalitie in persons unequal; I will live and die in defense of that equalitie; and honour arithmaticall proportion, as the only balance of justice, and sole standard of governement.[28]

Here, Harvey is expanding the brief mention of "proportion" in his 1580 letter to make the point that he was always an opponent of the social leveling that was perceived as a subliminal agenda of Martinism. Harvey's notion of "distributive justice" and "blessings" bestowed with "differ-ence" here owes something to Elyot and his emphasis on talent. Defending such distributive justice, Harvey professes a willingness to attack figures such as "Martin, and his applauders; Browne, and his adherents, . . . Kett and his sectaries" with the same vehemence that they have used against "judges, Bishops, Archbishops, Princes."[29] Harvey's implication is that the attacks upon judges, bishops, and other such luminaries come from frustrated aspirants to the same offices. He also makes the familiar point that attacks on church and state are hard to separate, despite Marprelate's claim that his last name did not make him a "Mar-prince" or "Mar-law."

This stigma of frustrated ambition, however, was applicable to Harvey himself in 1580. For not only was Harvey suspected of having satirized his betters in the 1580 letters to S. Immerito, but in 1592 Harvey admitted that his own satire was the result of disappointment over not having received the post of orator at Cambridge. Because of this satire, he had been summoned to the "Council Table" to "interpret" his "intention in more express terms."[30] Harvey's professed disgruntlement suggests that he did not always believe rewards were distributed in a fair manner or that the difference of blessings was necessarily equitable and proportional to merit.

Harvey also claimed that these letters between himself and S. Immerito were "privately written" and not meant to be "publicly divulged"[31]—a claim that, whether true or not, indicates Harvey's distinctly humanist awareness of the importance of context to meaning. Yet, after Harvey did not get the promotions that he desired, he, like Elyot before him, culti-vated the technology of divulgation, that is, printing. As Harvey con-fusingly explained it in *Pierces Supererogation,* "my writing, is but a private note for the publique advertisement of some fewe."[32] This public of "some few" is, however, belied by the clear efforts of Harvey and his detractors to attract widespread attention through their quarrel. The London printer, John Wolfe, dubbed "alias Machivill" by Marprelate for his role as Beadle of the Stationers Company,[33] may even have been Harvey's employer during the 1590s.

By refusing, however, to believe that arithmetical proportion could be the "balance of justice," Harvey resembles not only Elyot in 1531 but also Artegal encountering the egalitarian Giant and his balance in the 1596 *Faerie Queene.* As Spenser's knight of justice, whose name betokens equality but not necessarily equity, Artegal must also clear himself of any imputation of advocating the kind of crude leveling that the Giant represents. Similarly, as a pupil of Astraea, who teaches him to "weigh both right and wrong / In equal balance . . . / and equitie to measure out along" (5.1.7), Artegal must also show that he has no intention of bringing back the kind of golden age espoused by the communistic fox. Spenser most explicitly engages his strained relations with Lord Burleigh in the proem to book 4 of *The Faerie Queene,* but the encounter of Artegal and the egalitarian Giant in book 5 may also represent a revision, or, perhaps even retraction, of *Mother Hubberds Tale.* However, this revision would be necessary not because the Giant was entirely alien to Spenser but precisely because *Mother Hubberds Tale* as well as Spenser's printed connection to Harvey's public quarrels had made Spenser vulnerable to being confused with the kind of leveling that the Giant espouses.

In a broader sense, however, figures such as Harvey, Spenser, and even Cecil were vulnerable to the charge of political radicalism because of what we have seen to be a recurring difficulty of English humanism, that of distinguishing social mobility from egalitarianism. Even after Cecil's elevation to the peerage, the Cecils could be termed "pen-gent."[34] Likewise, Spenser, a poor scholar at the Merchant Taylor school, Harvey, the ropemakers son, and Nashe belonged to the aristocracy of "talent" whose titles were often those of books. "Printers take hede how ye play the Heralds," wrote Harvey in one of his assaults on "Sir Nash."[35] Moreover, print allowed writers to play their own heralds. Thus, the preface to the 1580 *Familiar Letters* invokes the topos of talent and refers to the "pleasaunte and witty Talente" of Harvey as well as the "good and divine gifts" of both correspondents.[36]

Harvey's own truncated career, however, indicates that the Tudor government lacked sufficient rewards to accommodate all of its talented and humanistically educated citizens. Frustrated aspirants to offices had, in turn, the potential to become authors with a less than absolute attachment to the status quo.[37] Spenser's own sojourn in Ireland scarcely counts as a Tudor success story. Given such widespread dissatisfaction, the market for subversive books, and the association of English humanism with ideal as well as actual polities, a poem whose supposed purpose was to exemplify social virtues such as friendship, justice, and courtesy was open to a wide range of political readings. Some of these readings might indeed narrow the distance between Faerie Land and, if not Utopia itself, the kind of radical alternatives to the English church and state for which Utopia had increasingly come to stand.

HEAVEN ON EARTH

Like More in his antiheretical works, Harvey saw an analogy between the confusion of real and ideal polities and what he perceived as the radical Protestant tendency to conflate earthly and heavenly churches. Thus, in the "Advertisement" Harvey ventriloquizes the views of the Martinists as follows: "What aile Religious handes, that they stay from building upp the Cittie of God? Can Plato's republic, and More's Utopia winne harts and cannot the heavenly Hierusalem conquer Soules? . . . Why forgetteth the grose Church that it ought to be the pure kingdom of heaven?" These kinds of questions, as Harvey recognizes, have the potential to lead to tumult. For the heirs to Plato and More will offer "new lands of promise" and "fools paradises" to their followers.[38]

Harvey was not alone in connecting Utopian polities to the attempt to reform the church. Thus, in his *An Admonition to the People of England* (1589), Thomas Cooper, who became Bishop of Lincoln in 1571 and Bishop of Winchester in 1584, responded to Martin Marprelate by linking Martinism to more dangerous and radical forms of leveling:

We may see therefore, and it is time to take heed of it, how Sathan under pretences seeketh to thrust the spirit of the Anabaptistes into this Church of England . . . either these sentences of the gospel touch bishops and ministers only and all else are left free, which is a very great absurdity . . . or else that the same doctrine . . . doth belong to all Christians, which with the Anabaptists taketh away all propertie and possessions of lands and goods, and . . . bringeth in a Platonical communitie. I say not that they which use these places doe mean it: but surely that inconvenience and daunger followeth upon it.[39]

Here, Cooper conflates Anabaptism, Platonic communism, and the Martinist desire to return to a more Gospel-based form of church government even as he admits that Martin may not "mean" what Cooper is ascribing to him. Nevertheless, Cooper's interesting point is that Martin has to take responsibility for what his arguments have the potential to mean as well as what they are explicitly intended to mean. The presence of *Utopia* as a subtext here is evident from Cooper's clarification elsewhere in *An Admonition* of the significance of his conjunction of Anabaptism and Platonic communism: "the phanatical spirits of the Anabaptistes, . . . not only taking away all possession and property, and allowing a Platonical community of all things: but also denying superiority and Lordship and dominion, and bringing in a general equality."[40] This "general equality" suggests that, when Cooper connects Anabaptism and a "Platonical communitie," he is using this connection as a kind of shorthand for the hybrid anti-Utopianism of Elyot, Cheke, and others.[41] Cooper has here traveled quite a distance from his proem to the 1548 *Bibliotheca Elyotae,* which celebrated the "commonwealth" as an ideal entailing, if not equality, at least an end to certain forms of economic oppression and monopoly.

Cooper's anti-Martinist prose needs to be compared to the influential political work of another survivor of the Edwardian years, Sir Thomas Smith, one of Harvey's mentors at Cambridge. For in his *De Republica Anglorum* (1565; published 1583) Smith rejects Plato's "common wealth," Xenophon's "kingdom of Persia," and More's *Utopia* as "feigned commonwealths, such as never was nor never shall be."[42] Moreover, Smith allies his own understanding of justice with that of Thrasymachus, the character in *The Republic* who advocates a might-makes-right approach to justice: "it must needes follow, that the definition which Thrasimachus did make, that is just which is the profite and most strong parte (if it be meante of the citie or commonwealth) is not so far out of the way (if it be civillie understood) as Plato would make it."[43] Smith's suggestion that Thrasymachus is the true victor in the dialogue of the *Republic* is a fascinating one, and it is roughly analogous to reading *Utopia* as the triumph of "More" over Raphael.[44]

This climate of retraction helps to explain why Spenser's letter to Raleigh rejects the goal of forming a perfect commonwealth in *The Faerie Queene:*

To some I know this Methode will seeme displeasaunt, which had rather have good discipline delivered plainly in way of precepts, or sermoned at large . . . then thus cloudily enwrapped in Allegorical devises. But such, me seeme, should be satisfide with the use of these dayes, seeing all things accounted by their showes and nothing esteemed of, that is not delightfull and pleasing to commune sence. For this cause is Xenophon preferred before Plato, for that the one in the exquisite depth of his judgement, formed a commune wealth such as it should be, but the other in the person of Cyrus and the Persians fashioned a governement such as might best be: So much more profitable and gratious is doctrine by ensample than by rule.

Despite Spenser's eschewal of "discipline sermoned at large," the voice here is that of the parodic preacher Folly, who was wont to appear in sermons or sermon-like discourses during times of national trouble and uproar. "Commune sence," which Spenser here opposes to "commune wealth," is a quality with which, as we have seen, both Chaloner's Folie and Erasmus' Stultitia identify themselves: "commune sense and the capacitie of all men (that is to saie) to folie." But the opposition of Chaloner's Folie in particular to Utopian commonwealths seems to be the subtext to Spenser's eschewal of ideal commonwealths in favor of common sense. Spenser's early interest in the figure of Folly is apparent from a Latin poem that appeared in *Two Other Very Commendable Letters* (1580), a continuation of his published correspondence with Harvey. In this poem, Spenser extols Harvey's more than Stoic "sapientia," but he claims that anyone who wants to please the "populus" must learn how to "desipere" and seek the "Stultitiae laus," the Latin title of the *Moriae Encomium*.[45] An ironic populism underwrites Spenser's use of Folly in this poem as it does one of E.K.'s notes to the June eclogue of *The Shepheardes Calender*. For there E.K. associates "the opinion of Faeries and elfes" with friars who use "feigned" inventions to keep the "comen people" from smelling out the "untruth" of their "Massepenie religion." Hence, a poet of fairie land would be a Catholic version of the kind of Menenius Agrippa figure that, in the words of Chaloner's Folie, "revoked the comminalitee of Rome, rebellyng against the Senate to agreement" as well as others such as Minos and Numa who "with feigned fayrie inventions bleared the gross multitudes eyes."[46] In Folie's formulation, Agrippa and his ilk represent the realistic alternative to attempting to find a nation governed by "those glorious institutions and rules of livying, that Socrates set forth."

The cloudy wrappings of allegory by definition entail some eye blearing and the rejection of doctrine by rule, but, more broadly, Spenser's emphasis upon appearances is reminiscent of Folly's message that illusion is the way of the world. All things are accounted by their shows in Spenser's letter just as in *The Praise of Folly* it is better to remain in Plato's cave than discover the truth of things. Indeed, making explicit the subtext of this letter, Redcrosse himself inaugurates the quest of book 1 by looking into a cave of deception—that of Error. The shift from the formation of ideal commonwealths to a monarchist poetics—Xenophon over Plato—emerges in the letter to Raleigh as an antiphilosophical and Folly-like concession to the world of appearances.[47]

As Thomas Nashe put it in *The Unfortunate Traveller,* Erasmus' message was to "swim with the stream," and in his avoidance of ideal commonwealths Spenser presents himself as doing just that. Yet, if taken at face value, the letter to Raleigh is almost as unreliable a guide to *The Faerie Queene* as E.K.'s glosses to *The Shepheardes Calender.* Nevertheless, as with E.K.'s glosses, the interpretive "solutions" offered in the letter to Raleigh serve to raise important problems, and thus we cannot dismiss them either. Spenser's eschewal of perfect commonwealths in favor of the best possible government should create expectations of this choice reappearing in the poem.

This choice does reappear in book 1 in the form of the New Jerusalem that Redcrosse and Contemplation behold:

> Faire knight (quoth he) Hierusalem that is,
> The new Hierusalem, that God has built
> For those to dwell in, that are chosen his,
> His chosen people purg'd from sinfull guilt, . . . (1.10.57)

The Redcrosse knight's vision of the "new Hierusalem" even puts Gloriana's Cleopolis to shame. But Redcrosse has to return to Cleopolis—a necessity that is more than a result of the familiar rivalry between the contemplative and active lives. Rather, Contemplation makes the point that the New Jerusalem is not even for the elect until they have been "purg'd from sinfull guilt." Contemplation's strictures apply both to Redcrosse and, by extension, to those contemporary radicals attempting to turn, as Harvey put it, the "gross church" into a celestial city. For as Contemplation sees it, the imperfections of earthly polities cannot be avoided. Thus, Contemplation goes on to observe that Cleopolis is "for earthy frame, / The fairest peece that eye beholden can" (1.10.59), and this observation, in particular, recalls Spenser's own professed preference of the best possible government to the perfect commonwealth. Like Xenophon and Plato, the City of God and that of Man irremediably diverge here; Redcrosse cannot occupy both at the same time.

The New Jerusalem that Redcrosse sees functions as something of a temptation, and it provides the political counterpart to his encounter with Despair in canto 9. To be sure, Redcrosse's visit to Contemplation is a part of the cure of pride and despair that he receives in the House of Holiness. Nevertheless, just as Despair nearly persuaded Redcrosse to die by offerinmg him desiderata such as "wished home" and "eternal rest" (1.9.39–40),[48] so, when Redcrosse sees the New Jerusalem, he wants to take yet another shortcut to heaven:

> O let me not (quoth he) then turne againe
> Backe to the world, whose joyes so fruitlesse are;
> But let me here for aye in peace remaine . . . (1.10.63)

The temptation of this New Jerusalem is also reminiscent of an earlier Renaissance Hagnopolis, that is, Utopia, and one of its more significant features, the way in which the irremediably ill are persuaded to die. Spenser thus specifies here the link that Harvey had suggested when he connected the Puritan desire to build the New Jerusalem on earth with Utopia. Like Raphael's description of Utopia, a vision of the New Jerusalem has the potential to cure the patient by killing him.

In both book 1 of *The Faerie Queene* and *Utopia* the irremediable illness whose only cure is death is fallen human nature. This ailment of human nature or "sinfull guilt" keeps Cleopolis from being the New Jerusalem and, as Raphael admits in his peroration, other countries from adopting Utopian institutions. Insofar as the commonwealth is, in addition to Redcrosse, the implied patient here, despairing of political structures of "earthly frame" is the only absolute cure. Thus, throughout *The Faerie Queene* provisional cures take the place of such absolute ones. Indeed, if Redcrosse is any indication, the House of Holiness is itself one such provisional cure. For during the fight with the dragon Redcrosse will endure still more "falls" and miraculous recoveries. How then can the New Jerusalem be a feasible goal for church or state if its exemplary citizen keeps getting knocked to the ground?

Fallen human nature is a theological ailment that defies political and narrative solutions in *The Faerie Queene*. But even as Spenser rejects the hope that Faerie Land could be a Utopia or that the New Jerusalem could ever be built on earth he continually raises this hope as a tantalizing possibility in *The Faerie Queene*. Spenser is especially tantalizing in books 4–6, whose subject is the creation and dissolution of the bonds that hold communities together. Thus, for instance, Telamond ("perfect world") never appears in book 4, though its title, "The Legend of Cambel and Telamond," promises that he will. But this title creates the expectation that an investigation of communal virtues such as friendship and in later books justice and courtesy will lead to a "perfect world," and indeed this expectation impels the reader through the story. More than any resolution of plot, which Spenser quite often does not provide, glimpses of an ideal social harmony, amidst incessant strife and bloodshed, constitute the narrative bait in the later books of *The Faerie Queene*.

Books 4–6, in particular, will prove Spenser to be something of a fox, profferring visions of a golden age and, at the moment of their potential consummation, failing to bring them to fruition. At issue again is the perfectibility of human nature. In the later books of *The Faerie Queene* "sinfull guilt" continues to make what "might best be" a more plausible goal than the establishment of an ideal polity or New Jerusalem. Yet the problem of sinful guilt is not merely Spenser's disinterested commentary on the human condition or the future of England. For we must remember that the possibly unauthorized publication of *Mother Hubberds Tale* as well the Harvey's "Advertisement to Pap-Hatchet and Martin Mar-prelate" separated the 1596 *Faerie Queene* from its 1590 predecessor. Thus, Spenser was addressing an issue involving what *The Shepheardes Calender* terms his "author self" as well as the English nation. Indeed, in the form of elderly female revilers such as Ate and Sclaunder, Spenser makes the vein of Mother Hubberd an explicit part of the 1596 *Faerie Queene*. In particular, Spenser associates the vein of Mother Hubberd with potentially seditious attempts to restore the perfection of a lost paradise or golden age.

Books 4–6 of *The Faerie Queene* waver between assertions of the ideal and flawed status of Spenser's own Faerie Land. Canto 8 of book 4 provides one of the more subtle examples of such wavering. Prince Arthur and two women, Amoret and Aemylia, must spend the night with an old woman, Sclaunder, who proceeds to abuse them verbally. But the problem of slander is not confined to this old woman; it also extends to the reader. For Spenser worries lest some "rash witted wight" read "with misregard" and conclude that the "conversing" of these ladies with the knight was not entirely innocent (4.8.29). This slander is of course particularly hard to resist since the two women have only just escaped from Lust.

Spenser's solution to this potentially slanderous reading is to argue that the world and age he describes is essentially a perfect one: "But Antique age yet in the infancie / Of time, did live then like an innocent." Hence, "Then loyal love had royall regiment / And each unto his lust did make a lawe / From all forbidden things his liking to withdraw" (4.8.30). This assertion leads to an equation of Faerie Land with the paradisiacal vision of Isaiah 11, which in the Geneva Bible figures as a foretelling of the coming of Christ:

> The Lyon there did with the Lambe consort,
> And eke the Dove sate by the Faulcons side,
> Ne each of other feared fraud or tort,
> But did in safe securitie abide,
> Withouten perill of the stronger pride:
> But when the world woxe old, it woxe warre old . . .
> And dared of all sinnes the secrets to unfold. (4.8.31)

Because each is a "law unto himself," Faerie Land is a place without predators or the need to use legal machinery to restrain such predators. Indeed, the Geneva Bible's gloss of Isaiah 11 makes explicit the reformation of human nature to which Spenser is referring: "Men because of their wicked affections are named by the names of beasts, wherein the like affections reigne: but Christ by his spirit shall reforme them, & work in them such mutual charitie, that they shall be like lambes, favoring and loving one another." Love and mutual charity replace strife and competition or, in legal terms, "fraud" and "tort" as Spenser himself returns briefly to pastoral.

All this seems well and good, but in the morning the sun "discovered heavens face / To sinful men with darknes overdight" (4.8.34). Who are these sinful men if not the same ones who a few stanzas earlier were without sin? Spenser seems to raise the hope of a restored paradise only to dash it immediately. A world where "mutual charity" prevailed would be a world of lambs—no difference of degree, domination, or hierarchy. As Thomalin puts it in the July eclogue, whose "Argument" highlights the "disprayse of proude and ambitious Pastors," the "first shepherd, / . . . lived with little gain" as well as "Humble, and like in each degree the flock" (125; 132). Such humility and equality, however, is a thing of the past in both the July eclogue and Arthur's encounter with Sclaunder.

Sclaunder turns Arthur's "loyal love" into lust, but Spenser's preemptive despoilation of his own paradise suggests that some "rash wight" could slanderously misread even the Christian love upon which this paradise is predicated. Thus, an implicit and overarching rivalry of Books 4–6 is that between Ate, the "mother of debate" (4.1.19), and Agape, mother of Priamond, Diamond, and Triamond. Agape is the Christian love to which the Geneva commentary on Isaiah is referring, and surely if Telamond ("perfect world") had made his promised appearance in book 4, he would have been her son. Indeed, as the Greek word that "charity" translates, Agape also recalls the maternal figure of Charissa in book 1.

But Agape and Ate are not merely opposing principles. Rather, like Una and Duessa in book 1, Agape, one kind of maternal figure, and Ate, another kind altogether, parody each another. Indeed, Ate is a slanderous misreading of Ate. That is, Agape is to Ate as lust is to love. But in the case of Ate the "forbidden things" that are the object of lust include not only potential paramours but also other kinds of belonging and property as well.

Erasmus, as we have seen, had shown that, in addition to denoting Christian love in general, *agāpe* also had a meaning specific to apostolic times. Defending the English church in the 1590s, Richard Hooker used this meaning of *agāpe* to criticize those who would hold this church too strictly to the apostolic norm:

In the Apostles times, that was harmless, which being now revived would be scandalous, as their oscula sancta. Those feastes of charitie, which being instituted by the apostles, were retained in the Church long after, are not now thought anywhere needful.[49]

Here, "feasts of charitie" is Hooker's translation of *agāpe,* and he uses such feasts to make what we have seen to be the familiar sixteenth-century argument that certain practices were appropriate to the time of the primitive church but are no longer possible. Communism is only indirectly Hooker's concern here, but, as the ultimate challenge posed by the apostolic to the English church, it constitutes a subliminal part of Hooker's critique of other features of English "disciplinarians." On the other hand, as we have seen, anti-Martinists such as Nashe and Cooper were not at all hesitant about suggesting that radically Protestant critics of the English church were social levelers and crypto-Anabaptists.

Spenser's Agape and her three sons, too, are meant to evoke apostolic Christianity. These sons, the "brethren" (4.2.41), are so "allyed / as if but one soul in them all did dwell" (4.2.43). The ultimate origin of this alliance is Acts 4, where the members of the early church are said to be, as the Geneva Bible puts it, "of one heart and one soul" (Acts 4:32), and this oneness in turn leads them to share their possessions. Agape, on the other hand, enables her sons to literalize unanimity. For the souls of Priamond and Diamond combine in the figure of Triamond as Cambel kills one after another. These three "brethren" have their lives in common. Yet, in typically Spenserian fashion, such apostolic communion does not last long. For the fight with Cambel uses two of Triamond's three spirits. We may infer that he only has his own left.[50]

Indeed, when Spenser portrays a feast of Agape in book 4, he redefines it and makes it more exclusive than the *agapai* of the primitive church. Thus, after Priamond and Diamond have been killed and Cambel and Triamond are the only survivors of the battle for Cambina's hand (4.3), Canacee, Triamond's sister, arrives to pacify the strife with Folly's drug of choice, Nepenthe:

> Nepenthe is a drinck of soverayne grace,
> Devized by the Gods, for to assuage
> Harts grief, and bitter gall away to chace,
> . . . Few men, but such as sober are and sage,
> Are by the Gods to drynck thereof assynd;
> But such as drinck, eternall happinesse do fynd. (4.3.43)

This drug makes Cambel and Triamond the best of friends and ultimately leads to Cambel, Triamond, Canacee, and Cambina living the rest of their lives as a kind of feast of love or Agape:

> Where making joyous feast theire daies they spent
> In perfect love, devoide of hatefull strife,
> Allide with bands of mutuall couplement . . . (4.3.52)

Yet, just as Canacee's Nepenthe is only available to "few men," so this feast of love is only open to a very small community. Unlike Erasmus' "Convivium Religiosum," the feast of the four lovers includes both genders, and indeed some of the "bands of mutual couplement" that unite the four are marital ones. Nevertheless, as with the "Convivium Religiosum," the feast of love here is a modified one, and it represents an enclosed version of the original *agapai* of the apostolic church. The "perfect love" of the four lovers does not translate into a "perfect world."

One indication of the modified character of the *agápe* of the four lovers is Canacee's arrival on the battlefield:

> And as she passed through th' unruly preace
> Of people, thronging thicke her to behold,
> Her angrie teame breaking their bonds of peace,
> Great heapes of them, like sheep in narrow fold,
> For hast did over-runne, in dust enrould, . . . (4.3.41)

This passage provides a grim alternative to shepherds and sheep living in "like degree." Since Nepenthe can only be given to a "few men," the way to pacify the rest is to overrun them like sheep in a fold. As a dispenser of Nepenthe, Canacee is a potential shepherd to the "preace of people." But their unruliness makes them unreceptive even to the opiates of Folly. The violence of her trampling steeds enacts a complete severance of shepherd from sheep, and it serves as a revealing prelude to the strictly limited sort of *agápe* that she is able to effect.

The figure of Ate, on the other hand, includes the threat of a radicalized humanism, one that would identify Faerie Land and Utopia as well as turn the desire to perfect the world into a source of chaos. Spenser's concern to depict her heinousness at every turn suggests that she constitutes a vulnerability of his own poem, that is, a misconstruction of the more limited possibilities of social harmony that he is trying to depict. Thus, one of Ate's triumphs is the "bloody feast" of the Centaurs and Lapiths (4.1.23), a triumph that served as a warning in Erasmus' "Convivium Religiosum" and that in Ovid's *Metamorphoses* includes the sacking of a palace by half-bestial figures. In *The Faerie Queene,* this "bloody feast" indicates the danger of taking *agápe* too far.

In Shakespeare's *A Midsummer Night's Dream,* Theseus immediately rejects—"We'll none of that" (5.1.46)—a play recounting the "Battle of the Centaurs" as an entertainment, and it is not hard to see why.[51] For Theseus, who, according to Ovid, was himself a participant in this battle, does not want to give ideas to the socially inferior players who are guests at his own wedding. The battle of the Centaurs and Lapiths took place at the nuptials of Pirithous and Hippodamia, and, in Golding's translation of Ovid, the "bloody frays" include an inventory-like description of the destruction of the contents of an aristocratic home. Bowls, dishes, trays, a "lampbeame full of lights," and even a "mighty altar" become part of the mélée.[52] Thus, if Agape evokes memories of early Christian feasts where rich and poor sit together, the battle of the Centaurs and the Lapiths suggests the dangers of such fellowship.

In *Pap with a Hatchet* Lyly shows that others beside Spenser saw the battle of the Centaurs and Lapiths as an apt metaphor for what might happen to the church:

I am ignorant of Martin and his maintainer, but my conscience is my warrant, to care for neither. For I know there is none of honor so carelesse, nor any zeal so peevish, . . . that will succor those that be suckers of the church, a thing against God and policie; against God in subverting religion, against policie in altering government, making in the church the feast of the Lapithes, where all shall be thrown upon another's head, because everie one would be the head.[53]

Lyly's premonitions concerning the effect of Martinism suggest, again, the degree to which defenders of the English church linked attacks upon religion and "policie." But, for the purposes of understanding Spenser, this quote also helps to explain the presence of so many "bloody feasts" in books 4–6 of *The Faerie Queene.* These feasts are to some extent eucharistic parodies,[54] but they also recall the primitive *agápe* and the kind of community for which it stood. Among such parodies, the "common feast" that the cannibals almost make of Serena is perhaps the most explicit (6.8.38), but also noteworthy is Lust's "bloudy banket," a fate that Amoret and Aemylia narrowly escape (4.7.20).

Ate demonstrates the truth of Lyly's connection between threats to religion and "policie." Thus, Ate's very body shape connotes social inequalities and the leveling tendencies—that is, the communistic Giant of book 5—to which those inequalities give rise. She has unequal hands, and, using them, she "great riches gathered manie a day, / . . . in short space did often bring to nought" (4.1.29). But even more importantly for Spenser as poet she cultivates both the "seedes of evill wordes, and factious deedes": her ears "fild with false rumors and seditious trouble, / Bred in assemblies of the vulgar sort" (4.1.25, 28) make her into an embodiment of the inflammatory potential of words. In contrast to Agape, who represents the true spirit of Christian love, Ate is a false preacher, sowing not the word of God but the germs of division.

The "vulgar" character of Ate's audience is an issue for Spenser, too. Although book 4 begins with Spenser's claim that he sings to his queen and she understands him perfectly (proem 4), the specter of "some rash witted wight"—potentially anybody—hovers over the poem as well. We have seen that the Lyly-Nashe-Harvey feud and the 1591 *Complaints* showed the vulnerability of a published author's words to being "drawn" in a direction that he might not have meant. Books 4–6 of the 1596 *Faerie Queene* reveal Spenser engaging this vulnerability even as he also to some extent continues the project of offering visions of a restored paradise.

As a corollary to the rash-witted wight who misinterprets love, Burleigh reappears in Spenser's poetry as the censurer of love in the proem to book 4. This censure, in turn, raises the problem of ideal commonwealths. For Burleigh is generally thought to be the "rugged forhead" who, in this proem, manages "affaires of state" and consequently cannot understand the importance of "lovers deare debate"—an oxymoronic conjunction of Ate and Agape. In comparison to the depiction of the Fox in *Mother Hubberds Tale,* Spenser's response to Burleigh in the proem to book 4 is subdued but pointed: "Witnesse the father of philosophie, / Which to his Critias, shaded oft from sunne, / Of love full manie lessons did apply, / The which these Stoic censours cannot well deny" (proem, 3). The reference here is a conflated one: Socrates discusses love with Phaedrus beneath a shady tree in the *Phaedrus* whereas the *Critias* is a proto-Utopian Platonic dialogue that among other things depicts a golden age of Athens in which the ideal city-state of the *Republic* actually existed. As such, the *Critias* is an interesting model for the *Faerie Queene* or at least those parts of it where Spenser claims to be representing the perfection of the antique world.[55]

According to Gabriel Harvey, Chaloner's *Praise of Folie* was a great favorite of Cecil's, and so he may have caught an allusion here to Folie's banishment of the Stoic wisemen to Plato's republic, Utopia, or Faerie Land.[56] For all his management of "affaires of state" Spenser's Burleigh here demonstrates a Stoic rigidity similar to that of Folie's ideal denizen of a philosophical nowhere. In books 4–6, however, the shady setting of the *Phaedrus* recurs in *The Faerie Queene* as an image of a vulnerability that extends beyond Burleigh. Throughout the poem and particularly in book 6, shade is where knights doff their armor and become open to attack—for instance, Aladine in canto 2 and Calepine in canto 3. Secrecy paradoxically leads to exposure and even violence, and this paradox is particularly true of lovers.

The problem of love in books 4–6, however, is quite different from that of erotic love in book 3. For although the chemistry between Britomart and Artegal has dynastic and political significance, it is nevertheless a bond between two people rather than the members of a community. The shift from the chaste erotic love of Britomart to friendship, on the other hand, is also a shift of emphasis from the couple to a form of love that is able to be extended beyond two people. Hence, the figure of Concord opens the gate to "Venus grace" when Scudamour approaches the Temple of Venus (4.10.35), and the paradise on which this temple is located includes "another sor Of lovers"—friends (4.10.26). In the latter books of the *Faerie Queene,* Spenser, then, shows much interest in the social context of love, and thus even lovers motivated by eros such as Aldus and Priscilla will prove to have carefully defined places in such a context.

But, like its strictly erotic counterpart, the love that makes social concord possible can be mistaken for its parodic double. The rivalry of Ate and Agape is Spenser's translation of the Platonic problem of distinguishing one kind of *eros* from another to Christian *agāpe.* For as in the *Phaedrus* the misinterpretation of love and the silence of writing are related difficulties, so that the same is true of *The Faerie Queene.* Spenser's warnings to overly "rash" readers provide one way of making a text speak, but such warnings are of limited efficacy. On paper, at least, or in other assemblies of the "vulgar" the threat of social tumult implicit in the religious struggles of the early 1590s was susceptible to being mistaken for an attempt to revive the unanimity of the apostolic church.

THE BEAST IN THE GARDEN

"One might ask, incidentally, what the poet had in mind when he picked those good humanist names, Calepine and Aldus," wrote Harry Berger in "A Secret Discipline."[57] Berger's perceptive question has never received the answer it deserves, and the presence of Aldus in particular, given the Blatant Beast's role as a disseminator of words, is suggestive. For Aldus Manutius was the heroic humanist exemplar of the power that the Beast wields so chaotically in book 6. Although the Beast does not make an explicit appearance in the Aldus episode, the function of Spenser's Aldus is to provide a standard against which the linguistic crimes of the Beast can be measured.

The Beast, for instance, has no sense of social decorum. His tendency to speak "reproachfully, not caring where or when" translates into attacks upon everyone: "And spake licentious words, and hatefull things / Of good and bad alike; low and hie / Ne Kesars spared he a whit, nor Kings" (6.12.28).[58] Aldus, on the other hand, upon seeing his son Aladine (Aldine letters?) wounded, makes the following observation: "This is the state of Kesars and Kings. / Let none therefore, that is in meaner place, / Too greatly grieve at any his unlucky case" (6.3.5). In other words, for Aldus death, the great leveler, replaces the possibility of those "in meaner place" attacking their kings and Caesars, either verbally or otherwise. Aldus' cautions against attacking social superiors are particularly interesting because his own son Aladine is described as "meaner borne" (6.3.7) in comparison to his paramour Priscilla. Thus, Priscilla undergoes the "hazard" of her "good fame" after consorting with Aladine (6.3.8).

In contrast to Aldus, on the other hand, the Blatant Beast reflects the changed attitude toward print, language, and the maintenance of the social order that Erasmus had demonstrated into the 1526 "Festina lente" as well as in *De Lingua*. Indeed, Thomas Warton has even suggested that the Beast's rampages are taken directly from *De Lingua:*[59]

> Through all estates he [Calidore] found that he [the Beast] had past,
> In which he many massacres had left,
> And to the clergy now was come at last;
> In which such spoile, such havocke, and such theft
> He wrought, that thence all goodnesse he bereft, . . .
> At length into a Monastere did light,
> Where he him found despoiling all with maine and might. (6.12.23)

In the preface to the 1526 *De Lingua,* Erasmus wrote the following:

In the same way we can now see how this deadly sickness of a malicious tongue has infected the whole world . . . pervading the courts of princes, the homes of commoners, theological schools, monastic brotherhoods, colleges of priests, regiments of soldiers, and the cottages of peasants.[60]

It is generally supposed that the Beast's despoliation of the monasteries refers to Henrician policies during the 1530s, but the presence of *De Lingua* as a subtext here indicates an additional possibility. For, as Erasmus and More both noted, monasteries were sacked and looted during the German Peasants' War, and thus the Beast's "maine and might" could be that of rebelling subjects rather than a power-hungry monarch. Certainly, "massacres" fits the scale of bloodshed in the German Peasants' War better than the more limited violence of the Henrician Reformation.

Nevertheless, the historical referrent for the Beast's massacres is probably meant to be ambiguous. For although different in kind, the German Peasants' War and the Henrician Reformation were part of the same historical upheaval. Both were assaults upon clerical power, and during the uproars of the 1590s such assaults could have looked equally dangerous, no matter what their source. For the intertwinement of "policie" and prelacy that Martinism underscored would make any attack upon the latter appear to threaten the stability of the social order, too. Nor could learned poets necessarily remain above the fray represented by the Beast. Thus, as part of his condemnation of "scholars" in Nashe's *Summer's Last Will and Testament* (published 1600 but performed in the early 1590s), the character of Winter ascribes the invention of ink to Cerberus, who "head-long drawn from hell, / . . . voided a black poison from his mouth, / Called acconitum, whereof ink was made." This genealogy of writing is not too far from that of the hellish Blatant Beast, who according to one of Spenser's accounts, is the offspring of Cerberus and Chimaera.[61] In *Summer's Last Will,* moreover, Winter's lengthy rebuke of scholars leads to the most canicular of philosophers, the Cynic Diogenes and his tub.[62]

The connection between tumult and the dissemination of discontent is most evident in the figure of the egalitarian Giant and the "vulgar" who "about him flocke" (5.2.33). For the Giant's speech is an appeal to the grievances of the have-nots, and thus he is a Kett-like figure of the danger of "divulgating" Utopia or related ideas.[63] That is, the Giant indicates what we have seen to be a primary vulnerability of English humanism—its susceptibility to being taken out of context and, as Nashe put it, "drawn" to seditious meanings. Artegal's destruction of the Giant will prove to be Spenser's attempt to kill off this interpretive problem as far as his own poetry is concerned. Yet, the unequivocal character of the Giant's destruction—a rather drastic palinode on Spenser's part—is again testimony to the genuineness of the uncertainties that the Giant evokes.

As the "mother of debate" and social strife, Ate, in a sense, gives birth to the egalitarian Giant of book 5. Just as she frequents "assemblies of the vulgar sort," so the "vulgar" who "flocke" around the Giant are also said to form a "great assembly" (5.2.29). He promises to draw "all the wealth of rich men to the poore" (5.2.38), and thus he provides a means of carrying out Ate's program of bringing "great riches gathered manie a day to nought." His balance, too, is clearly one of, as Harvey put it, "arithmetical proportion," for his goal is to "reduce unto equality" (5.2.32) all things.

But the "vulgar" who "flocke" around the Giant also mark him as something of a pastor figure, and indeed Ann Imbrie has linked the Giant to such parodic preachers as Despair and Mammon, who use Scripture for their own diabolical ends.[64] Like Ate—also a parodic preacher—the Giant sows the "seeds of evil words and factious deeds," but interestingly the Giant is the only parodic preacher in *The Faerie Queene* whose chief text—Esdras 2—is from the Apocrypha. Indeed, 2 Esdras 4 in particular resembles Tobit because an angel (in the case of Esdras, Uriel) offers a theodicy of sorts to a mere mortal. But, as a book that explicitly addresses the Babylonian captivity as a repercussion of Adam's loss of paradise, Esdras also engages what we have seen to be a preoccupation of Spenser's poetics: the place of paradise in Faerie Land.

English Puritans were known for their resistance to the inclusion of the Apocrypha in the Bible, but this resistance did not prevent opponents from using the Apocrypha to stigmatize them. Indeed, the practice of stigmatizing Protestant radicals as the possessors of an apocryphal or dubious authority dated from the early Reformation. Thus, for instance, in the *Responsio* More had called Luther a "novus Esdras,"[65] and, in the early years of the Reformation, Esdras had in fact been a crucial text for radical Continental reformers, including Melchior Hofmann, an important influence on the Muenster revolt.[66] In his "Advertisement," on the other hand, Harvey had used the Apocrypha as a figure for the difficulties that radical reformers experienced when attempting shift from "types in abstracto" to more concrete political change. One particular difficulty was that of variability:

If the precisest, and most scrupulous Treatises, have much adooe to uphold the credit of any perfection, or estimation, with their own associats; (how many heads, so many plottes) what may reason conceive of the assurance, or maturitie of their judiciall, or other morall proceedings *in esse?* When His and His Scripture, after some prettie pausing, is become Apocryphal with his, and his owne adherents, whose writing was Scripture with many of them, how can any of them ascertaine or resolve themselves of the Canonicall incorruption or autenticall omnisufficiencie of his, or his actuall government?[67]

Here, what Puritan ("precisest") critics defined as the gulf separating scripture and Apocrypha serves as a measure of these critics' own giddy reading habits. Harvey also connects such reading habits to an inability to negotiate the passage between ideal perfection and "actual government."

The apocryphal and egalitarian Giant of book 5 may or may not prove unable to make the same passage, but, whatever one decides, words provide the measure of his success or failure. The importance of language becomes clear from the way in which the Giant and Artegal reenact the debate between Uriel and Esdras. Thus, Esdras complains that the Babylonians, who are no less sinful than the Israelites, nevertheless have dominion over them:

Do those who live in Babylon really do any better? And has it for that reason subdued Zion? But when I arrived there and observed innumerable vices, . . . I was utterly perplexed. . . . [H]as any other nation except Israel known you? (2 Esdras 3:28–32)

The Angel then challenges Esdras to "weigh" the "weight of fire," "measure" the "measure of the wind," or "recover" the "day that is past" (2 Esdras 4.5). If Esdras cannot perform these feasts, he has no right to weigh the wickedness of various nations. Similarly, the Angel asks Esdras to determine the "ways of Paradise" (2 Esdras 4:7). Not knowing these things, Esdras is unfit to judge God. Yet, Esdras can, to some extent, "open . . . up for me closed chambers" (2 Esdras 5:37) to discover God's judgment. For God does offer a vision to Esdras in which the wicked are punished and the godly enjoy felicity. Indeed, God finally admits to having "opened" "paradise" to Esdras and "built" a "city" for him (2 Esdras 8:52).

Artegal is less willing to make a vision of paradise available to the Giant, and, instead of this vision, a focus of the episode becomes language. Thus, just as the angel reproves Esdras's presumption, so Artegal castigates the Giant's desire to "weigh the world anew," but Artegal repeats this rebuke with a significant difference:

> For take thy ballaunce, if thou be so wise,
> And weight the winde, that under heaven doth blow;
> Or weigh the light, that in the East doth rise;
> Or weigh the thought, that from mans mind doth flow.
> But if the weight of these thou canst not show,
> Weigh but one word which from thy lips doth fall.
> For how can thou those greater secrets know,
> That does not know the least thing of them all? (5.2.43)

The weighing of words is Spenser's addition to his source, and it raises a problem similar to Harvey's point that those who constantly confuse scripture and Apocrypha are unfit for actual government. Thus, the Giant's supposed failure to weigh his own utterances serves as evidence of his inability to wield the balance that he intends to use to redistribute the substances of the world, including riches. Incapable of distinguishing the relative weight of words, the Giant cannot tell his own apocryphal utterances from scripture, and thus he will prove singularly incapable of making the transition from theory to practice. Yet the problem of weighing words in the balance is complicated by the point that Artegal's own words have as apocryphal an origin as those of the Giant. Artegal is the Uriel of this episode, and Uriel is an angel of as dubious scriptural authority as Raphael. The balance that the reader must use to adjudicate the dispute, therefore, may show an uncomfortable equality between the two speakers.

Although derogated in stereotypical ways, the "vulgar" followers of the Giant are at the center of the episode. For like the reader, the Giant's audience must wield scales of their own and balance the words of Artegal against those of the Giant: "The eare must be the ballance, to decree / And judge, whether with truth or falshood they agree," claims Artegal (5.2.47). But the episode suggests that even this inner balance may tilt in what Artegal would identify as the wrong direction. Thus, on the one hand, the Giant proves unable to weigh words in his balance because he weighs the "false" against the "true" rather than, after locating the true in the center of his balance, weighing one falsehood against another. More problematically, however, the "vulgar" fail to weigh correctly the words of Artegal against those of the Giant. Hence, they become rebellious even after hearing Artegal and seeing the death of their leader.

The Giant and his followers literalize the desire for a Telamond or perfect world. Hence, the Giant's ambition to "weigh the world anew" leads to the need to redistribute its parts and "restore" them to equality. The depradations of sea and fire must be repaired, and thus the Giant promises to perform impossible feats such as "all the earth [to] uptake, and all the sea." The Giant's retrospective vision, however, is not entirely distinct from the narrator's idealization of the "antique age" in book 4 or implication that the *Critias,* with its discovery of an ideal city in Athen's past, is a model for Faerie Land. The Giant's goal of economic and social equality is an offshoot of the possibility that turns up throughout the last three books of *The Faerie Queene*—that of restoring a lost perfection.

Whereas the Fox is merely "uncased" at the end of *Mother Hubberds Tale,* the Giant is utterly destroyed. His bones are "timbered" and his balances "battered"—a conclusion that would seem to leave little room for doubt. Yet bits and pieces of the Giant and his too egalitarian balance turn up later in the poem. Thus, for instance, book 6 features another giant, Disdain, who is said to be the "sib to Orgoglio" (from book 1). Disdain's lineage, however, ultimately leads back to the mythological Giants who, because they did "warres darrain Against the heaven," became a standard trope of rebelliousness in the Renaissance (6.7.41–42). In Nashe's *The Unfortunate Traveller* Jack Wilton accuses Protestant radicals, too, of trying to take the "Kingdom of Heaven" by storm, and thus of enacting a contemporary version of the revolt of the giants against the Olympians.[68] Even Mt. Acidale, the poetic paradise that allows Spenser's authorial persona, Colin Clout, to achieve some proximity to heaven, displays traces of the rebellious aspirations of the Giants. In particular, Acidale's "wood / Of matchless hight, that seem'd the earth to disdaine" (6.10.6) makes such gigantic aspirations a part of its grandeur.

The problem of discontent from below, on the other hand, reappears in disguised form when, just before encountering Acidale, the courtly Calidore tries to flatter his shepherd host Meliboe with the wish that his "fortunes might transposed bee / From pitch of higher place, unto this low degree" (6.9.28). Meliboe's response to Calidore rebukes Calidore's desire to be lower than he is, but it could also double as a criticism of those who aspire to be higher than they are:

> In vaine (said then old Meliboe) doe men
> The heavens of their fortunes fault accuse . . .
> For not that, which men covet most, is best,
> Nor that thing worst, which men do most refuse;
> But fittest is, that all contented rest
> With that they hold. (6.9.29)

Here, Meliboe, the humble shepherd, seems to demonstrate an immunity to Calidore's courtly efforts at ingratiating himself. Yet Meliboe is himself an ex-courtier, and the point of his strictures may be as cloaked as Calidore in his lowly shepherd's outfit. For not only conniving courtiers but also followers of the egalitarian Giant would be placated by the content that Meliboe espouses. Like Chaloner's Folie, Meliboe offers a kind of nepenthe or opiate of disgruntlement, and he thus shows that the threat represented by the Giant does not fully vanish with the Giant's destruction.

Acidale is itself not quite the vacation from menaces such as the Giant and the poetic responsibility of countering them that critics have sometimes taken it to be. Nor is Colin Clout a solitary or withdrawn figure there. Indeed, Acidale is a rather crowded place—with its nymphs, faeries, graces, and Calidore hovering at the margins. Acidale, to be sure, is said to be "far from all peples troad" (6.10.5), but it is not far from the tread of the numerous foot-thumping maidens (6.10.10) that surround Colin. Harvey's claim that his writing was a "private note for the publique advertisement of some few" provides a good gloss on the contradictory qualities of secrecy and exposure that seem to inform Acidale. Likewise, Acidale's concentric circles, leading finally to Colin and the four Graces, recall the gardens within gardens of Eusebius' semi-public domain in Erasmus' "Convivium Religiosum."

Acidale is said to be impervious to the approach of "wylde beastes" or the "ruder clowne," and these categories would presumably include the Blatant Beast (6.10.7). Nevertheless, Acidale's exclusion of such beastliness does not necessarily amount to isolation. The Hermit of Canto 6, not Colin, represents such isolation in the poem, and, though his "art of words" (6.6.6) does facilitate the cures of Serena and Timias, his advice to them is singularly inept:

> The best (sayd he) that I can you advize
> Is to avoide the occasion of the ill:
> . . . Abstaine from pleasure, and restraine your will
> . . . Shun secresie, and talke in open sight. (6.6.14)

This best is not all that good, and, to follow it, the hermit's patients would effectively have to remain with the hermit. But Serena and Timias, not surprisingly, leave the hermitage and thereby get into further trouble.

Colin is no hermit at Acidale, though it is a place of secrecy as well as open sight. Indeed, when the onlooker Calidore abandons the "covert of the wood" for the "open greene" (6.10.11), Colin's vision at Acidale dissolves. But Acidale is also a place of desire and pleasure, whose reigning deity is Venus. Indeed, the name Acidale was originally the designation of a venereal "fons." The Renaissance knew of this "fons" through Servius, who, annotating a reference to "Acidalian" Venus in *The Aeneid,* gave as one explanation of the epithet "Acidalian" the "fonte Acidalio . . . in quo se Gratiae lavant" (*ad Aeneid,* 1.720). Among others, Boccaccio and Nicolas Perotti repeat this Servian gloss. Although Spenser's transference of the epithet from fountain to hill makes Acidale into something of a Parnassus, too, traces of its origin as a fountain linger in the topography of the mountain and, in particular, its "gentle flud" (6.10.7).[69]

But pleasure and desire do not necessarily entail a dereliction from care and obligation. Editions of *The Faerie Queene* regularly gloss Acidale as meaning "careless," and Spenser criticism has often succumbed to the temptation of reading Mt. Acidale as a kind of truancy on the parts of Calidore, Colin, and Spenser himself. Nevertheless, Servius' other influential explanation of the epithet Acidale gives it exactly the opposite meaning: "Acidalia Venus dicitur vel quia iniciit curas, quas Graeci *akidas* dicunt" [Venus is called Acidalian because she inflicts care that the Greeks term *akidas*]. Whether this gloss is accurate or not, it is repeated throughout Renaissance dictionaries and compendia of mythology, and Spenser would certainly have expected his readers to know of it.

For all of its pleasures, then, Acidale is the site of cares that are central to Spenser's poetry. In particular, Acidale is the final place where Spenser opens paradise to his own readers, and he is scrupulous in his depictions of its limitations. For instance, as if the Giant were still exerting his pressures, the Graces at Acidale are said to bestow, among other things,

> . . . all gracious gifts . . .
> Which decke the body or adorne the mynde, . . .
> They teach us, how to each degree and kynde,

> We should our selves demeane, to low, to hie;
> To friends, to foes, which skill men call Civility. (6.10.23)

Colin's Graces are the dispensers of what Harvey termed differences in blessings, and they implicitly stand opposed to any attempt to redistribute those blessings in a way that eliminates differences of low and high. Yet the gifts distributed by the Graces are also those of "mynde," and such gifts recall the familiar trope of talent. That is, the status quo upheld by the Graces here is not necessarily one of inherited land, wealth, or power. Their civility is based upon a different and more distinctly humanist kind of birthright.

The possibility, however, of an egalitarian reading of humanist civility is one of the cares at Acidale, and thus the feast of the Lapiths and Centaurs makes an appearance in the midst of the dance of the Graces:

> Looke how the Crowne, which Ariadne wore
> Upon her ivory forehead that same day,
> That Theseus her unto his bridale bore,
> When the bold Centaures made that bloudy fray
> With the fierce Lapithes, which did them dismay,
> Being now placed in the firmament,
> Through the bright heaven doth her beams display . . .
> Such was the beauty of this goodly band. (6.10.13–14)

This image of the harmony of the graces is, like Redcrosse's vision of the New Jerusalem, an admonitory as well as beatific one. The gap between the "Crowne" in the firmament and the battle of the Centaurs and the Lapiths is another version of the difference between the possibilities of harmony on heaven and earth. Spenser's desire to juxtapose an image of celestial harmony with one of earthly chaos helps to explain why he conflated the two originally distinct parts of this allusion, the Ariadne story and the battle of the Centaurs and Lapiths. Thus, the battle of the Centaurs and Lapiths, in which Theseus fought as a wedding guest rather than a bridegroom, figures as the conspicuous sign of the limits of social cohesion in the City of Man. The wedding should be a unifying occasion, but it is all too vulnerable to the forces of disintegration.

As we know from book 1, however, Spenserian weddings also have Christian and even apocalyptic significance, and thus a perfectly consummated marriage (such as Una's and Redcrosse's never is) would mark the passage from the church miltant to the church triumphant in heaven. But, beginning with nuptials of Scudamour and Amoret, weddings are particularly prone to go awry in books 4–6. Indeed Spenser's revision of Hesiod's story of the conception of the Graces has the union of Jove and

Eurynome occurring on Jove's way back from the "feastfull glee" of Thetis and Peleus (6.10.22), the occasion of the introduction of the apple of discord, or Ate. Spenser associates the origin of the Graces with the nuptials that produced the Trojan War. He thus suggests the provisional nature of the social harmony that even the Graces create.

The harmonies of poetry, too, are provisional. At Acidale poetry can span the distance between heaven and earth but only briefly. If Spenser constructs Acidale as yet another paradise only in order to demolish it, the point may be to keep readers from ever thinking that they can enjoy an unmediated relationship to the perfect worlds that poetry builds on the page. Rather, the mediations of history, language, and, most important, the Fall keep Spenser's readers from ever quite getting where they are going. Nevertheless, an ability to read visions of perfect harmony in a less rash or immediate way than Calidore does is an important part of the "art of words" that Spenser himself is trying to teach at Acidale. Without these visions, large portions of books 4–6 and perhaps history itself, would be hard to distinguish from an extended bloodbath, punctuated only by intermittent resolutions of narrative tangles. Nowheres such as Acidale and the Temple of Venus are the primary "places" of poetry in books 4–6, and they arguably provide the real goals of quests that otherwise do not seem to be progressing. Yet such goals are never entirely separable from the background of strife and contention out of which they emerge. They prove New Jerusalems of all too earthly frame.

"Master of his own Book"

From Radical to Liberal Humanism

The second translator of *Utopia* into English was a defender of property, liberty of conscience, and the Glorious Revolution of 1688. In his "A Sermon Preached before the House of Commons on the 31st of January, 1688. Being the Thanksgiving-Day for the Deliverance of this Kingdom from Popery and Arbitrary Power, by his Highness the Prince of Orange's Means," Gilbert Burnet clarified the threat of popery and arbitrary power as the

breaking through a Man's inclosure, or, in a word, the violating these two sacred things, Liberty and Property, and the Constitution of this August Body, which is the great fence to both. When the only use that was made of laws, was to find a colour to break them. . . . When no Man's Fence was strong enough to resist precarious Judges, and suborned Juries; When adhering to law and religion was become a crime. . . . In a word, when no Man was safe in his innocence, nor secure in his Property.[1]

Burnet's latitudinarian views on religious toleration and his belief in the protections afforded by law to property converge here in the language of fenced enclosures. But Burnet's translation of *Utopia,* including Raphael's attack upon enclosures, was published in 1684, and it would seem to offer a striking contrast to Gilbert's 1688 sermon. For as Raphael puts it in Gilbert's translation, only "where no man has any property, all men do zealously pursue the good of the publick."[2] Burnet's translation, which first appeared in print without his name, provides a good measure of the degree to which the 1688 revolution was not a Utopian one. As John Locke, another defender of the 1688 revolution, put it, "The great and chief end therefore, of Men's uniting into Commonwealths, and putting themselves under Government, is the Preservation of their Property."[3]

Nevertheless, Burnet's own translation of *Utopia* shows that "possessive individualism" was not necessarily, as C. B. Macpherson has influentially argued in his analysis of the origins of liberalism, a rooted assumption of seventeenth-century political theory. In Burnet's case such individualism was rather a conscious choice, taken despite an awareness of alternatives.[4] Such alternatives included more than the vanished forms of community once available during the medieval period, as in the classic Marxist accounts of the transition from feudalism to capitalism. Rather, as one such alternative, More's Utopian society was a sophisticated and self-conscious intellectual construction. Moreover, unlike Macpherson's largely secular liberalism, the radical humanism that informed More's *Utopia* had decidedly religious sources, and the changes in its own reception were often a function of religious controversy.

Utopia provided Burnet with a way of understanding the political and religious struggles of England's recent past. In his anonymous preface to the 1684 *Utopia,* Burnet argued that More could not have gone "in heartily to that which is the chief Basis of his *Utopia,* the taking away of all *Property,* and the levelling the *World*" but rather that More "only intended to set many Notions in his Reader's way, and that he might not seem too much in earnest, he went so far out of all Roads to do it the less suspected."[5] In Burnet's translation of book 1, on the other hand, Raphael adduces Plato's conclusion that "setting all upon the Level, was the only way to make a Nation happy; which cannot be obtained as long as there is Property."[6] "Setting all upon the Level" translates the Latin "rerum aequalitas," which Robinson renders "equalitie of all thynges."[7] Burnet's emphasis on leveling suggests that, when reading *Utopia,* he is conscious of the upheavals of the Civil War. In particular, he is aware of the degree to which this period favored the development of Utopia and utopian ideas.

Macpherson has argued that the Levellers who debated the franchise at Putney in 1647 were no opponents of property,[8] but these Levellers were not the only possible referent for Burnet's "levelling the *World.*"[9] For in his *The True Levellers Standard Advanced* (1649), Gerrard Winstanley had argued that in the "beginning of Time, the great Creator Reason, made the Earth to be a Common Treasury" but that the "coming in of bondage" was called *A-Dam* because a "ruling and teaching power without, doth dam up the Spirit of Peace and Liberty." Winstanley further claimed that from "the coming in of the stoppage, or the A-dam the Earth hath been inclosed."[10] Winstanley's communistic ideas, advanced in a series of publications between 1648 and 1652, are significant in their own right and as a reminder of the considerable ferment of the Civil War years. When Burnet associated Utopian communism with leveling in 1684, he probably meant not only Winstanley and his ilk but more generally ideas that, although not explicitly communistic, nevertheless had the potential to lead to what could be construed as a dangerous equality. For as the sixteenth-century reception of Utopian communism and radical Erasmian ideas has shown, early modern writers were often held responsible for the implications as well as the overt contents of their publications.

In 1688 Burnet constructed the individual English subject as a sacrosanct enclosure in danger of being violated by the monarch. But his translation of *Utopia* demonstrates his consciousness of the persistence of other threats to enclosure, specifically, that of communistic leveling. Likewise, Burnet's rather proprietary understanding of authorship demonstrates a similar knowledge of alternative practices. Thus, in his preface to the 1684 *Utopia,* Burnet writes that *Utopia*

> was once translated into English not long after it was written; and I was once apt to think it might have been done by Thomas More himself: for as it is in the English of his Age, and not unlike his stile, so the Translator has taken a liberty that seems too great for any but the Author himself, who is Master of his own Book, and so may leave out or alter his original as he pleases: which is more than a Translator ought to do, I am sure it is more than I have presumed to do.

More himself might have agreed in principle with Burnet's contention that an author ought to be the "Master of his own Book," but More also knew that such mastery was not the norm. As we have seen, More's statements concerning the reception of *Utopia* show considerable nervousness over the ability of readers to make *Utopia* their own. Burnet, too, knows that the first translator of *Utopia* has appropriated it for purposes of his own and has made it a different book than the Latin original. Burnet's application of the principle of possessive individualism to authorship, then, may resemble an assumption never fully defended, but it is also a deliberate reaction to a more communal state of affairs. Like More before him, Gilbert wants to make authors masters of their own books precisely because *Utopia* provides evidence that they are not.

Despite Burnet's distancing of *Utopia* from the ferment of the Civil War period, however, his translation was not without its own agenda of political criticism. Burnet, who wrote an unflattering letter to Charles II in 1679–80 and later likened this king to the decadent Roman emperor, Tiberius, had lost royal favor when *Utopia* appeared in 1684. Indeed, Burnet would soon go into exile and only return with William of Orange. Burnet's preface to *Utopia* shows his particular interest in the problem of criticizing the monarch, as it is represented in book 1. Thus, Burnet labels "the representation he gives of Henry the Seventh's Court" as the "tenderest part of the whole work," where his "disguise is so thin, that the Matter would not have been much Plainer if he had named him." Burnet is referring to Raphael's discussion of how his advice would be received if he ventured to oppose the policies of a monarch bent upon extorting money from his subjects. Burnet's identification of this unnamed monarch as Henry VII then leads him to wonder how More could "write so freely of the Father in the Son's Reign, and to give such an Idea of Government under the haughtiest Prince, and the most impatient of uneasy Restraints that ever reigned in England." Burnet, whose dissidence over political and religious matters did not endear him to Charles' brother, James II, either, is clearly suggesting an application of many of Raphael's antimonarchical strictures to his own time.

But Burnet also made use of *Utopia* when exhorting James' successor to virtue. Thus, in addition to celebrating the Glorious Revolution before the House of Commons, Burnet preached the sermon at William of Orange's coronation in 1689. This sermon, which delineates the "character of a Just Prince" and contains many warnings against tyranny, combines the apocalyptic and the Utopian:

When we see Kings become thus truly Christian philosophers, then we may expect to see the City of God, the New Jerusalem, quickly come down from Heaven to settle among us.[11]

As we have seen, Guillaume Bude had identified Utopia with the New Jerusalem, and later sixteenth-century figures such as Gabriel Harvey and Edmund Spenser had expressed concern over conflations of Platonic and Utopian polities with the heavenly city. According to More's Raphael, however, Plato was right to say that, unless kings become philosophers, no improvement was possible. Gilbert Burnet is thus recasting what had been conceived of as either a dangerous program or an impossibility and situating the earthly heaven at court. Burnet himself then becomes the antidote to the kind of courtiers whom Raphael attacks in book 1. These courtiers are like bad preachers, but, urging William to be a Christian philosopher, Burnet is doing what Raphael claims cannot be done. That is, Burnet is acting the part of a good courtier and a bold rather than compromising preacher.

But Burnet's *History of the Reformation* provides a further enclosing of Raphael's dangerous religiosity and still another application of More and his *Utopia* to Burnet's own time. For the third volume of this massive work, published in four volumes over the course of several decades, casts More's *Utopia* as an anticipation of the Reformation and, in particular, of Burnet's own attitudes toward religious toleration:

167

Those of the church of Rome look on him [More] as one of their glories, the champion of their cause, and their martyr. . . . He wrote that book [*Utopia*] probably before he had heard of Luther; the Wicklevites and the Lollards being the only heretics then known in England. In that short, but extraordinary book he gave his mind full scope, and considered mankind and religion with the freedom that became a true philosopher. By many hints, it is very easy to collect what his thoughts were of religion. . . . I will lay together such passages as give clear indications of the sense he had of these matters.[12]

Burnet goes on to note that More calls the abbots who enclose common land in book 1 "holy men in derision," and he argues that Raphael's comparison of bad courtiers to preachers constitutes More's "severe censure" of preachers. Burnet also points out that Utopian churches lack images—"no obscure hint of his opinion in that matter"—and that the Utopians are inclined to elect their own priests. Burnet sees this latter point in particular as an illustration of More's "largeness of thought," for it "must have appeared one of the most dangerous of all heresies." Burnet admits that all this occurs in a "fable of his Utopians." But, according to Burnet, Utopia "was a scene dressed up by himself, in which he was fully at liberty to frame every thing at pleasure; so here we find in this a scheme of some of the most essential parts of the Reformation." Burnet's argument here seems to be that we must interpret Utopian society and religion as the fulfillment of More's deepest wishes. Nevertheless, Burnet does not apply this method of interpretation to Utopian communism. More's willingness to entertain dangerous "heresies" can only go so far.

Most important, however, Utopia anticipates Burnet's belief in limited religious toleration:

And whereas persecution and cruely seem to be the indelible characters of popery; he . . . makes it one of the maxims of the Utopians, "that no man ought to be punished for his religion, . . ." but for inflaming the people to sedition . . . And though there were many different forms of religion among them, yet they all agreed in the main point of "worshipping the Divine Essence so that there was nothing in their temples, in which the several Persuasions among them might not agree. . . ."
. . . by all which he carried not only toleration, but even comprehension further than the most moderate of our divines have ever pretended to do. (46)

Here, Burnet assimilates More to the incipient Enlightenment as well as the Reformation. Burnet's More anticipates and outdoes even the most moderate of divines, and this ability to do so depends upon what Burnet has already identified as More's largeness of thought and philosophical spirit. In Burnet's formulation, More's moderation and tolerance also make him dispassionate. Thus, Burnet calls More's religious beliefs, as expressed in *Utopia,* his "first and coolest thoughts," and this coolness echoes Burnet's own translation of *Utopia,* where Utopus is said to have instituted religious toleration because of the destruction wrought by "daily contentions and irreconcilable heats in these matters."[13] Burnet's view of *Utopia* confuses the authorial More with both Raphael and Utopus, and it thereby creates not only a topical *Utopia* but a progressivist one. *Utopia* is the harbinger of a series of developments that lead inevitably to Burnet's own enlightened historical moment.

Not surprisingly, however, Burnet has trouble with More, the hunter of heretics: "[I]f he had died at that time [i.e., right after writing *Utopia*], he would have been reckoned among those, who, though they lived in the communion of the Church of Rome, yet saw what were the errors and corruptions of that body, and only wanted fit opportunity of declaring themselves more openly for a Reformation." But, unfortunately for Burnet, More did not die "at that time." He went on to exemplify everything Burnet abhors:

It is not easy to account for the great change that we find afterwards . . . he not only set himself to oppose the Reformation in many treatises . . . but when he was raised to the chief post in the ministry, he became a persecutor even to blood. . . . [H]ow a man who had emancipated himself, and had got into a scheme of free thoughts, could be so entirely changed, cannot be easily apprehended; . . . It cannot indeed be accounted for, but by charging it to the intoxicating charms of that religion, that can darken the clearest understandings, and corrupt the best natures. (47)

Ultimately, Burnet relies upon a demonized Catholicism to account for the contradictions in More's life. In doing so, however, he overlooks much. Most importantly, *Utopia* itself is a work of at times violent contradictions rather than cool moderation, and More's attacks upon the Reformation do not diverge from the spirit of *Utopia* to the degree that Burnet would like. Thus, Burnet pays little attention to the Utopian punishment of a seditious preacher. More broadly, Burnet's ability to separate the communism of *Utopia* from More's enlightened views on religious subjects depends upon a distinction between the religious and political that was at best nascent in the early sixteenth century. Given Burnet's implicit reliance upon this distinction, his inability to comprehend More's "great change" during the Reformation is not surprising.

In Burnet's More, we can see radical humanism turning into the more familiar liberal and secular variety. Burnet's More is an "emancipated" individual, one who is therefore master of himself in addition to his book.

Hence, Burnet can only explain More's contradictions by resorting to the agency of a powerful and intoxicating institution that for Burnet is tantamount to an oppressive government. However, as Burnet's comments about Robinson's translation of *Utopia* would indicate, such mastery was not really possible for early modern writers. Their interpretive property was not a secure enclosure but rather one vulnerable to constant plundering. Aware of this vulnerability, writers such as More, Elyot, and Spenser did not so much strive to maintain a course of moderation as oscillate between antitheses. The opposition between persecutor and radical was no less vehement for being confined to the writings of a single figure.

By contrast, John Milton's *Areopagitica* (1644), a text frequently assimilated to "liberal humanism," is more akin to the radical variety. Indeed, Milton's career as a polemicist bore a resemblance to several of the writers that I have examined in this book. As we have seen, in the preface to *Eikonoklastes* (1649), Milton cited the printed debate between Henry VIII and Luther as one precedent (albeit not a favorable one) for his own controversy with the royal author of *Eikon Basilike*.[14] As the writer of anonymous attacks upon episcopacy, on the other hand, Milton may have been influenced by the Marprelate pamphlets, which were reprinted in the early 1640s. Nevertheless, despite such uses of anonymity, Milton's publications are generally marked by an extreme willingness to display the talents of John Milton. Finally, like More, Milton took actions that apparently contradicted his writings and thus became, as it were, his own persecutor. For, after arguing against prepublication licensing of books in *Areopagitica,* Milton then became a licenser under Cromwell.

Areopagitica was published one year after the birth of Gilbert Burnet, and it reflects the tumultuous revolutionary atmosphere that Burnet probably meant to denote by the word "levelling." Most conspicuously, the toleration that Milton advocates in *Areopagitica* is not a particularly moderate or cool one. Rather, the dominant mode of *Areopagitica* is combat or, as Milton puts it, the "wars of Truth."[15] The gates of the Temple of Janus, with his two "controversal faces," have been set open.[16] Truth, ever outstripping the "pace of method and discourse," controverts herself even within *Areopagitica*.[17] Thus, toleration can extend only so far: "I mean not tolerated Popery, and open superstition . . . that also which is impious or evil absolutely against faith or manners."[18]

The place of controversy and contradiction within Milton's own writings was particularly evident to those who attempted to make a mockery of those writings. Thus, the anonymous *Censure of the Rota upon Mr. Milton's Book, intitled, "The ready and easy Way to establish a free Commonwealth"* (1660) not only satirized the *Ready and Easy Way* but addressed more generally the problem of reading Milton. Thus, one "young gentleman" present at this imaginary meeting of the Rota club argues that Milton's "writings are best interpreted by themselves." This remark leads to a discussion of Milton's use of Sidney's *Arcadia* in *Eikonoklastes.* Another participant then responds that "such a sense was quite contrary" to Milton's purpose. This objection then leads to the conclusion that "it was no new thing" for Milton "to write that, which is as well against as for your purpose."[19] Here, the two controversial faces on the gates of the Temple of Janus prove to belong to John Milton.

This conclusion of the *Censure of the Rota* is particularly acute when applied to Milton's supposed utopianism. Thus, the *Censure* makes the point that

[f]or though you brag much of the people's managing their own affairs, you allow them no more share of that in your Utopia [i.e., the commonwealth of the *Ready and Easy Way*], as you have ordered it, than only to set up their throats and bawl . . . once in an age, or oftener, as an old member drops away and a new is to succeed, not for his merit . . . but because he is able the greatest and most deep-mouthed pack of the rabble in the field.[20]

The immediate reference is to Milton's proposal in the *Ready and Easy Way* for a Grand Council whose members enjoy life terms, but this accusation that Milton does not allow the English people to manage their own affairs soon gives way to the charge of having envisioned a too democratic Utopia. In the revisions to the *Ready and Easy Way,* Milton is particularly careful to respond to the objection that he intends to give any power to the "rabble." Thus, elections to the Grand Council are not subject to the "shouting of a rude multitude" but rather to the decisions of the "rightly qualifi'd" as well as those of a "better breeding."[21] Here, Milton, like Burnet after him, responds to the possibility of Utopia's having a leveling effect, or, as the *Censure* put it, being "written to the elevation of that rabble."[22] But Milton is also attempting to adjudicate a controversy within his own writings, that is, their simultaneously democratic and antidemocratic character.

In addition to attacking Milton as a Utopian, the *Censure* castigates Milton for wanting to see the "commonwealth of Heaven" established on earth.[23] This accusation has a definite basis in the *Ready and Easy Way,* where Milton argues that a "free Commonwealth" was "enjoyed" by Christ himself. In Milton's interpretation, Christ's admonition to his disciples that they not be like the kings of the gentiles pertains to civil government. When Christ says that "he that is greatest among you, let him be as the younger," he is describing the true character of a commonwealth, where, according to Milton, the "greatest are perpetual servants and drudges to the publick at their own cost and charges . . . and are not elevated above their brethren."[24] In the poem, "On the Morning of Christ's Nativity," Milton had rejected the possibility of Christ's birth ushering in an "age of gold" and a return of "Truth, and justice" (see stanzas xiv and xv). In the *Ready and Easy Way*, however, Milton depicts the restoration of such justice as viable political option.

Milton's *Ready and Easy Way* does not present itself as a proposal for Utopia. On the contrary, Milton repeatedly insists that he is being realistic throughout the *Ready and Easy Way*. Nevertheless, Utopia is a vulnerability of Milton's project there, and the *Censure* exploits this vulnerability. Indeed, as a purportedly realistic plan, the *Ready and Easy Way* demonstrates the difficulty of disentangling the extravagantly idealistic from the less far-fetched elements of Milton's politics.

Such inextricability is particularly evident in *Areopagitica*, which purports to be opposed to the idea of Utopia. Thus, on the one hand, Milton refuses to "sequester out of the world into Atlantick and Eutopian polities,"[25] and an emphasis on the world as it is rather than an ideal perfection pervades *Areopagitica*. When telling the story of the dismemberment of Truth, Milton writes of how she "came once into the world with her divine Master, and was a perfect shape." Yet, captured and hacked to pieces by a "wicked race of deceivers," she loses her perfection as a consequence of entering the world.[26] Likewise, the Temple, built of "many schisms and many dissections made in the quarry," cannot be "united into a continuity" but rather must be "contiguous in this world."[27] So Milton's author is one who "writes to the world," presumably this one.[28]

Nevertheless, Milton's tropes of dismemberment and schism are reversible. Thus, if the stones of the Temple can only be contiguous in this world, nevertheless, much of the building of the Temple does take place there. Similarly, if the body of Truth cannot be completely reconstituted until her "Masters second coming," the "sad friends of Truth" can recover many of the pieces before he arrives.[29] History is not just a matter of waiting for its own dissolution. Rather, structures anticipating and even constitutive of a final union and harmony of warring parts can find a place amidst the contentions of seventeenth-century England. The world to which Milton's writer addresses his words has otherworldly elements.

This world of schism relieved by a certain degree of cohesion also possesses democratic features. Thus, Milton accuses licensing of being tantamount to esteeming the "people for an untaught and irreligious gadding rout."[30] Licensing is to the "common people" nothing "lesse than a reproach."[31] Elsewhere, Milton would himself esteem the people for a rout in need of guidance, but here they too are part of the spiritual architecture of a reformed English. Not only are the common people worthy readers of books, but they are worth listening to as well. Thus, writing in a more apocalyptic vein, Milton claims that the time has arrived when "all the Lords people are become prophets."[32] This biblical allusion suggests that the gap between writers, who, like Milton himself, adopted a prophetic vein, and their readers has closed.

Such a time entails the distribution of Truth to all the Lord's people. Thus, "Truth and understanding are not such wares as to be monopoliz'd," nor are they meant to be stored in barns. Hence, Milton further criticizes licensers as an "Oligarchy of twenty engrossers" that would hoard learning and bring a "famin upon our minds again."[33] Indeed, Milton here applies to the food of the mind the rather Utopian strictures of the Lady in *Comus:* "If every just man that now pines with want / Had but a moderate and beseeming share / Of that which lewdly-pampered luxury heaps upon some few. . . . / Nature's full blessings would be well-dispensed" (lines 768–73).[34] Likewise, the "wealthy man addicted to his pleasure," who resigns to a clergyman the keys to the "whole ware-house of his religion," is another figure of the attempt to restrict the goods of religion and truth to a private enclosure.[35]

Such opposition to monopolizations of truth does not mean that the construction of the author as a possessive individual is not, to some degree, occurring in *Areopagitica.* Milton criticism with a focus on ideology has found Macpherson's model a useful point of departure.[36] Indeed, when in *Areopagitica* Milton calls a good book the "life-blood of a master spirit," he perhaps anticipates Burnet's desire to see authors the masters of their own books. Nevertheless, in *Areopagitica* as in Burnet's defenses of property, the enclosed individual is less an ideological given than a deliberate reaction to more collective possibilities. These texts at least define liberal humanism in contrast to its more radical counterpart, and we would do well to attend to the struggle of the two as well as its more familiar outcome.

In *Areopagitica,* moreover, the emergence of the master author out of the collectivity of a nation of prophets is not so assured as it is for Burnet. Parts of *Areopagitica* still have the potential to overpower their author rather than demonstrate his autonomy. As a work that controverts itself, *Areopagitica* has much in common with the More that Burnet cannot understand. Burnet's moderate tolerance and inclusiveness may have been the historical destiny of the humanism of More and Milton, but it was not the point of origin for such humanism. Nor could moderation provide a way of fully understanding a controversial past. In the end, More's own Janus-like countenance remains impervious to Burnet's enlightened scrutiny.

Notes

Abbreviations

ASD: Erasmus, Desiderius. *Opera Omnia*. Amsterdam: North Holland, 1969– .
CWE: *Collected Works of Erasmus*. Toronto: University of Toronto Press, 1974– .
FQ: *The Faerie Queene*
LB: *Erasmi Roterdami Opera Omnia*. Edited by J. LeClerc. 10 volumes. Leyden:
   P. Van Der Aa, 1703–06.
WA: Luther, Martin. *Werke*. Weimar: H. Bohlau, 1883– .

Introduction

1. See *The Unfortunate Traveller* in *Thomas Nashe,* ed. Stanley Wells (London: Edward Arnold, 1964), 191.
2. Nashe, *The Unfortunate Traveller,* 218–19.
3. For this observation and an examination of the complex reception of More during the English Renaissance, see Prescott's introduction to Jackson Campbell Boswell, *Sir Thomas More in the English Renaissance* (Binghamton, N.Y.: Center for Medieval and Renaissance Studies, 1994), xi–xxxiv and in particular p. xxxiii. The classic argument against More allowing his authorial point of view to collapse into that of Raphael is Richard Sylvester, " 'Si Credimus Hythlodaeo': Vision and Revision in Thomas More's *Utopia,"* in *Essential Articles for the Study of Thomas More,* ed. R. Sylvester and G. P. Marc'hadour (Hamden, Conn.: Archon, 1977), 290–302.
4. See *Utopia,* ed. J. H. Hexter and Edward Surtz ((New Haven: Yale University Press, 1965), 98. All future references to the Latin *Utopia* are to this Yale edition. As the editors note, persona "More" is quoting Erasmus' Stultitia quoting Lucian here.
5. J. Collins' edition of Robinson's 1551 translation of *Utopia* (Oxford: Oxford University Press, 1904), 140. For the Latin, see the Yale *Utopia,* 240. Robinson's translation is itself close to More's Latin here.
6. *The First Tome or Volume of the Paraphrase of Erasmus on the New Testamente,* ed. John N. Wall Jr. (1548; rpt., New York: Delmar Scholar's Facsimiles, 1975), sig. Biii.
7. Taverner, *Proverbes or Adages* (London, 1539; rpt., DaCapo Press, Amsterdam, 1969), fol. xiiii. See, however, LB 2:748A–D for the adage "Contra torrentem niti," where Erasmus, among other things, includes a quote from Juvenal praising the "prudentia" of submitting to the violence of the emperor Domitian. See also "Contra stimulum calces" in LB 2:131A–C, where Erasmus applies the adage to a number of disparate goads, including quarrelsome spouses and God. Taverner has combined the two adages to create a more coherent message of compliance than is in the original. For more on Taverner's politics, see his version of "Ne quid nimis," where Taverner sets the adage against both those who would "over do, ether in the redresse of the abuses in the church" or "without choise styffely defende, . . . all customes, ceremonies & traditions be they never so detestably abused, and gone from the fyrst institucion" (fol. xxi). This may sound Erasmian, but it is not in the original adage. See also Taverner's rendition of "Multae regum aures, atque oculi," which advises subjects "not only to kepe theyr Princes lawes . . . in the face of the worlde, but also

prevely" (fol. iiii). Erasmus, on the other hand, uses this adage to address the monstrosity of tyranny in LB 2:69E–70A. But see also the first adage of Taverner's *Proverbs*, "Nemo bene imperat, nisi qui paruerit imperio," where Taverner urges kings to obey their tutors and governors (fol. ii). Here, Taverner's emphasis on the authority of tutor over king is really only implicit in Erasmus' original (LB 2:25F–26C).

8. See also Shakespeare's source for *The Winter's Tale,* Robert Greene's *Pandosto,* ed. P. G. Thomas (New York: Duffield & Co., 1907), 9, for a related usage of the same proverb:

> Franion, seeing that to persuade Pandosto any more was but to strive against the stream, consented, as soon as the opportunity would give him leave, to dispatch Egistus.

Since Pandosto is Franion's king and he is trying to persuade Pandosto to change his plan of having Egistus murdered, this usage raises the same kind of issues as in *The Unfortunate Traveller.*

9. Thus, I disagree with Margo Todd's point in *Christian Humanism and the Puritan Social Order* (Cambridge: Cambridge University Press, 1987), 187. As she puts it, "for Erasmus the appellation 'common' or 'vulgar' was not related to social class but level of understanding." Erasmus' notion of "vulgarity" could refer to social class, but it did not necessarily do so. See Elizabeth Eisenstein, *The Printing Press as an Agent of Change: Communications and Cultural Transformations in Early Modern Europe* (Cambridge: Cambridge University Press, 1979), 63, however, for a warning against the opposite fallacy of assuming that superior learning necessarily entailed a higher social status while those who read "popularizations" were necessarily of a lower social status.

10. David Cressy, *Literacy and the Social Order: Reading and Writing in Tudor and Stuart England* (Cambridge: Cambridge University Press, 1980), 43–44. For More's estimate of English literacy, see *The Apology,* ed. J. B. Trapp (New Haven: Yale University Press, 1979), 13. For critiques of Cressy's own low estimates of literacy, see Keith Thomas, "The Meaning of Literacy in Early Modern England," in *The Written Word: Literacy in Transition,* ed. Gerard Bauman (Oxford: Oxford University Press, 1986), 97–133, and Tessa Watt, *Cheap Print and Popular Piety: 1550–1640* (Cambridge: Cambridge University Press, 1991), 6–8. Eamon Duffy has argued that a literate laity was the result of the dissemination of vernacular religious texts before the Reformation. See *The Stripping of the Altars: Traditional Religion in England, c. 1400–1580* (New Haven: Yale University Press, 1992), 68–87. Part of the problem with Cressy's low estimates is that they are based on writing ability, although in the sixteenth century reading was taught before writing.

11. Trapp, *Apology,* 163–65.

12. Duffy, *Stripping of the Altars,* 432–33, on this act.

13. *Dialogue Concerning Heresies,* ed. Thomas M. C. Lawler, Germain Marc'hadour, and Richard C. Marius (New Haven: Yale University Press, 1981), 333.

14. Thomas Chaloner, ed., *The Praise of Folie,* Early English Text Society (Oxford: Oxford University Press, 1965), 4.

15. Eisenstein, *Printing Press as an Agent of Change,* 353. More generally, her analysis of the impact of print on historical periodization has influenced my work (pp. 163–303).

16. See Duffy, *Stripping of the Altars,* 53–89.

17. Latin, of course, allowed humanists to reach a broader international market.

18. See John King, *English Reformation Literature: The Tudor Origins of the Protestant Tradition* (Princeton: Princeton University Press, 1982); Annabel Patterson, "The Peasant's Toe: Popular Culture and Popular Pressure," in *Shakespeare and the Popular Voice* (Oxford: Basil Blackwell, 1989), 32–51; and David Norbrook, "Introduction," "The

'Utopia' and Radical Humanism," and "The Reformation and Prophetic Poetry," in his *Poetry and Politics in the English Renaissance* (London: Routledge, 1984), 1–59. Helen White, *Social Criticism in Popular Religious Literature of the Sixteenth Century* (1944; rpt., New York: Octagon Books, 1965), 110–32, still, however, offers the most comprehensive and detailed treatment of these years.

19. Norbrook, *Poetry and Politics,* 8. For an example of the kind of reading of *Utopia* to which Norbrook's strictures would apply, see John Perlette, "Of Sites and Parasites: The Centrality of the Marginal Anecdote in Book I of More's *Utopia,*" *English Literary History* 54 (summer 1987): 231–53.

20. Norbrook is particularly secular in his approach to humanist radicalism. Though he notes the overlap between humanism and Protestantism, his use of phrases such as "radical rationalism" (*Poetry and Politics,* 26) and his identification of humanism as a shift to a more "secular and individualistic world-view" (23) suggest that his humanists are proto-Enlightenment figures. For a more religious perspective, see Todd, *Christian Humanism and the Puritan Social Order,* which emphasizes continuities between Erasmian humanism and later Puritan social criticism. See in particular pp. 176–205. Todd's arguments are often compelling, but she pays insufficient attention to the conservatism of sixteenth-century humanists when confronted with social upheavals. Thus, trying to explain More the heretic-hunter, Todd writes that the Reformation led More to "repudiate humanism" as if no distinctly humanist continuities between the pre-Reformation and Reformation More existed. Helen More, however, distinguishes perhaps too sharply between a "religious tradition of social criticism" and the "commonwealth tradition" inaugurated by *Utopia* (*Social Criticism,* 41).

21. See my epilogue for more on Burnet.

22. Trapp, *Apology,* 12. Of course, More's well-known interest in monasticism and Erasmus' indebtedness to the *devotio moderna* as well as his education at the Brothers of Deventer school also militate against an overly secular approach to the radical elements of humanism.

23. Trapp, *Apology,* 249. For more on the rebellions of this period, see Steven Justice, *Writing and Rebellion: England in 1381* (Berkeley: University of California Press, 1994).

24. For the evolving law of heresy in England, see the introduction to *The Debellation of Salem and Bizance,* ed. John Guy, Ralph Keen, Clarence H. Miller, and Ruth Mcgugan (New Haven: Yale University Press, 1987), xlvii–lxvii.

25. Lawler, Marc'hadour, and Marius, *Dialogue Concerning Heresies,* 315.

26. Lawler, Marc'hadour, and Marius, *Dialogue Concerning Heresies,* 315.

27. See White, *Social Criticism,* 1–41, for more on the medieval tradition of social and religious criticism in England. On Langland, see also Andrew McRae's *God Speed the Plough: The Representation of Agrarian England, 1550–1650* (Cambridge: Cambridge University Press, 1996), 26–28. As McRae points out, though *Piers Plowman* addresses the issue of poverty, Langland's emphasis is on individual regeneration rather than social reformation. But see Justice, *Writing and Rebellion,* 102–40 for possible appropriations of Langland by the rebels.

28. See *Piers Plowman,* B, 20, pp. 273–75.

29. Jerry Bentley, *Humanists and Holy Writ: New Testament Scholarship in the Renaissance* (Princeton: Princeton University Press, 1983), 187.

30. See Udall's letter to Katherine Dowager in Wall, *Paraphrase.*

31. In her book *Erasmus, Man of Letters: The Construction of Charisma in Print* (Princeton:

Princeton University Press, 1993), Lisa Jardine takes a somewhat different approach to Erasmus' attempts to fashion himself in print:

> The story I tell is one of Erasmus' consummate mastery of his chosen medium, print. The most vivid way I can find to convey the intellectual thrust of this study is to characterize it as uncovering a fully fashioned portrait, cunningly contrived . . . on the printed page . . . the typographical equivalent to the draughtsman's pen and link. (9)

Jardine's detailed study of Erasmus' immersion in and manipulation of his chosen medium is important to my own work, but my focus is Erasmus' growing sense that the medium might be mastering him. That is, I do not think that Erasmus' self-portrait always came out the way he wanted it, and thus I will be paying particular attention to the defensiveness that Erasmus displays in so many of his published works. This defensiveness provides clues to the other forces, besides Erasmus himself, that went into the making of Erasmus' portrait.

32. See Luther's *De Servo Arbitrio* in WA 18:601.

33. For an argument in favor of the hypothetical and interior status of Renaissance "second worlds," see Harry Berger, *Second World and Green World: Studies in Renaissance Fiction-Making* (Berkeley: University of California Press, 1988), 39–40:

> Plato treats his Critias and Atlantis very much as More treats Hythloday and his Utopia, as Spenser treats Faerie, Sydney poetry, and Shakespeare the green world. All are useful only if they proclaim their hypothetical status and are understood to have literal existence . . . "deepe within the minde."

But at moments of looming social disorder the hypothetical or sequestered state of such second worlds often began to look more real.

34. Stephen Greenblatt, *Learning to Curse: Essays in Early Modern Culture* (London: Routledge, 1990), 99–130 and especially 101 and 109. See Merritt Hughes, "Spenser and Utopia," *Studies in Philology* 17 (1920): 132–46. For Greenblatt's most powerful "containment" argument, see "Invisible Bullets" in *Shakespearean Negotiations: The Circulation of Social Energy in Renaissance England* (Berkeley: University of California Press, 1988), 22–66. Greenblatt's argument that subversion is only thinkable as the thought of another is at least complicated by what I am contending was the pervasive fear among humanist writers that such subversive thoughts of others would be read as their own.

35. For a good example of the emphasis on school and state that the "revisionist" approach entails, see the introduction to Mary Crane, *Framing Authority: Sayings, Self, and Society in Sixteenth-Century England* (Princeton: Princeton University Press, 1993), 5–6.

36. See Paul Oscar Kristeller, *The Classics and Renaissance Thought* (Cambridge: Harvard University Press, 1955), 8–15.

37. See Jardine, *Erasmus, Man of Letters,* passim, and Kristeller, "Renaissance Humanism and Its Significance," in *Reconsidering the Renaissance,* ed. Mario di Cesare (Binghamton, N.Y.: Medieval and Renaissance Texts and Studies, 1992), 32–37.

38. See Erika Rummel, *The Humanist-Scholastic Debate in the Renaissance and Reformation* (Cambridge: Harvard University Press, 1995), 96–126, for an analysis of these kinds of polemics. Jardine discusses the intersection of the printing press with academic disputes at Louvain in *Erasmus, Man of Letters,* 14–23.

39. See the Harvey section of "Pragmatic Humanism," in Grafton and Jardine, *From*

Humanism to the Humanities: Education and the Liberal Arts in Fifteenth- and Sixteenth-Century Europe (Cambridge: Harvard University Press, 1986), 184–200.

40. For a somewhat different perspective on Harvey, see my fifth chapter and Norbrook, *Politics and Poetry in the English Renaissance,* 79–81.

41. See my second chapter for this remark and my reading of it.

42. For the Latin of this adage, see LB 2:13–14. For a good English translation that indicates Erasmus' alterations of this adage, see John Olin, "Erasmus' *Adagia* and More's *Utopia,*" in *Miscellanea Moreana,* ed. Clare Murphy, Henri Gibaud, and Mario A. Di Cesare (Binghamton, N.Y.: Medieval and Renaissance Texts and Studies, 1989), 127–36. See p. 129 in particular:

> He [Plato] also says that a society will be happy and blessed where the words "mine" and "not mine" are never heard. But it is amazing how displeasing, yes, how hateful that community of Plato's is to Christians, although nothing ever said by a pagan philosopher is more in keeping with the mind of Christ.

43. On Muntzer see James Stayer, *The German Peasants' War and the Anabaptist Community of Goods* (Kingston, Ont.: Queen's University Press, 1991), 107–23, and "Heaven on Earth for the Common Man," in Frank Manuel and Fritzie Manuel, *Utopian Thought in the Western World* (Cambridge: Harvard University Press, 1979), 181–205.

44. See Parente, "Erasmus, La Republique de Platon et la Communauté des Biens," in *Erasmus of Rotterdam: The Man and the Scholar,* ed. J. Sperna Weiland (Leiden: E. J. Brill, 1988), 40–48. See also Erasmus' "Diversoria," in the *Colloquia,* where Erasmus comically situates what he terms the "vetus aequalitas," or "old equality," of Christ and his disciples as well as "civitas Platonica" in a German inn. See LB 1:715–18.

45. Taverner, *Adages,* fol. liii.

46. See Duffy, *Stripping of the Altars,* 425–27, for more on Taverner's attempts to use, among other things, condemnations of Anabaptism to demonstrate his orthodoxy.

47. Quoted from *Religion and Society in Early Modern England: A Sourcebook,* ed. David Cressy and Lori Anne Ferrell (London: Routledge, 1996), 70.

48. See Hexter, "A Window to the Future: The Radicalism of *Utopia,*" in the Yale *Utopia,* cv–cxxiv, cxvi. For Hexter's Cold War agenda, see Hexter, *More's Utopia: The Biography of an Idea* (Princeton: Princeton University Press, 1952, 1965), 77. See also Margo Todd, *Christian Humanism and the Puritan Social Order,* 176–205 and especially p. 185, where she argues that the Reformation gave More good reason to "repudiate humanism" as if no distinctly humanist continuities between the More of 1516 and 1529 existed. But More's *Dialogue Concerning Heresies* (1529) recalls *Utopia* at numerous points, not the least of which is its being cast as a dialogue—a favorite humanist form. Likewise, although Todd makes much of Juan Luis Vives' *De Subventione Pauperum* (1526) and its espousal of poor relief, she does not mention Vives' 1539 *De Communione Rerum*—an anti-Anabaptist tract.

49. Karl Kautsky, *Thomas More and His Utopia,* intro. Russell Ames (New York: Russell & Russell, 1959), 143–46.

50. Hexter "A Window to the Future," cxxi.

51. See the Yale *Utopia,* 136, 178.

52. *A View of the Present State of Ireland* in *Spenser's Prose Works,* ed. Rudolf Gottfried (Baltimore: Johns Hopkins University Press, 1949), 146–47.

53. See ASD 2.4, pp. 190–91, for this adage and textual apparatus denoting the changes that it underwent.

54. See also James Stayer, *The German Peasants' War and the Anabaptist Community of Goods*, 134–35. Stayer argues that Anabaptist Munster contained some Utopian features, and he thus provides a counterpart in modern historiography for the kind of reading of *Utopia* that Erasmus was doing in the 1526 "Ut fici."
55. *The Unfortunate Traveller*, 216.
56. *The Unfortunate Traveller*, 210–16.
57. See *The Works of Thomas Nashe: Notes*, ed. R. B. McKerrow, vol. 4 (Oxford: Oxford University Press, 1908), 268. The book from which Nashe took his account was *A Famouse Chronicle of oure time, called Sleidanes Commentaries* (1560).
58. *The Unfortunate Traveller*, 210.
59. *The Unfortunate Traveller*, 213.
60. See Thomas Greene's "Introduction" and "Erasmus' 'Festina Lent': Vulnerabilities of the Humanist Text," in his *The Vulnerable Text: Essays on Renaissance Literature* (New York: Columbia University Press, 1986), xi–xx, 1–18. Greene's antagonist in *The Vulnerable Text* is Terence Cave, *The Cornucopian Text: Problems of Writing in the French Renaissance* (Oxford: Clarendon Press, 1979).
61. Greene, *The Vulnerable Text*, 6–7.
62. See Greene, *The Vulnerable Text*, 8.
63. For an English translation of "Festina lente," see Margaret Mann Phillips, *Erasmus on His Times: A Shortened Version of the Adages* (Cambridge: Cambridge University Press, 1967), 3–17. For the Latin see LB 2:397–404. For Aldus' world library, see Phillips, p. 10, and LB 2:403: "Once this was the task of princes, and it was the greatest glory of Pompey. But his library was contained between the narrow walls of its own house [domesticis & angustis parietibus], and Aldus is building up a library which has no other limits but the world itself."
64. See CWE 29:348 and for the Latin ASD 4.1A, p. 116.
65. See Phillips, *Erasmus on His Times*, 12, and LB 2:404, where printing "threatens the authority [collabitur auctoritas] of senate, council, school, legal expert or theologian."
66. See Phillips, *Erasmus on His Times*, 12, and LB 2:404:

    So in the study of Holy Scripture [literae sacrae], someone may detect points which escaped the notice of Chysostom or Jerome; but I do not think there will be anyone who will accomplish what they did over the whole field [in summa].

67. See *In Defense of Humanism: Letters to Dorp, Oxford, Lee, and a Monk*, ed. Daniel Kinney (New Haven: Yale University Press, 1986), 279.
68. Phillips, *Erasmus on His Times*, 4, and LB 2:398–99. I have checked the 1508 Aldine and the 1515 Froben editions of the *Adagia* as well since the Leyden edition does not mark clearly Erasmus' many changes and revisions. See also *De Lingua*, where Erasmus turns this Homeric story into a decidedly Christian parable:

    What Pallas Athene does for Achilles in Homer, reason should provide for us. And yet that Homeric Pallas only holds him back from fighting, quite content if he limits his resentment to verbal abuse, whereas our Pallas Athene does not allow us even to vent our passion against a man in abuse, even if we do keep our hands clean. No, if we want to heed the spirit of Christ, whenever he plucks at our ears, we must return blessings for curses.

    See CWE 29:390 and ASD 4.1a, p. 157.
69. See LB 2:402A, 404.

70. Derrida, "Plato's Pharmacy," in *Dissemination,* trans. Barbara Johnson (Chicago: University of Chicago Press, 1981), 65–173 and, in particular, 144–45.

71. See Arthur Kinney, *Continental Humanist Poetics: Studies in Erasmus, Castiglione, Marguerite De Navarre, Rabelais, and Cervantes* (Amherst: University of Massachusetts Press, 1989), 45, 67. See ASD 4.3, p. 110 for Erasmus' reference to Theuth.

72. The Listrius commentary on the 1515 Froben edition of the *Moria* links Stultitia's discussion of medicine to Plato—specifically, the *Gorgias.* See Erasmus, *Moriae Encomium* (Basel: Froben, 1515), sigs. H–H2.

73. See ASD 4.1A, p. 25 and CWE 29:262.

74. See Eisenstein, *Printing Press as an Agent of Change,* 113–26.

75. The Listrius commentary reads as follows in the 1515 Froben *Moria:*

> De hoc Theuto Socrates apud Platonem in Phaedro ita loquitur, audivi equidem, circa Naucratim Aegypti, priscorum quendam fuisse deorum, cui dicata sit avis, quam ibim vocant. Daemoni autem ipsi nomen Theuth, hunc primum numerum, geometriam, astronomiamque invenisse, praeterea lusus talorum, alearum, literasque. Erat tunc totius Aegypti rex Thamius, & in amplissima eminentissimaque civitate. . . . Ad hunc Theuth profectus, artes demonstravit suas, dixitque eas distribui Aegyptis caeteris opportere. In hunc fere modum Plato. Unde cum idem daemon, qui talorum & tessararum ludorum pestiferorum, inventor fuit, humanas has scientias commentus est, constat haec non minus graviter, quam iocose dicta esse (sig. H).

76. See CWE 29:288 and ASD 4.1a, p. 54.

77. See Edgar Wind's *Pagan Mysteries in the Renaissance* (London: Faber and Faber, 1958; rpt., 1968), 1–17, 18–26, 97–113. For more on Neoplatonism and the *Phaedrus,* see the "introduction" to Michael Allen, *Marsilio Ficino and the Phaedran Charioteer* (Los Angeles: UCLA, Center for Medieval and Renaissance Studies, 1981), 29–49. See also pp. 209–11 for Ficino's commentary on the Theuth myth from his 1496 *Commentaria in Platonem.*

78. See "Academic Dreams" in Martin Lowry, *The World of Aldus Manutius: Business and Scholarship in Renaissance Venice* (Ithaca: Cornell University Press, 1979), 180–217.

79. See ASD 1.1, pp. 65–66 for this quote and, more generally, the use of the *Phaedrus* as a model for the *Antibarbari.*

80. See the *Republic,* 416d–417a as well as 423e.

I. VULNERABILITIES OF HERCULES

1. For work on Erasmus' approach to language, rhetoric, and scriptural interpretation, see Marjorie O'Rourke Boyle, *Erasmus on Language and Method in Theology* (Toronto: University of Toronto Press, 1977) and *Rhetoric and Reform: Erasmus' Civil Dispute with Luther* (Cambridge: Harvard University Press, 1983). See also " 'Sancte Socrates Ora pro Nobis': Erasmus' *Encomium Moriae* and the Poetics of Wordplay," in Arthur Kinney, *Continental Humanist Poetics: Studies in Erasmus, Castiglione, Marguerite de Navarre, Rabelais, and Cervantes* (Amherst: University of Massachusetts Press, 1989), 46–87; "Erasmus: Prudence and Faith," in Victoria Kahn, *Rhetoric, Prudence, and Skepticism in the Renaissance* (Ithaca: Cornell University Press, 1985), 89–115 as well as Kahn, "Humanism and the Resistance to Theory," in *Literary Theory/Renaissance Texts,* ed. David Quint and Patricia Parker (Baltimore: Johns Hopkins University Press, 1986), 373–97; Kathy Eden, "Rhetoric in the Hermeneutics of Erasmus' Later Works," *Erasmus of Rotterdam Society Yearbook* (1991): 88–104; Eden, *Hermeneutics and*

the Rhetorical Tradition: Chapters in the Ancient Legacy and Its Humanist Reception (New Haven: Yale University Press, 1997), and "Interpretation" in Terence Cave, *The Cornucopian Text: Problems of Writing in the French Renaissance* (New York: Oxford University Press, 1979), 78–125.

2. For a modern translation of the *Paraclesis,* see *The Praise of Folly and Other Writings,* trans. Robert Adams (New York: Norton, 1989), 118–27. For the Latin, see LB 16:3–5.

3. See Marjorie O'Rourke Boyle, "Erasmus' Prescription for Henry VIII," *Renaissance Quarterly,* no. 31 (1978): 161–72.

4. See Erasmus' letter to Martin Dorp in Adams, *The Praise of Folly and Other Writings,* 228–51. Thus, for instance, Erasmus claims that the "jokes of Folly" are much more in accordance with the "teachings of the evangelists and the apostles" than the reasoning of theologians. See also Erasmus' claim that the *Moria* "says, though jokingly, precisely the same thing as the *Enchiridion*" (p. 231). For the Latin, see Michael Allen, *Erasmi Epistolae* (Oxford: Oxford University Press, 1910), no. 337, 2:93 and 96.

5. See CWE 28:408.

6. I mean, again, to distinguish my emphasis on rhetoric from Lisa Jardine's work on Erasmus' constructions of himself in print. I assume that Erasmus' chosen medium, that is, print, posed real threats as well as opportunities, whereas Jardine emphasizes, for instance, the degree to which Erasmus' print controversies were staged (see for instance her analysis of the Erasmus/Dorp quarrel [*Erasmus, Man of Letters* (Princeton: Princeton University Press, 1993), 112–22]). This staged quality might seem to mitigate the animosities evinced during such controversies, but attack and collaboration may not be as mutually exclusive as Jardine makes them. However rigged, the Erasmus/Dorp quarrel was part of a larger debate, which, as Erika Rummel has recently shown in *The Humanist-Scholastic Debate in the Renaissance and Reformation* (Cambridge: Harvard University Press, 1995), 63–95, involved real rivalries and acrimony. But Jardine's point that the Dorp/Erasmus quarrel was a "performance" is borne out by what we will see is the extensive language of masking and theatricality that Erasmus everywhere uses to describe his approach to print and writing. On the other hand, see Elizabeth Eisenstein, *The Printing Press as an Agent of Change: Communications and Cultural Transformations in Early Modern Europe* (Cambridge: Cambridge University Press, 1979), 341, where Eisenstein argues that before he became aware of the scope of the Reformation, Erasmus was blind to the power of print and the degree to which it separated him from past restorers of the Christian tradition such as Jerome:

> Despite his [i.e., Erasmus'] close collaboration with printers (or, perhaps, just because he was so close that perspective was lacking) he did not take full stock of the powers he commanded; powers that had not been envisaged by the Church fathers and that he wielded most skillfully before Luther turned them to other ends.

Eisenstein may underestimate Erasmus here. Rather, the Reformation seems to have exacerbated Erasmus' sense of the press as both a problem and a tool, but it was not the origin of Erasmus' always keen awareness of the volatile power of print.

7. See for instance *Cornucopian Text* (91), where Cave argues that the Erasmian "germanus sensus" is a "figure of authenticity (rather than a precise theoretical concept) by means of which Erasmus attempts to close the fissure between . . . the text and what it signifies" and that "in proposing the interchangeability of a hermeneutic

model and a rhetorical model, the text of Erasmus discloses the ineradicable element of licence which is germane to his theory and its figures." This license in turn leads to a "plurality of interpretive transgressions" and a "new liberty of the reader."

8. See Wesley Trimpi, "Reason and the Classical Premises of Literary Decorum," *Independent Journal of Philosophy* 5/6 (1988): 103–13. Trimpi shows how "the conception of decorum, and more broadly of mimesis as an activity continually resisting imbalance, is fundamental to Aristotle's defense of the mimetic arts against Plato's criticism." Part of such criticism is "Plato's reservations about written language in the *Phaedrus.*"

9. See Eden, "Rhetoric," 94–95:

> It is precisely by means of this principle of decorum—and not by means of allegory—that Erasmus generates an interpretation accommodated to his own audience, one situated in a time and place so different from Paul's. . . . Elaborating the more summary treatment in the *Methodous,* the *Ratio* reminds the exegete that meaning can only be determined by context, where context includes not only the nature of the speaker and the audience, the time, the place, the occasion, . . . but also what comes before the passage in question and what follows it.
>
> To illustrate this rule Erasmus adduces the rhetorical practice of Jesus, whose style both befits (decet) him as a speaker, . . . and takes account of his changing audience.

See also Victoria Kahn, "Humanism and the Resistance to Theory," 377–78. Kahn argues that humanist decorum was a rule that could never be theorized and thus distinguished from its application. Rather, such decorum was a "practice of examples" or an "exemplary practice" that involved the reader "in a practice of interpretation . . . essential for the active life." While I agree that humanists did not theorize decorum in Kahn's sense, I will also be trying to show that they gave it a more specific and less indeterminate meaning than Kahn allows. Likewise, the willingness of sixteenth-century humanists to leave interpretive decisions to their readers had as its corollary anxieties over and attempts to curtail this interpretive freedom.

10. See Boyle, *Erasmus on Language and Method in Theology,* 26.
11. See the chapter "Sermo" in Boyle, *Erasmus on Language and Method in Theology,* 3–22.
12. See LB 9:119C.
13. See LB 9:113D–F.
14. See C. A. Jarrott, "Erasmus' 'In Principio erat Sermo': A Controversial Translation," *Studies in Philology* 61 (1964): 35–40.
15. See LB 9:112E–F:

> Haec seu bene habent, seu male, quid seditiosus, quam vociferari apud imperitam multitudinem? Nos illa doctis scripsimus, non populo: privatim legi cupimus, non publice. . . . Non hoc umquam postulavimus a Romano pontifice Leone, (cuius hortatu laborem hunc primum *evulgavimus,* cuius authoritate freti denuo recognivimus) ut tolleret veterem ac receptam translationem, sed ut ex nostra hac domi collata, illa & dilucidior esset & minus depravata. . . .
>
> Nunc *evulgant,* quod erat inter eruditos disputantdum . . . apud coriarios, apud textores, apud mulierculas.
>
> [Whether or not these things are good, what is more seditious than to proclaim them among the inexperienced multitude? We wrote those things for the learned, not the people: we want them to be read privately, not publicly. . . .
>
> Neither have we ever asked Pope Leo (by whose exhortation we first *divulgated* this labor, by whose authority we at last have corrected it) to remove the old and received translation. Rather, we sought by a comparison of our translation to the vulgate at home, to make the Vulgate clearer and less corrupt. . . . Now they *divulgate* what was to be disputed among the learned to tanners, weavers, and women.] (my translation and emphases)

Note Erasmus' shifting uses of *evulgo* in this passage. The word denotes a legitimate activity sponsored by the pope as well as the unwarranted dissemination of Erasmus' translation to an unsuitable audience.

16. In *Rhetoric and Reform,* Boyle does discuss the issue of civility and, more generally, the civic realm as one that Erasmus tried to make Luther aware of during their debate. See especially pp. 26, 31, and 33 as well as 101–3 on the Peasants' Revolt.

17. See Allen, *Erasmi Epistolae,* no. 1033, vol. 4: "Multa scripsit Lutherus imprudenter magis quam impie." Erasmus also makes the point that he had himself advised Luther not to write anything "seditiose." Although it is clear from the letter to Albert that Erasmus does not agree with the strictures of many of Luther's critics, he also admits to having tried to keep Froben from publishing Luther's works.

18. For the English, see "The Luther Affair," in *The Erasmus Reader,* ed. Erika Rummel (Toronto: University of Toronto Press, 1990), 194–215 and in particular p. 207. The Latin can be found in Allen, *Erasmi Epistolae,* no. 1202, 4:487–88, part of which I reproduce here:

> Porro cuum prudentis oeconomi sit dispensare veritatem, hoc est promere cum res postulat, et promere quod satis est, et cuique promere quod sit accomodum, ille tot libellis praecipitatis simul effudit omnia, nihil non evulgans, ac cerdonibus etiam communia faciens quae solent inter eruditos ceu *mystika* et *aporreta* tractari.

(I have Latinized the Greek letters here.)

19. See *Luther's Works,* ed. Walter Brandt, (Philadelphia: Muhlenberg Press, 1962), 45:109, where Luther attacks temporal lords as being without "justice, integrity, or truth" and behaving "worse than any thief or scoundrel."

20. See *Utopia,* 38, where More uses *oeconomia* as an equivalent to *dispositio.*

21. See Allen, *Erasmi Epistolae,* no. 1202, 4:492, where Erasmus claims that his "literae" serve no faction but that of Christ, who is "communis . . . omnium."

22. See Allen, *Erasmi Epistolae,* no. 1202, 4:489.

23. See Allen's introduction to epistle 1033, 4:96–97.

24. See Rummel, *The Erasmus Reader,* 212:

> From my own books, written before I ever dreamt of Luther's appearing, they have made a selection [decerpserunt] of troublesome statements [odiosa] and published them [publicarunt] in a German translation, that they might be thought to approximate to some of Luther's opinions [quae viderentur affinia quibusdam Lutheri dogmatibus]. And the men who do this wish to be thought my friends. . . . This weapon they have put into the hands of my opponents, so that now they can hold forth in their public sermons on points of agreement between me and Luther. As though falsehood were not very close to truth on either side if you overstep the line.

See also Allen, *Erasmi Epistolae,* no. 337, 2:1515 the letter to Martin Dorp, for a similar discussion of "calumniatores" of the *Moria* who, making use of a technique of Quintillian's, pluck out [decerpere] two or three words from an author's "sermo" and quote them out of context (p. 102). For more on Erasmus' response to the charge that he supported Luther, see also ibid., no. 1218. There, in a letter to Richard Pace, Erasmus makes reference to a critic who ascribed Luther's *Babylonian Captivity of the Church* to Erasmus!

25. See Allen, *Erasmi Epistolae,* no. 472, vol. 2.

26. See, for instance, Allen, no. 801, vol. 3, *Erasmi Epistolae,* where Froben is expressing his gratitude to Erasmus for the right to print the second edition of Erasmus' New Testament.

27. See Allen, *Erasmi Epistolae,* no. 802 and 815, vol. 3.

28. See Allen, *Erasmi Epistolae,* no. 815, vol. 3, where Erasmus vehemently urges Jodocus Badius to convince the printer not to go ahead with his edition.

29. For the English *Moria,* I have used the Robert Adams translation in *Praise of Folly and Other Writings.* For the Latin I am indebted to Clarence Miller's edition of the *Moria*—ASD 4.3—in the Amsterdam *Opera Omnia* as well as the 1515 Froben edition (Basel), which includes the Listrius commentary. See Adams, *Praise of Folly,* 54–55, and ASD 4.3, p. 142.

30. The quote is from John Owen, *Epigrammatum Libri Decem* (1612) as found in Jackson Campbell Boswell's "The Reception of Erasmus' *Moria* in England," *Erasmus of Rotterdam Society Yearbook* 7 (1987): 83. For the reference to Stultitia pointing to herself, see the 1515 Froben *Moria,* sig. B.

31. See *The Answer to a Poisoned Book,* ed. Stephen Merriam Foley and Clarence H. Miller (New Haven: Yale University Press, 1985), 12.

32. See *The Answer to a Poisoned Book,* 13.

33. See Allen, *Erasmi Epistolae,* no. 337, 2:28.

34. See Jardine, *Erasmus: Man of Letters,* 41–44. She discusses the changes that Erasmus made in the adage over time.

35. For the English, see Margaret Mann Phillips, *Erasmus on His Times: A Shortened Version of the Adages* (Cambridge: Cambridge University Press, 1967), 19, and ASD 2.5, p. 26.

    Siquidem nullorum benefactis malignius respondet gratia quam eorum, qui de vulgo bene merentur.
    [Seeing that nobody gets less thanks for their benefaction than those who have served the common people.]

36. See Phillips, *Erasmus on His Times,* 19–20, and ASD 2.5, pp. 26–27.

37. See ASD 2.6, p. 582, and LB 2:1–7.

38. See LB 9:120F.

39. See LB 10:1252C–D, where Erasmus suggests that Luther must have had help writing *De Servo Arbitrio* since it showed uncharacteristic rhetorical astuteness: "Soles enim *ten leonten endusamenos* clava rem gerere." (I have Latinized the spelling of the Greek words.) In fact, Erasmus insinuated that the help had come from someone who had learned his eloquence from Erasmus' writings.

40. See LB 2:265C–D.

41. See LB 2:990D.

42. See Adams, *The Praise of Folly and Other Writings,* 83, and, for the Latin, ASD 4.3, p. 190. See also the letter to Martin Dorp in *The Praise of Folly and Other Writings,* where Erasmus discusses why he had Folly don the lion's skin at near the close of her oration: "I'm surprised your hypercritical friends haven't noticed how cautiously I express myself and how careful I am to soften my words with modifiers. For example, Folly says, 'Now that I've "got on my high horse" [again, the Latin has "put on the lion's skin"], I want to take the next step and argue that the happiness after which Christians strive so passionately is nothing but a certain kind of folly amounting to madness.' You hear what she says? First because she is Folly and discussing such an arcane topic, I temper her boldness with a proverb to indicate that she's already embarked on a lofty theme." The tempering of boldness is a strategy, I would argue, that Folly shares with Erasmus.

43. See, for instance, ASD 4.3, pp. 132, 78, and 88.

44. Thus, Marjorie O'Rourke Boyle notes that, although Erasmus did receive a doctorate

in theology in 1506 from the University of Turin, he did not receive this degree from one of the universities—that is, Oxford, Paris, etc.—from which such a degree really counted. See *Erasmus on Language and Method in Theology,* p. 4. The letter to Dorp also evinces some diffidence on this subject: "Really, I have so much respect for theological learning that it's the only sort I allow to be learning at all. I admire and reverence this order so much, that it's the only one in which I aspire to be enrolled. Only modesty prevents my laying claim to such a splendid title" (p. 237).

45. See Allen, *Erasmi Epistolae,* no. 1634: "Si me venditarem pro magno theologo aut philosopho, merito mihi detrahat aliquis leonis exuvium." [If I were trying to pass myself off as a great theologian or philosopher, someone rightly might remove the lion's skin.]

46. See ASD 4.3, p. 178 and LB 9:1219E. See M. A. Screech, *Ecstasy and the Praise of Folly* (London: Duckworth, 1980), 30–33, on the New Testament significance of this word. The important New Testament references that Screech gives are Matthew 11:25 and Luke 10:21.

47. See ASD 4.3, p. 72.

48. See WA 18:626:

> Hos igitur tumultus velle sedare aliud nihil est quam velle verbum dei tollere et prohibere. Sermo enim Dei venit mutaturus et innovaturus orbem, quoties venit.

49. See LB 9:1217E–18B: Paul "novit discrimen inter ea quae licent et ea quae expediunt. Licet verum dicere, verum non expedit apud quoslibet, nec quovis tempore, nec quovis modo." On the other hand, the divulging [evulgari mundo] of Luther's paradox of the will to the world could open a window to "impietas." For this paradox will be subject to the interpretation of the many [plerique]. Erasmus also calls Paul a "prudens dispensator sermonis divini." This "eadem prudentia" befits [decet] those who have undertaken the "part" of dispensing this "sermo."

> Proinde tales materias fortassis tractare licuerat in colloquiis eruditorum aut etiam in scholis theologicis, quamquam nec hic quidem expedire putarim, ni sobrie fiat; ceterum hoc genus fabulas agere in theatro promiscuae multitudinis mihi videtur non solum inutile, verum etiam perniciosum.

50. See WA 18:629:

> Et quomodo posses, qui nec personarum nec temporum nec modorum rationem ullam noris? Ac si maxime noris, hominum corda tamen, non nosti. nisi is sit tibi modus, hoc tempus, haec persona, ut sic doceamus verum, ne Papa indignetur, Ne Caesar irascatur, ne moveantur pontifices et principes, tum ne tumultus et motus fiant. . . . lpse [i.e., God] enim novit quid, quando, quomodo cuique dicendum est. Nunc vero sic praescripsit ut Evangelion suum omnibus necassarium, nullo loco, nullo tempore, praescriberetur sed apud omnes, omni tempore, omni loco praedicaretur. Et supra probavi ea, quae in Scripturis prodita sunt, talia esse, quae omnibus exposita et invulganda necessaria et salubria sunt, sicut et in tua Paraclesi meliore tunc quam nunc consilio, ipse statuisti.
>
> Eadem *prudentia* est, qua deinde consulis, non debere profiteri, si quid perperam in conciliis esset definitum, ne ansa contemnendi praeberetur autoritatem patrum.

51. See LB 10:1282E–83A:

> Atqui hic ingeritur mea Paraclesis, in qua volo neminen secludi a lectione sacrorum voluminum . . . Si permitto omnibus ut legant sacros libros, ideone de quibuslibet difficultatibus, apud quosvis, & quovis modo disputandum est in utramque partem?

52. See LB 10:1282E.
53. See Kahn, *Rhetoric, Prudence, and Skepticism in the Renaissance,* 90–96 and, for the connection between rhetoric in utramque partem and deliberative rhetoric, pp. 38–40. Erasmus, writes Kahn, "was concerned above all with preserving a realm of prudence or responsible human action" and this concern meant that as an author Erasmus wanted to educate "his readers to a certain notion of praxis by means of the rhetorical practice of literature" (pp. 90–91). But he did not want to educate all readers at all times.
54. See LB 10:1278B.
55. See LB 10:1558–74 for the complete text.
56. See LB 10:1559D:

> Atque huius calumniae proemium hoc facit quod ego prior in omnibus libris meis arguerim & Pontificias, & omnes humanas constitutiones: velut in *Moria,* in *Enchiridio,* in *Annotationibus in Novum Testamentum,* in *Adagiis,* . . . quod idem me secutus fecerit Lutherus, sed fortius & apertius. . . . Nullus est locus in omnibus libris meis, qui damnat omnes humanas constitutiones: alioqui damnarem & leges civiles.

57. See LB 10:1559E.
58. See LB 10:1563D.
59. See LB 10:1563E.
60. See Clarence Miller's discussion of the Listrius commentary in his introduction to ASD 4.3 and J. Austin Gavin, "The Praise of Folly in Context: The Commentary of Gerard Listrius," *Renaissance Quarterly* 24 (1971): 193–209.
61. On Erasmus' own opinion of this commentary, see Allen, *Erasmi Epistolae,* no. 641, 3:63.
62. See Adams, *The Praise of Folly and Other Writings,* 5.
63. See Adams, *Praise of Folly and Other Writings,* 233. See Allen, *Erasmi Epistolae,* no. 337, 2:95, for the Latin: "Quis nescit quam multa dici potuerint in malos pontifices, in improbos episcopos et sacerdotes, in vitiosos principes, breviter in quemvis ordinem, si ad Juvenalis exemplum non puduisset ea mandare literis."
64. See Adams, *The Praise of Folly and Other Writings,* 239, and Allen, *Erasmi Epistolae,* no. 337, 2:102. The Latin is as follows:

> O si tibi liceret, mi Dorpi, tacitis oculis animi mei cogitationes intueri; nimirum intelligeres quam multa prudens hoc reticeam loco. At horum aut nihil attigit Moria, aut certe levissime attigit, ne quem offenderem.

65. See Erasmus, *Moria Encomium* (Basel: Froben, 1515), sig. B.
66. See volume 12 of *The Interpreter's Bible,* ed. George Buttrick et al. (New York, 1952–57), 329.
67. See Erasmus, *Annotationes in Novum Testamentum* in LB 6:1090F.
68. See Boyle, *Rhetoric and Reform,* 5–6, which discusses Luther's characterization of Erasmus as a flatterer of princes. See also my chapter on More for a similar characterization of Erasmus on the part of Tyndale.
69. See Adams, *The Praise of Folly and Other Writings,* 234, and for the Latin, Allen, *Erasmi Epistolae,* no. 337, 2:97.

> "Why don't we allow this little pamphlet the liberties that even marketplace audiences [idiotae] allow to popular comedies [vulgaribus istis comediis]?

70. I am grateful to Margaret Ferguson for first suggesting to me the importance of the Apocrypha to sixteenth-century humanist texts. Also helpful to me has been Mark

Wollaeger's article on Milton's use of the angel Raphael in *Paradise Lost*—"Apocryphal Narration: Milton, Raphael, and the Book of Tobit," *Milton Studies* (1985), 137–57. For a textual history of the Apocrypha, see Robert Pfeiffer, "Literature and Religion of the Apocrypha," in Buttrick, *Interpreter's Bible,* 1:391–402. For two widely divergent views on the Apocrypha of a humanist translator of the Bible, see *The Prefatory Letters of Jacques Lefevre D'etaples,* ed. Eugene Rice (New York: Columbia University Press, 1972), 310–12 and 514, where Lefevre justifies their inclusion in his French translation of the Bible. Jerome's statement on the Apocrypha can be found in *Praef. in libros Sam. et Malach. (ML,XXVIII {1865}, 600B–602A.* Jerome's distinction between the Apocrypha and the canonical works was translated into the Articles of Religion (1553) in England as one between "example of life and instruction of manners" and the establishment of "doctrine." For Luther and the Apocrypha, see *The Cambridge History of the Bible: The West from the Reformation to the Present Day,* ed. S. L. Greenslade (Cambridge: Cambridge University Press, 1963), 94–100.

71. See LB 9:1221A and LB 10:1340C for Erasmus on the Apocrypha.

72. LB 9:1217B.

73. See Adams, *The Praise of Folly and Other Writings,* 26–27, and ASD 4.3, pp. 100–102. The references to Numa and Minos can be found in Livy 1.19.5 and Plato's *Minos,* 320D.

74. See ASD 4.3, p. 32.

75. See ASD 4.3, p. 88, and Adams, *The Praise of Folly and Other Writings,* 28–29.

76. See Phillips, *Erasmus on His Times,* 79–81, and ASD 2.5, pp. 162–64:

> Another Silenus was Diogenes, whom the mob considered a dog [vulgo canis habitus]. But it was about this dog that a divine observation was made by Alexander the Great.... "If I were not Alexander, I would wish to be Diogenes." But is not Christ the most extraordinary Silenus of all? But if one may attain a closer look at this Silenus image, ... what unspeakable riches ... in such humility, what grandeur [in quanta humilitate, quantam sublimitatem].

> See at the Folger Shakespeare Library, *Here folowith a Scorneful image or monstrus shape of a marvelus strange figure, called Sileni Alcibi . . . Presentying . . . the Spiritualitie how farre they be from the perfite Trade and Lyfe of Christe* (London: Gouge, 154?).

77. See ASD 2.5, p. 178, and Phillips, *Erasmus on His Times,* 87.

78. See ASD 2.5, p. 178, and Phillips, *Erasmus on His Times,* 88.

79. For the *Convivium,* see LB 1:330–38. In the Listrius commentary, Diogenes, by means of "porrecto medio" [a raised middle finger], provides a variation on the tendency of bystanders to point to published authors. See the Froben *Moria,* sig. N3.

80. See ASD 2.5, p. 162, and Phillips, *Erasmus on His Times,* 79.

81. See Phillips, *Erasmus on His Times,* 62, and ASD 2.6, p. 413.

82. See Phillips, *Erasmus on His Times,* 63, and ASD 2.6, p. 415.

83. See "Images of the Material Bodily Lower Stratum," in Bakhtin, *Rabelais and His World,* trans. Helene Iswolsky (Bloomington: Indiana University Press, 1984), 368–437.

84. For the theologian reference, see ASD 4.3, p. 179, where Stultitia summons the spirit of Scotus to help her act the part of a theologian [theologum agere].

85. See Screech, "The *Moriae Encomium* of 1511 and 1512," in *Ecstasy and the Praise of Folly,* 1–12.

86. See ASD 4.3, p. 80.

87. See Adams, *The Praise of Folly and Other Writings,* 20–21, and ASD 4.3, p. 92.

88. See Adams, *The Praise of Folly and Other Writings,* 9, and ASD 4.3, p. 74.

89. Thus, for instance, see ASD 4.3, p. 134, where Stultitia appears to the "vulgus" as a synonym for "plebecula." But see also the "optimatum et sapientum vulgus" (p. 72) as well as the "vulgus oratorum" (p. 74).
90. See LB 6:1087.
91. LB 6:1091.
92. See Stephen Foley's "Erasmus and the Sacramentarians," in the introduction to More, *The Answer to a Poisoned Book,* xxxvii–xlvii.
93. See Erasmus' commentary on 1 Corinthians 11 in *Erasmus' Annotations on the New Testament: Acts, Romans, I and II Corinthians,* ed. Anne Reeve and M. A. Screech (Leiden: E. J. Brill, 1990), 492–93. For further evidence of Erasmus' interest in the social significance of eucharistic ritual, see pp. 282–83, where Erasmus, annotating Acts 2, identifies "communio" not with the breaking of bread as in the Vulgate but rather with "mutua charitas, quae faciebat inter eos omnia communia."
94. See Adams, *The Praise of Folly and Other Writings,* 6–7, and ASD 4.3, p. 71, where a draught of nepenthe combined with nectar makes Stultitia's audience the equal of the Homeric gods—"pariter deorum homericorum nectare non sine nepenthe temulenti, esse videamini."
95. See ASD 4.3, p. 150:

   Idem [i.e., Paul] ut charitatem optime praestitit, ita parum dialectice vel dividit vel finit in priore ad Corinthios epistola, capite decimoterio.

96. See ASD 4.3, pp. 160–62.
97. See Adams, *The Praise of Folly and Other Writings,* 61, and ASD 4.3, pp. 156–58.
98. See ASD 4.3, p. 190.
99. See ASD 4.3, p. 191.
100. See "The Religious Feast," in Adams, *The Praise of Folly and Other Writings,* 182. For the Latin see LB 1:672D.
101. See LB 1:672C.
102. See LB 1:676E.
103. See LB 1:673–74.
104. See Adams, *The Praise of Folly and Other Writings,* 193.
105. See Adams, *The Praise of Folly and Other Writings,* 212.
106. See Adams, *The Praise of Folly and Other Writings,* 186.
107. See Adams, *The Praise of Folly and Other Writings,* 183, and LB 1:673A.
108. See Adams, *The Praise of Folly and Other Writings,* 192 and LB 1:678B.
109. See More, *Responsio ad Lutherum,* ed. John M. Headley (New Haven: Yale University Press, 1969), 270–75.
110. See Adams, *The Praise of Folly and Other Writings,* 196–97, and LB 1:680–81.
111. See Adams, *The Praise of Folly and Other Writings,* 191, and LB 1:677E.
112. See LB 1:685A. Eusebius for instance eschews marble in the home, but this material is presented as being conspicuous in monastic establishments.

2. HERESY AND UTOPIA

1. See the beginning of *Thomae Mori . . . Omnia . . . Latina Opera* (Bogard: Louvain, 1566). This epitaph is also in the 1563 Basel *Lucubrationes,* but it is less prominently displayed there. More's "Tabula Affixa ad Sepulchrum" can also be found in Allen, *Erasmi Epistolae,* no. 2831, 10:260. The reference to More as an "omnium horarum hominem" comes from the prefatory letter to the *Moria.* See ASD 4.3, p. 68. The

English translation, "man for all seasons," can be found in the 1520 *Vulgaria* of Richard Whittington. See *Vulgaria,* ed. Beatrice White, Early English Text Society, no. 187 (London, 1932), 64–65.

2. See Allen, *Erasmi Epistolae,* no. 2831, 10:259.

3. See Allen, *Erasmi Epistolae,* no. 2831, 10:260.

4. John M. Headley discusses this possibility in part 2 of his edition of the *Responsio ad Lutherum* (New Haven: Yale University Press, 1969), 718–21.

5. See *The Correspondence of St. Thomas More,* ed. Elizabeth Frances Rogers (Princeton: Princeton University Press, 1947), 387–38.

6. See Allen, *Erasmi Epistolae,* no. 2831, 10:259.

7. See Allen, *Erasmi Epistolae,* no. 2659, 10:33.

8. On More's complex self-representations within *Utopia,* see Elizabeth McCutcheon's *My Dear Peter: The Ars Poetica and Hermeneutics of More's Utopia* (Angers: Editions Moreana, 1983), 23–37. Stephen Greenblatt has brilliantly charted the relation between the More of *Utopia* and More the controversialist in his "At the Table of the Great: More's Self-Fashioning and Self-Cancellation," in *Renaissance Self-Fashioning: More to Shakespeare* (Chicago: University of Chicago Press, 1980), 11–74. Greenblatt examines More as one of the first artfully constructed selves in the English Renaissance, and he extends this examination to both *Utopia* and the antiheresy works. Greenblatt also notes the way in which More's caricatures of Luther and Tyndale seem to be extreme versions of Raphael Hythlodaeus. Nevertheless, Greenblatt is ultimately interested in the epistemological angst that underlies More's self-fashioning and his demonizing of Protestant opponents, whereas my focus is rather the actual religious and political issues that both divided More from and linked him to Luther and Tyndale.

9. See *The Confutation of Tyndale's Answer,* ed. Louis Schuster et al. (New Haven: Yale University Press, 1973), 179. See also More's translation, *The Life of John Picus Erle of Myrandula,* for a possible early model for this quote. Pico in More's translation burned "bokes, that in his youth of wanton verses of love with other like fantasies he had made in his vulgar tonge." See *The Workes of Sir Thomas More* (London: Cawood, 1557), 4.

10. See Allen, *Erasmi Epistolae,* no. 2659, 10:33.

11. See *In Defense of Humanism: Letters to Dorp, Oxford, Lee, and a Monk,* ed. Daniel Kinney (New Haven: Yale University Press, 1986), xxiii, for this overlap in time.

12. See the Yale *Utopia,* 218–19.

13. See the Yale *Utopia,* 220–21.

14. See the Yale *Utopia,* 98–99. The Yale translation of "locus" as "room" does not capture the pun.

15. See Yale *Utopia,* 100–101.

16. For Erasmus' "In angulos," see LB 2:1069:

> ... in angulo, fieri dicitur, quod sit in occulto. Quod, usurpatum in Evangelis a domino Jesu Christo, reperitur esse apud Platonem in Gorgia ... reliquum vitae degere cum adolescentis ... in angulo susurrantem. ... Sic & illud in Evangelicis literis proverbialiter est dictum super tectum praedicare, pro eo, quod est, palam & in publico praedicare.
>
> [What is hidden is said to be "in a corner." This saying, used in the Gospels by Lord Jesus Christ, is discovered to be in Plato's *Gorgias:* "to spend the rest of your life whispering in a corner with adolescents." Thus, also that Gospel saying is proverbial: "to preach on the roof," meaning openly and in public to preach.] (my translation)

Note Erasmus' opposition between "whispering in a corner" and "preaching on the rooftop."

17. See Yale *Utopia*, 101.

18. See LB 2:217C:

> Lesbia regula, dicitur, quoties praepostere, non ad rationem factum, sed ratio ad factum accommodatur. Et cum lex moribus applicatur, non mores ad legem emendantur: aut quoties princeps se populi moribus accommodat, cum contra conveniat plebem ad principis arbitrium vitam instituere, si modo princeps ipse ad honesti regulam ac scopum respiciat.

See also Kathy Eden, "Rhetoric in the Hermeneutics of Erasmus' Later Works," *Erasmus of Rotterdam Society Yearbook* (1991): 94–96, where she makes reference to this passage from *Utopia* and discusses the ways in which Aristotle's "Lesbian rule" at times mutates into the overly soft "Lydian rule" in the works of Erasmus and More. For the Aristotle, see the *Nicomachean Ethics*, 5.10.3–8.

19. Richard Marius discusses the importance of the Hunne case in *Thomas More: A Biography* (New York: Knopf, 1984), 123–41.

20. For the significance of Raphael's name, see Elizabeth McCutcheon, "Thomas More, Raphael Hythlodaeus, and the Angel Raphael," *Studies in English Literature* 9 (1969): 21–38. McCutcheon emphasizes the angel Raphael's association with both healing and travel. She also notes the degree to which More uses medical metaphors throughout *Utopia* and how such metaphors reinforce the significance of Raphael Hythlodaeus' name (pp. 31–32). McCutcheon, however, argues that the Raphael Hythlodaeus' links to the angel Raphael and healing generally work to validate Raphael Hythlodaeus' positions in *Utopia* whereas I will make the case that the medical metaphor, in particular, is double-edged.

21. See the Yale *Utopia*, 176–77, where Raphael describes the Utopian enjoyment of food as a natural pleasure:

> Such pleasures they hold should not be highly valued and only insofar as they are necessary. Yet they enjoy even these pleasures and gratefully acknowledge the kindness of mother nature who, with alluring sweetness, coaxes her offspring to that which of necessity they must constantly do. In what discomfort [taedium] should we have to live if, like all other sicknesses which less frequently assail us, so also these daily diseases [morbi] of hunger and thirst had to be expelled by bitter poisons and drugs [venena ac pharmaca]?

It is not evident from the translation that "pharmaca" can mean "poisons" as well as "drugs." More uses this kind of Greek-Latin doublet elsewhere. See, for instance, "fundamentum omnium ac basim" on p. 172.

22. See in Gombrich, *Symbolic Images: Studies in the Art of the Renaissance* (London: Phaidon, 1972), 27.

23. See CWE 31:45 and for the Latin ASD 1.4, p. 178. See also Rudolph Arbesmann, "The Concept of 'Christ Medicus' in Augustus," *Traditio* 10 (1954): 1–29. Erasmus owes a good deal to Augustine and other patristic sources here.

24. See the Yale *Utopia*, 186.

25. See the Yale *Utopia*, 104–7.

26. See the Yale *Utopia*, 106.

27. See the Yale *Utopia*, 50.

28. See the Yale *Utopia*, 112–13.

29. See the Yale *Utopia*, 12–13.

30. See the Yale *Utopia*, 10–12.
31. See the Yale *Utopia*, 236.
32. See the Yale *Utopia*, 224.
33. See *A Dialogue of Comfort against Tribulation*, ed. Louis L. Martz and Frank Manley (New Haven: Yale University Press, 1976), 121–58. See also Augustine's *City of God*, 1.16–27. Some of More's examples—for instance, Cato—come directly from Augustine.
34. See *City of God*, 1.27.
35. See the Yale *Utopia*, 244–45:

> Quae [i.e., superbia] quoniam pressius hominibus infixa est, quam ut facile possit evelli, hanc Reipublicae formam, quam omnibus libenter optarim, Utopiensibus saltem contigisse gaudeo, . . . Extirpatis enim domi cum caeteris vitiis ambitionis, & factionum radicibus, nihil impendet periculi ne domestico dissidio laboretur.
>
> [Pride is too deeply fixed in men to be easily plucked out. For this reason, the fact that this form of commonwealth—which I should gladly desire for all—has been the good fortune of the Utopians fills me with joy. . . . At home they have extirpated the roots of ambition and factionalism along with all the other vices.]

36. In the Vulgate, this crucial scene of revelation includes the following:

> Tum dixit eis occulte. . . . Etenim sacramentum regis abscondere bonum est: opera autem dei revelare & confiteri honorificum est. Bona est oratio cum jejunio, et eleemosyna magis quam thesauros auri recondere: . . . Manifesto ergo vobis veritatem, et non abscondam a vobis occultam sermonem.

The translation is from Caxton, *The Golden Legend* (London: J. M. Dent, 1928), 74. For the Latin, see *Biblia Latina Cum Glossa Ordinaria: Facsimile Reprint of the Edition Princeps, 1480/81* (Brepols: Turnhout, 1992), 340–41.

37. The Utopians have *principes*, although their form of government is clearly republican. For more on this apparent paradox, see my article, " 'First among Equals': The Utopian *Princpeps*," *Moreana* 30 (December 1993): 33–46. To my knowledge, Russell Ames was the first to note the lack of a Utopian monarch in *Citizen Thomas More and His Utopia* (Princeton: Princeton University Press, 1949), 86–87.
38. See the Yale *Utopia*, 42–45. As the editors point out (p. 294), More's farewell to his book ("I nunc . . .") is probably a direct allusion to "Herculei labores."
39. See the Yale *Utopia*, 45.
40. See LB 2:147.
41. See this preface in *Doctrinal Treatises and Introductions to Different Portions of the Holy Scriptures by William Tyndale*, ed. Rev. Henry Walter (Cambridge: Cambridge University Press, 1848), 395–96.
42. See David Daniell, *William Tyndale: A Biography* (New Haven: Yale University Press, 1994), 83–84.
43. See the Yale *Utopia*, 46–47. See also Daniell, *William Tyndale*, 397, which lists the places where Erasmus does praise Tunstall.
44. See Lisa Jardine's "Self-Portrait in Pen and Link" and "Inventing Rudolph Agricola: Recovery and Transmission of the *De Inventione Dialectica*," in *Erasmus, Man of Letters: The Construction of Charisma in Print* (Princeton: Princeton University Press, 1993), 3–27 and 83–99. Jardine shows how humanists manipulated print to fabricate public associations between "men of letters."
45. See WA 18:628:

Nec ista pars concilii vel remedii tui valet, ubi dicis: licet verum dicere, sed non expedit apud quoslibet nec quovis tempore nec quosvis modo. . . . Non enim Paulus de doctrina aut docenda veritate ibi loquitur, sicut tu eius verba confundis et trahis quo libet. . . . Veritas et doctrina semper, palam, constanter praedicanda, numquam obliquanda caelandave est, nullum est enim in ea scandalum. Est *virga rectitudinis.* Et quis tibi fecit potestatem aut ius dedit doctrinae Christianae locis, personis, temporibus, causis alligandae, cum Christus eam velit liberrimam in orbe vulgari et regnare? (my emphasis)

See also p. 631:

Scilicet, Creator tuus a te creatura discet, quid utile et inutile sit praedicatu, ac ille stultus ille vel imprudens Deus hactenus nescierit, quid doceri opporteat, donec tu magister eius modum illi praescriberes sapiendi et mandandi, quasi ignorasset, nisi tu docuisses, sequi ad hoc paradoxon. . . . Si igitur Deus talia voluit palam dici et *invulgari,* nec spectari, quid sequeretur, . . . tu quis es, qui vetes? Paulus Apostolus in Epistola ad Rom. non *in angulum, sed in publicum* ac coram toto mundo . . . palam disseruit. . . . [my emphasis]

46. See Walter, *Doctrinal Treatises and Introductions,* 153–54.
47. For More's response to the Protestant appropriation of the Lesbian rule, see *A Dialogue Concerning Heresies,* ed. Thomas M. C. Lawler, Germain Marc'hadour, and Richard C. Marius (New Haven: Yale University Press, 1981), 129, 135.
48. See *Eikonoklastes,* ed. William Haller, vol. 5 in *The Works of John Milton* (New York: Columbia University Press, 1931–38), 63.
49. Walker, *Doctrinal Treatises and Introductions,* 179. See also Greenblatt, *Renaissance Self-Fashioning,* 89–93, for more on the ambiguities of the obedience espoused by Tyndale in *The Obedience of a Christian Man.* See Lawler, Marc'hadour, and Marius, *Dialogue Concerning Heresies,* 369, for More on Tyndale's "boke of dysobedience" and the relation of religious reformation to peasant revolt.
50. Luther was aware that Henry probably did not write the *Assertio* by himself. For since it was published [vulgatur] under Henry's name, Luther asserted that Henry must suffer the brunt of Luther's "impetus." See WA 10/11:183.
51. See WA 10/11:183.
52. WA 10/11:184.
53. See Headley, *Responsio ad Lutherum,* 19.
54. See Headley, *Responsio ad Lutherum,* 18–19.
55. See Headley, *Responsio ad Lutherum,* 436–39.
56. See the Yale *Utopia,* 80–83.
57. As evidence of Erasmus' own insecurity on the subject of the English perceptions of his allegiances in 1526, see Allen, *Erasmi Epistolae,* no. 1697, 6:322–23, where Erasmus defends his *Colloquia* to Wolsey and Longland as containing "nothing impious, nothing obscene, nothing seditious." The letter shows that Erasmus believed that the distribution of the colloquia had been forbidden in England. More generally Erasmus criticizes those who confuse the cause of "good letters," that is, humanism, with Lutheranism.
58. See More, *Translations of Lucian,* ed. Craig R. Thompson (New Haven: Yale University Press, 1974), 4–5, 10–24.
59. See Headley, *Responsio ad Lutherum,* 180, 62.
60. See the Letter to Bugenhagen, in Rogers, *The Correspondence of Sir Thomas More,* 325–65 and, in particular, 364. See also Lawler, Marius, Marc'hadour, *Dialogue Concerning Heresies,* 369, and Schuster, *Confutation of Tyndale's Answer,* 59–60, for More on the direness of the Peasants' Revolt and its implications for England.

61. See WA 7:720–23.
62. See Headley, *Responsio ad Lutherum,* 118–19:

> Nam si posset obscurum aliquem angulum reperire (quod, opinor, non potest): tamen angulus ille non esset cum reliqua comparandus ecclesia: quae non Christo solum subest: sed et propter Christum, unico Christi vicario . . . et ordinem credit esse sacramentum. . . . Quos populos omnes [i.e., all other nations] quum de Christi tollat ecclesia: necesse est: ut aut ecclesiam Christi fateatur esse nusquam: aut more Donatistarum, ecclesiam Christi catholicam, ad duos aut tres hereticos redigat, de Christo susurrantes in angulo.

63. See Headley, *Responsio ad Lutherum,* 118–19. To be sure, since the reference to Utopia belongs to the marginalia of the *Responsio,* it is unclear whether More or the printer is responsible for it. Yet frequent punning in the *Responsio* on "nusquam" suggests that the reference to Utopia was at least in accord with More's intentions. Stephen Greenblatt also refers to this annotation in *Renaissance Self-Fashioning,* p. 59, but he does not emphasize the theological connection between Utopia and Lutheranism. Rather, he argues that Utopia is being "invoked . . . as an image of a madman's fantasy."
64. See Rogers, *Correspondence of Sir Thomas More,* 338.
65. See the Yale *Utopia,* 116–17.
66. See the Yale *Utopia,* 178–79.
67. See the Yale *Utopia,* 218–19.
68. Yale *Utopia,* 226. See Edward L. Surtz, S.J., *The Praise of Wisdom: A Commentary on the Religious and Moral Problems and Backgrounds of St. Thomas More's* Utopia (Chicago: Loyola University Press, 1957), 150–52. Surtz takes a much more orthodox view of the Utopian priesthood than the one I am maintaining.
69. See Yale *Utopia,* 42–43.
70. See Daniell, *William Tyndale* for more on Tyndale's debt to Erasmus for this and other translations of key New Testament terms.
71. See Luther's *Contra Henricum,* WA 10/11:221:

> Ego ordinem negavi sacramentum esse, id est promissionem et signum gratiae adjectum, quale est Baptismus et panis, non negavi, imo asserui esse vocationem et institutionem ministri et concionatoris, sive hoc fiat autoritate unius Apostoli vel pontificis sola, vel populis eligentis et consentientis simul, nihil refert. Quamquam rectius fiat populo eligente et consentiente, quo modo Apostoli Act.4 septem Diacones instituterunt.

Luther hedges a bit here, but he ultimately comes down in favor [rectius] of popular elections. Likewise, Erasmus notes in his *Annotationes:*

> Rabanus opinor admonet hunc esse modum in conferendis sacris ordinibus, ut populus eligat, episcopus ordinet. Ea certe consuetudo diutissime perseverarit in ecclesia verum ob tumultus populares recte mutata est. (*Erasmus' Annotations on the New Testament: Acts, Romans, I and II Corinthians,* ed. Anne Reeve and M. A. Screech [Leiden: E. J. Brill, 1990], 290)

This annotation, added in 1527, does *not* show Erasmus in favor of the election of priests, but he does attest to its having been a practice of the early church. See Lawler, Marius, and Marc'hadour, *Dialogue Concerning Heresies,* 289, for More's complaint against Tyndale as a translator of *presbuteros:*

> Now as touchnge the cause why he chaunged the name of preste in to senyor ye must understande that Luther and his adherentys holde this heresy that all holy order is nothynge. And that a preste is nothyng els but a man chosen amonge the people to preche. . . . Where sooever the scrypture speketh of the prestys that were amonge the Jewes there dothe he in his transla-

cyon call them styll by the name of prestys. But where so ever the scrypture speketh of the prestys of Crystes chyrche there dothe he put away the name of preste in his translacyon bycause he wolde make it seme that the scrypture did never speke of any prestes different from ley men amonge Crysten people.

72. See Schuster, *Confutation,* 194–95.
73. See William Tyndale, *An Answer to Sir Thomas More's Dialogue,* ed. Rev. Henry Walter (Cambridge: Cambridge University Press, 1850), 176. For More's response to this jibe, see p. 191 in Schuster, *Confutation.* More basically claims that God's providence would insure that such a situation never occurred. For more on Protestant appropriations of More and *Utopia,* see Anne Lake Prescott's introduction to Jackson Campbell Boswell, *Sir Thomas More in the English Renaissance* (Binghamton, N.Y.: Center for Medieval and Early Renaissance Studies, 1994), xxiii–xxiv. Prescott focuses on the Protestant association of *Utopia* with indentifiably Catholic entities such as Purgatory and images, but I am trying to make the case for Tyndale's awareness of the overlap between *Utopia* and aspects of the Reformation.
74. Yale *Utopia,* 228, 546.
75. Yale *Utopia,* 194–95.
76. Yale *Utopia,* 230.
77. Yale *Utopia,* 216–19.
78. Kinney, *In Defense of Humanism,* 278–79.
79. See the Yale *Utopia,* 82–83.
80. I am grateful to Kathy Eden for pointing this out to me. On the "germanus sensus" as an Erasmian standard of scriptural interpretation, see Eden, *Hermeneutics and the Rhetorical Tradition: Chapters in the Ancient Legacy and Its Humanist Reception* (New Haven: Yale University Press, 1997), 76–77, and Terence Cave, *The Cornucopian Text: Problems of Writing in the French Renaissance* (New York: Oxford University Press, 1979), 71.
81. See the prefatory material in LB 6.
82. See the Yale *Utopia,* 144.
83. See the Yale *Utopia,* 130–33.
84. Yale *Utopia,* 226:

> Eorum tamen haereses duae sunt, Altera caelibum . . . altera coniugium praefert. . . . Huiusmodi ergo sunt, quos illi peculiari nomine sua lingua Buthrescas vocant, quod verbum latine religiosos licet interpretari.

Here the Yale translation renders "haereses" as "schools," which is philologically correct—a *haeresis* could denote a philosophical sect or school—but does not work in the context. For the Buthrescae are said to be those who, motivated by "religio," neglect "literae" and the contemplative life in general in favor of an active life of service to others. The translation obscures the clearly religious significance of the word *haeresis.*

85. See Reeve and Screech, *Annotationes,* 325–26:

> Cum haeresis apud Graecos, nihil aliud sit quam secta, quid venit interpreti in mentem, ut Latinam vocem interpretaretur per Graecam sed idem significantem? . . . Caeterum haeresis, apud veteres non erat tam odiosum vocabulum, quam est hodie apud Christianos. Quibus cum summa competat concordia, utpote eiusdem corporis membris, iure videlicet optimo invisum est sectae vocabulum, divisionem sonans.

See also Erasmus' critique of contemporary usage of the word "heresy" in "Sileni Alcibiades":

They call it heresy [haeresim appellant] to say or write anything which differs in any way from the petty propositions of the Masters of Theology, or even to disagree on matters of grammar; but it is not heresy [haeresis non est], to proclaim the chief part of human felicity to lie in precisely the very thing which Christ always teaches us to set aside; it is not heresy, to encourage a mode of life quite unlike the teachings of the Gospel.

(Margaret Mann Phillips, *Erasmus on His Times: A Shortened Version of the Adages* [Cambridge: Cambridge University Press, 1967], 87)

86. See Kinney, *In Defense of Humanism,* 143.

87. See Marius, *Thomas More: A Biography,* 178–79.

88. For more on More's complex attitude toward the role of the Bible in Christianity, see Kinney, *In Defense of Humanism,* 88, where More contrasts the living gospel of faith to any writing-based gospel. See as well Headley, *Responsio ad Lutherum,* 232–33, where More defines the role of the Bible as a whole in a way that recalls both traditional justifications for reading the Apocrypha, that is, that of inculcating moral precepts, and the kind of Christianity that Raphael brings to Utopia.

89. See the Yale *Utopia,* 72–73.

90. Headley, *Responsio ad Lutherum,* 275–77.

91. See the Yale *Utopia,* 195, for the relative paucity of laws in Utopia.

92. See Headley, *Responsio ad Lutherum,* 276; see also Headley's very useful discussion of this passage on pp. 756–57. Headley notes the resemblance to Utopian communism here, but he sees the resemblance as being less problematical for More than I do.

93. See Lawler, Marc'hadour, and Marius, *Dialogue Concerning Heresies,* 32.

94. See Martz and Manley, *Dialogue of Comfort against Tribulation,* 172–73.

95. See Lawler, Marc'hadour, and Marius, *Dialogue Concerning Heresies,* 338. The Bible, More notes, was originally written in a

vulgare tonge such as the hole peple understode nor in no secret cyphers but suche comen letters as almost every man coulde rede. For neyther was the hebrewe nor the greke tonge nor the latyn neither any other speche than such as all the people spake.

96. See Lawler, Marc'hadour, and Marius, *Dialogue Concerning Heresies,* 343.

97. See Lawler, Marc'hadour, and Marius, *Dialogue Concerning Heresies,* 342.

98. See the Yale *Utopia,* 222.

99. This prohibition creates interesting problems for the reception of Lucian, one of the Greek authors that Raphael brings to Utopia and whose brand of satire is one source of *Utopia.* For, as More wrote in the preface to his and Erasmus' translations of Lucian, Lucian was "disposed to doubt his immortality" [ut non satis immortaliti suae confideret] (see More, *Translations of Lucian,* 4–5). Given the Utopian reception of Greek books and their discovery of printing, how will they keep these doubts from being disseminated "apud vulgus"?

3. "To Devulgate or Sette Fourth"

1. See Crane, *Framing Authority: Sayings, Self, and Society in Sixteenth-Century England* (Princeton: Princeton University Press, 1993), 112–14. Crane's view of Elyot is in accord with that of Alistair Fox, "Sir Thomas Elyot and the Humanist Dilemma," in Fox and John Guy, *Reassessing the Henrician Age: Humanism, Politics, and Reform, 1500– 1550* (New York: Blackwell, 1986). Fox argues that *The Governour,* with its panegyric of monarchy, represents Elyot's attempt to reinstate himself at court. But, "[h]aving

failed a second time to secure permanent advancement, Elyot fell back upon the certitudes of his own moral vision. From playing the part of Morus, in other words, he adopted the stance of Hythlodaeus" (62). Fox and Crane are right as far as they go. But the panegyric of monarchy represents only a small portion of *The Governour,* and is, as we shall see, qualified in important ways. In fact, the audience and rhetorical strategies of *The Governour* are far more complex than either Fox or Crane, with their too exclusively monarchical world-pictures, admits. Fox, in particular, is hampered by his reliance on overly rigid intellectual categories such as "neo-Stoic, Erasmian, moral absolutism" (62).

2. For a complete bibliography of Elyot's works, see S. E. Lehmberg, *Sir Thomas Elyot: Tudor Humanist* (Austin: University of Texas Press, 1960), 197–98. Editions of *The Boke Named the Governour* appeared in 1531, 1537, 1544, 1546, 1553, 1557, and 1565. Elyot's *Dictionary* and *Castle of Health* also underwent numerous reprintings in the sixteenth century.

3. See Duffy, *The Stripping of the Altars: Traditional Religion in England, c. 1400–1580* (New Haven: Yale University Press, 1992), 385–86.

4. See *Tudor Royal Proclamations,* ed. Paul Hughes and James Larkin (New Haven: Yale University Press, 1964), 1:271.

5. Elyot discusses his promotion and fall in a 1532 letter to Thomas Cromwell. See "The Letters of Sir Thomas Elyot," ed. K. J. Wilson in *Studies in Philology* 73 (winter 1976): 12.

6. See Wilson, "The Letters of Sir Thomas Elyot," 14.

7. See Lehmberg, *Sir Thomas Elyot,* 14–19 and 30–31, on the vexed question of the More-Elyot relationship. The primary documentary evidence supporting the existence and importance of this friendship is Elyot's 1536 renunciation of it in a letter to Thomas Cromwell. John Major, however, has argued that Elyot's satirical works, *Pasquil the Playne* and *Of the Knowledge Which Maketh a Wise Man,* were written to enlist support for the persecuted More. See Major, *Sir Thomas Elyot and Renaissance Humanism* (Lincoln: University of Nebraska Press, 1964), 97.

8. See *The Boke Named the Governour,* ed. H. H. Croft, 2 vols. (London: C. Kegan Paul & Co., 1880), 1:144–45.

9. John Major distinguishes between the "intellectual aristocracy" that rules More's Utopia and Elyot's governors, who combine features of an intellectual aristocracy with characteristics of a landed one. This distinction would seem a good description of Elyot's position, too. See Major, *Sir Thomas Elyot and Renaissance Humanism,* 114. For the categorization of Elyot as a member of the "New Tudor Aristocracy," see Paul Siegel's "English Humanism and the New Tudor Aristocracy," *Journal of the History of Ideas* 13 (1952): 455. See also S. E. Lehmberg's rebuttal to this identification in *Sir Thomas Elyot,* 187–93. Lehmberg has a somewhat tendentious appendix, showing the "deepness of Sir Thomas's roots in West Country gentry stock." Nevertheless, even Lehmberg acknowledges that Elyot's literary activities were unusual for a member of the gentry. More recently, however, in Quentin Skinner's chapter, "Political Philosophy," in *The Cambridge History of Renaissance Philosophy,* ed. Charles Schmitt and Quentin Skinner (Cambridge: Cambridge University Press, 1988), 447–49, Elyot becomes a champion of virtue rather than lineage as the criterion of nobility.

10. See Stephen Foley, "Coming to Terms: Thomas Elyot's Definitions and the Particularity of Humanist Letters," *English Literary History* 6.2 (1994): 212.

11. See Lehmberg, *Sir Thomas Elyot,* 151.

12. See Lehmberg's *Sir Thomas Elyot,* 148–54 and 108. See also Constance Jordan's

"Feminism and Humanists: The Case of Sir Thomas Elyot's *The Defense of Good Women*," *Renaissance Quarterly* 36 (summer 1983): 181–202, which uses Elyot's *Defense of Good Women* to support the conclusion that Elyot was privy to the conspiracy to depose Henry.

13. Elyot, however, was recalled early. See Lehmberg, *Sir Thomas Elyot*, 95–115.

14. See Eisenstein, *The Printing Press as an Agent of Change: Communications and Cultural Transformations in Early-Modern Europe* (Cambridge: Cambridge University Press, 1979), 361:

> Protestant objections to veiling Gospel truths were adopted by the translators and used for more secular ends. For example, they argued that the liberal arts and sciences should not be "hidden in Greek or Latin tongue" but made familiar to the "vulgar people." In "blunt and rude English," they set out to "please ten thousand laymen" instead of "ten able clerks." They sought to close the gap not so much between priest and laity as between academic or professional elites and "common" readers who were variously described as "unskillful," "unlettered," and "unacquainted with the Latin tongue."

15. See Ted Brown, "Word Wars: The Debate over the Use of the Vernacular in Medical Writings of the English Renaissance," *Texas Studies in Language and Literature* 37 (spring 1995), 98–113, and in particular, 106.

16. See G. R. Elton's discussion of the tricky question of what constituted propaganda during this period in *Policy and Police: The Enforcement of the Reformation in the Age of Cromwell* (Cambridge: Cambridge University Press, 1972), 171–216. Elton argues for two criteria of propaganda: it is either "specifically known to come from government-employed pens" or it was "published by the king's printer, Thomas Berthelet" (173). *The Governour* does not pass the first test, but it does pass the second since it was printed by Thomas Berthelet. Nevertheless, as applied to Elyot, the Berthelet test fails as a measure of propaganda since all of Elyot's books were printed by Berthelet. It is hard to reconcile the caustic satires of court life in *Of the Knowledge Which Maketh a Wise Man* (1533) and *Pasquil the Playne* (1533) with royal propaganda. Neither does the medical advice dispensed in *The Castle of Health* (1539) seem to have anything to do with such propaganda.

17. One purpose of *The Governour* is to make the attributes of the monarch more widely accessible. Thus, Elyot justifies his shift in focus from monarch to inferior governors by claiming that these governors have "theyr education and vertue in maners" in "commune with princes" (1:26). See also Elyot's exposition of "majesty":

> More over towarde the acquiring of maiestie, thre thinges be required to be in the oration of a man havyng authorite; that it be compendious, sententious, and delectable. (2:16)

Majesty can be acquired, and it can adhere to any man having authority. See Croft's notes for Elyot's use of his sources, Erasmus and Patrizi (2:12–13). When in *Institutio Principis Christiani* and *De Regno e Regis Instituto* Erasmus and Patrizi discuss *majestas*, they are explicitly defining royal behavior. Elyot, however, is interested in "majesty" as a quality belonging to anyone in authority.

18. See this preface in Wilson, "The Letters of Thomas Elyot," 71.

19. See Wilson, "The Letters of Sir Thomas Elyot," 71.

20. See Max Weber, *The Protestant Ethic and the Spirit of Capitalism*, trans. Talcott Parsons (New York: Scribner's Sons, 1958), 163.

21. *The Governour* (1:cxci–cxcii). For other appearances of this topos in *The Governour*, see

where Elyot refers to his own "talent" and the "account" he has to render to God for its use (1:306). For other humanist usages of the topos of the talent, see Erasmus' *Antibarbari* in the ASD 1.1, p. 105, as well as More's "Letter to a Monk" in *In Defense of Humanism: Letters to Dorp, Oxford, Lee, and a Monk,* ed. Daniel Kinney (New York: Yale University Press, 1986), 302–3. In these passages from More and Erasmus, a refusal to bury one's talent serves as a defense of the secular and civic character of humanist learning against those who would try to confine learning to the more sequestered environment of the monastery.

22. See *The Governour,* 2:5.

23. For purposes of contrast, see Elyot's discussion of the easily counterfeited coin or "noble" in the *Governour,* 2:36–37.

24. See Brown, "Word Wars," 101, for more on charity as the frequently invoked rationale for the popularization of medical knowledge.

25. See William Tyndale, *Doctrinal Treatises and Introductions to Different Portions of the Holy Scriptures,* ed. Rev. Henry Walter (Cambridge: Cambridge University Press, 1848), 60.

26. See *The Governour,* 2:89.

27. See Brown, "Word Wars," 101, for more on the importance of charity for translators of medical treatises during the sixteenth century.

28. See *The Governour,* 2:99–100.

29. Wilson, "The Letters of Sir Thomas Elyot," 59–60.

30. See also *The Governour,* for an allusion to "Festina lente," which Elyot interestingly buries in a discussion of dancing and treats apart from its use by Erasmus (1:242–45).

31. Elyot's point is that Latin was "propre" and "maternal" to the Romans but not to the English.

32. See Wilson, "The Letters of Sir Thomas Elyot," 57.

33. Wilson, "The Letters of Sir Thomas Elyot," 76–77.

34. On such Cromwellian preachers and the havoc they wreaked, see G. R. Elton, *Reform and Reformation: England, 1509–98* (Cambridge: Harvard University Press, 1977), 160–61, and Duffy, *The Stripping of the Altars,* 387–88.

35. See *The Governour,* 2:96–98.

36. See both these prefaces in the twentieth-century reprint of the *Dictionary* (Menston, U.K.: The Scolar Press, 1970). For the English preface, see also Wilson, "The Letters of Sir Thomas Elyot," 60–65.

37. See Wilson, "The Letters of Sir Thomas Elyot," 61.

38. See *The Governour,* 2:224–27. See also Elyot's *Defence of Good Women* (1540), in *The Feminist Controversy of the Renaissance,* ed. Diane Bornstein (Delmar, N.Y.: Scholar's Facsimiles and Reprints, 1980), where the name of the misogynist character, Caninius, is suggestive of Cynic or doglike railing.

39. See also the "argument" in the *Defence of Good Women,* where the detractor of women is named Caninius because he, "like a curre, at womens condicions is always barkyng." The defender of women, however, is named "Candidus," which, Elyot writes in the "argument," "maie be interpreted, benigne or gentill." Currishness and benignity constitute the two sides of Elyot's public persona, and his deployment of them for and against women suggests that the triumph of feminism in the *Defence* is an ambiguous one. As Constance Jordan writes in "Feminism and Humanists," it is tempting "to think that Elyot, who had nothing to say about courageous and intelligent women in any of his other works, wrote the *Defence* somewhat half-heartedly and to fulfill an

obligation" (p. 196). As we have seen, the pro-feminist Candidius must support his position by disparaging poetry, and he even dismisses it as "railing." This dismissal alone makes him less than a complete spokesman for Elyot's views.

40. For this dialogue, see More, *Translations of Lucian,* ed. Craig Thompson (New Haven: Yale University Press, 1974), 11–25.

41. See *Pasquil the Playne* in Elyot, *Four Political Treatises,* ed. Lilian Gottesman (Gainesville, Fla.: Scholars Facsimiles and Reprints, 1967), 42–43, 59.

42. Alistair Fox examines the ways in which Pasquil and Gnatho replay the conflict between More and Raphael in "Sir Thomas Elyot and the Humanist Dilemma," 66–67. But Tyndale and Luther's rejection of the Lesbian rule of compromise indicates that Pasquil's inflexibility was not necessarily tantamount to ineffectuality, as Fox argues.

43. *Pasquil,* 49.

44. *Pasquil,* 50–51.

45. *Pasquil,* 55–56.

46. *Pasquil,* 97.

47. During their debate, Luther interestingly implies that Erasmus is a Gnatho, a character originally from Terence's *The Eunuch.* In *The Eunuch* (l. 252) Gnatho signifies his willingness to assent to anything as follows: "Aiunt, aio, negant nego." So Luther accused Erasmus of imitating the one who said "Aiunt, aio, negant nego" because he was not willing to risk the peace of the world for the word of God. See Luther, WA 18:605.

48. See *Pasquil,* 61, 47.

49. See *Pasquil,* 42.

50. Pasquil further displays his allegiances by referring to Rome as the "heed of the world." See *Pasquil,* 98.

51. See Lehmberg, *Sir Thomas Elyot,* 48–54, and Wilson, "The Letters of Sir Thomas Elyot," 30.

52. See *The Governour,* 2:400. For more on Elyot's use of the category of "history," which includes Scripture, including the Apocrypha, pagan philosophy, and poets such as Homer, see also 2:385–89.

53. See also the "prologue" to Elyot's *The Banquet of Sapience,* where Elyot describes his project of juxtaposing the "wise sayings" of both the "gentiles" and the "faithful" (in *Four Political Treatises,* 104).

54. See *Pasquil,* 48.

55. See *Pasquil,* 48.

56. See *Pasquil,* 99.

57. See *Pasquil,* 97.

58. See *Pasquil,* 43.

59. See *Pasquil,* 60–61.

60. Wilson, "The Letters of Sir Thomas Elyot," 46–47.

61. See Wilson, "The Letters of Sir Thomas Elyot," 31. The original adage can be found in LB 2:748b–d. See also K. J. Wilson's *"Usque ad Aras:* Thomas Elyot's Friendship with Thomas More," in *Acta Conventus Neo-Latini Sanctandreani,* ed. I. D. McFarlane (Binghamton, N.Y.: Medieval & Renaissance Texts and Studies, 1986), 531–57.

62. See Wilson, "The Letters of Sir Thomas Elyot," 26.

63. For this proclamation, see Hughes and Larkin, *Tudor Royal Proclamations,* 1:235–37.

64. Wilson, "The Letters of Sir Thomas Elyot," 26–27.

65. Wilson, "The Letters of Sir Thomas Elyot," 27.

66. Wilson, "The Letters of Sir Thomas Elyot," 27.
67. For the Latin translation to which Elyot is referring, see "Contio quam anglice habuit reverendus pater Ioannes Roffensis episcopus . . . verso in Latinum per Ricardum Pacaeum" (Cambridge: Ioannem Siberch, 1521). This text interestingly likens Henry to one of Plato's philosopher-kings (p. Diiii).
68. See Wilson, "The Letters of Sir Thomas Elyot," 26. As Wilson notes, Elyot is getting the phrase "similitude of studies" from Cicero. For an example of Erasmus' similar definition of friendship, see Erasmus' letter to Peter Giles, which introduces the *Parabolae* in LB 1:561. Erasmus defines "animorum conjunctio" and "societas studiorum" as the basis of true friendship.
69. Wilson, "The Letters of Sir Thomas Elyot," 26.
70. See also Wilson, "The Letters of Sir Thomas Elyot," 26, where Elyot even declares his willingness to excise the "offensive" parts of the questionable volume. This gesture shows the fragmentation of "studies" at the level of the book as material object.
71. *The Governour,* 2:129.
72. For *The Governour* as "anti-*Utopia,*" see chapter 3 of J. Major, *Sir Thomas Elyot and Renaissance Humanism* and, in particular, p. 109. Major makes the case that Elyot's goal in *The Governour* is to make his ideal republic reflect English realities to a greater degree than More's had. For *The Governour* as a "Utopian" work, see Thomas Baldwin, *William Shakespere's Small Latin and Lesse Greeke* (Urbana: University of Illinois Press, 1944), 198–99. Baldwin calls *The Governour* "Utopian" to distinguish it from works that had an impact on the pedagogic practices of English grammar schools. Baldwin finds that *The Governour* had no influence on such practices. I find Baldwin's notion of a Utopian *Governour* an attractive one because it demonstrates the need to examine *The Governour* apart from the current emphasis on the grammar school as the primary site for the transmission of humanism in England. *The Governour,* however, appealed to autodidacts such as Elyot himself, who, in the Latin preface to his *Dictionary,* claims to have been self-educated as far as the liberal arts were concerned. *The Governour* also appealed to beneficiaries of the grammar school education who were autodidacts, too—for example, William Shakespeare. An attention to the dissemination of humanism outside of the grammar school, i.e., in the form of popularizations such as *The Governour,* broadens the range of the political meanings that this humanism could have. For examples of recent books that confine humanism to the grammar school, see Richard Halpern, "A Mint of Phrases," in his *The Poetics of Primitive Accumulation: English Renaissance Culture and the Genealogy of Capital* (Ithaca: Cornell University Press, 1991), 19–61. Halpern argues that the humanist emphasis on style and copiousness made the often politically threatening content of classical literature manageable. See also pp. 85–100 for an analysis of the ways in which a "discourse of capacities" functioned within schools. Halpern's argument depends upon the assumption that "subjects" internalized the ideological conditioning of the grammar school, but, as I have tried to show, frequent anxieties over "misconstruction" suggest that Renaissance writers were less sure that they were writing for such a properly conditioned audience. See also Mary Crane, *Framing Authority,* p. 55, for an application of Pierre Bourdieu's rubric of "cultural capital" to the educational institutions of the English Renaissance. While her remarks about cultural capital could apply to "talent," too, I have been trying to avoid the former phrase since its premise is a tighter institutional control of such wealth than is evident from Elyot's works.
73. See the Yale *Utopia,* 236–40.
74. *The Governour,* 1:2. It is worth noting, however, that Elyot himself uses "common-

wealth" as the English equivalent of *respublica* in *The Governour.* See, for instance 1:26, where Elyot is describing the need for magistrates or lesser governors: "That in every commune weale ought to be a great nombre of suche maner of persons it is partly proved in the chapter nexte before written."

75. *The Governour,* 2:88–89.
76. See *The Governour,* 2:96.
77. See *Noctes Atticae,* 13:16.
78. See *The Governour,* 1:1. Elyot generally assumes that some of the readers of *The Governour* know Latin and Greek and some do not. Thus, at the outset of book 2, Elyot describes his advice to the future governors as "nat of myn owne heed devised, but excerpted or gathered as well out of holy scripture as out of the warkes of other excellent writars of famouse memorie, as they shall sone perceive whiche have radde and perused good autours in greke and latine" (2:2). Elyot seems to recognize here that not all his readers were able to have "perused good autours in greke and latine." See also *The Governour,* where Elyot translates some verses of Latin poetry and suggests that they be "in a table, in suche a place as a governour ones in a daye maye beholde them, specially as they be expressed in latine by the said poete, unto whose eloquence no translation in englisshe may be equivalent" (2:11). This sentence seems to leave open the question of whether the governor will need to read these verses in Elyot's translation or will be able to study them in the original.
79. See, for instance, *The Governour.* After detailing all the poets that a future governor should master, Elyot writes:

> Here I wolde shulde be remembred, that I require nat that all these warkes shud be throughly radde of a childe in this tyme, whiche were almost impossible. But I only desire that they have, in every of the saide bokes, so moch instruction that they may take therby some profite. (1:70)

But *The Governour* is itself filled with profitable examples taken from the poets, and the child could presumably read Elyot instead of the originals. See also *The Governour,* where Elyot details all the books of rhetoric his student should read and then suggests that they are really not necessary for the student who possesses Erasmus' *De Copia:*

> And in good faythe, to speake boldly that I thinke: for him that nedeth nat, or doth nat desire, to be an exquisite oratour, the litle boke made by the famous Erasmus . . . which he calleth *Copiam Verborum et Rerum,* that is to say, plentie of wordes and matters, shall be sufficient. (1:73)

80. *The Governour,* 1:24.
81. *The Governour,* 1:27.
82. Throughout this discussion of nobility Elyot keeps introducing virtue as a qualification of the supposed link between the landed gentry and the qualities that make good governors. See, for instance:

> And excepte excellent vertue and lernynge do inhabile a man of base astate of the communalitie, to be thought of all men worthy to be so moche avaunced: els suche governours wolde be chosen out of that astate of men whiche be called worshipfull, if amonge them may be founden a sufficient nombre, ornate with vertue and wisedome, mete for suche a purpose. (1:26)

83. See the Yale *Utopia,* 112–13.
84. See Wilson, "The Letters of Sir Thomas Elyot," 67.
85. See Wilson, "The Letters of Sir Thomas Elyot," 67.
86. During the 1530s Elyot was not alone in his concern to supervise the divulgation of dangerous knowledge and books. See Hughes and Larkin, *Tudor Royal Proclamations,*

1:196–97, for proclamations that prohibit the "divulgation" of both Tyndale's translation of the Bible and papal bulls.

87. See *The Governour*, "*Plebs* in englisshe is called the communaltie, which signifieth only the multitude, wherin be contayned the base and vulgare inhabitauntes not avanced to any honour or dignite" (1:2). See also where Elyot uses the "vulgare people" as a synonym for "communalitie" (1:8).

88. See Plutarch's *Life of Aristides*, chap. 2.

89. The source of Aristides' surname is Plutarch's *Life of Aristides*, chap. 6.

90. See *The Governour*, 2:224–25. For Erasmus' and Cicero's versions of the same story, see ASD 29:292, and *De Officiis*, book 3.49. See also Plutarch's *Life of Themistocles*, chap. 20, and his *Life of Aristides*, chap. 22. For more on Elyot and this story, see my article, "'To divulgate or set forth': Humanism and Heresy in Sir Thomas Elyot's *The Book Named the Governor*," *Studies in Philology* 90 (winter 1993): 46–57.

91. Thus, Aristides in Elyot's account tells the people that "the counsayle of Themistocles was very profitable, but the enterprise was dishonest and agayne justice." The people "heringe that the acte was nat honest or juste, all cryed with one voyce, nor yet expedient." But Aristides does not tell the people what the counsel is. He merely gives them a choice between two abstractions.

92. Earlier in *The Governour* Elyot shows his awareness that Aristides was not always in accord with democratic Athens:

> But to retourne agayne. Athenes and other cities of Grece, whan they had abandoned kynges, and concluded to lyve as it were in communaltie, whiche abusifly they called equalitie, . . . what noble man had they whiche avanced the honour and weale of theyr citie, whom they dyd not banisshe or slee in prison? Surely it shall appiere to them that wyll rede Plutarche, or Emilius probus, in the lyves of Milciades . . . Themistocles, Aristides, and divers other noble and valiant capitaynes. (1:17–18)

93. See Plutarch's *Life of Aristides*, chap. 22.

94. See *The Governour*, 2:187–89.

95. See *The Governour*, 1:5–6.

96. *The Governour*, 1:1.

97. See *The Governour*, 1:119–20. Elyot is criticizing the belief that rhetoric without knowledge is sufficient to an orator. For *logodaedali*, see the *Phaedrus* 51.

98. See Hughes and Larkin, *Tudor Royal Proclamations*, 1:227–28.

99. See Hughes and Larkin, *Tudor Royal Proclamations*, 1:272.

100. *The Governour*, 2:210–12. For the original adage, see LB 2:258D. Erasmus' adage does not at all resemble Elyot's version.

101. Wilson, "The Letters of Sir Thomas Elyot," 3.

102. See *Erasmus' Annotations on the New Testament: Acts, Romans, I and II Corinthians*, ed. Anne Reeve and M. A. Screech (Leiden: E. J. Brill, 1990), 282:

> Fractione panis . . . id est, Et in fractione panis, ut sint quatuor, doctrina, communio, fractio panis, & precationes . . . . Illud quod animadvertendum primo loco posuit doctrinam, sed evangelicam proximo mutuam charitatem, quae faciebat inter eos omnia communia, tertio symbolum illud sacrum Christianae conspirationis, quarto precationes. (1522)

In other words, the Vulgate omitted the "et" and made "communio" seem an appositive of "fractio panis." So Erasmus continues in 1527:

> Nostra lectio [i.e., the Vulgate] tria duntaxat ponit, doctrinam, fractionem panis, quam vocant communionem & preces.

For another place where Erasmus uses "nostra lectio" to mean the Vulgate, see p. 275. For more on "communion," which in the 1552 Book of Common Prayer, replaced the Mass as the designation for the central service of the Reformed English religion, see John King, *English Reformation Literature: The Tudor Origins of the Protestant Tradition* (Princeton: Princeton University Press, 1982), 137.

103. See Wilson, "The Letters of Sir Thomas Elyot," 2.

104. Arthur Ferguson, *The Articulate Citizen and the English Renaissance* (Durham: Duke University Press, 1965), 225–26; on the Pilgrimage of Grace, see 322–23 in Penry Williams' *The Tudor Regime* (Oxford: Clarendon Press, 1979) and Ferguson, *The Articulate Citizen,* 223–27.

105. See Richard Morison, *A Remedy for Sedition,* in *Humanist Scholarship and Public Order,* ed. David Berkowitz (Washington, D.C.: Folger Shakespeare Library, 1984), 111–12.

106. Morison, *A Remedy for Sedition,* 115.

107. Morison, *A Remedy for Sedition,* 116.

4. TOPICAL UTOPIAS

1. See Helen White, *Social Criticism in Popular Religious Literature of the Sixteenth Century* (1944; rpt., New York: Octagon Books, 1965), 41–83, 110–32; and David Norbrook, "The Reformation and Prophetic Poetry," in his *Poetry and Politics in the English Renaissance* (London: Routledge, 1984), 32–59. In contrast to my notion of a "topical Utopia," see Fredric Jameson, "Of Islands and Trenches: Neutralization and the Production of Utopian Discourses," in *The Ideologies of Theory: Essays, 1971–86* (Minneapolis: University of Minnesota Press, 1988), 75–103. Jameson discusses the ways in which utopias neutralize history. But Robinson's *Utopia* reverses this process.

2. A. F. Pollard's *England under Protector Somerset: An Essay* (London, 1900; rpt., New York: Russell & Russell, 1966) is still a good history of the period. But see also S. L. Greenslade, "English Versions of the Bible, 1525–1611," in *The Cambridge History of the Bible,* vol. 3, *The West from the Reformation to the Present Day,* ed. Greenslade (Cambridge: Cambridge University Press, 1963), 141–74. See also "Vox Populi, Vox Dei," in John King, *English Reformation Literature: The Tudor Origins of the Protestant Tradition* (Princeton: Princeton University Press, 1982), 122–60. For more on Henrician shifts in policy toward the English Bible, see David Scott Kastan, "'The Noyse of the new Bible': Reform and Reaction in Henrician England," in *Religion and Culture in Renaissance England,* ed. Claire McEachern and Debora Shuger (Cambridge: Cambridge University Press, 1997), 46–69.

3. See this dedication in J. H. Lupton's edition of *Utopia* (Oxford: Clarendon Press, 1895), 15–17, and *Utopia* (London: Abraham Vele, 1551), where it is unpaginated. With the exception of the preface, my citations of Robinson's 1551 translation will come from the more readily available J. Collins edition of Robinson's translation (Oxford: Clarendon Press, 1904). Both Collins and Lupton use the 1551 as opposed to the 1556 edition of Robinson's translation, but for some reason Collins does not include Robinson's prefatory letter to Cecil, which Robinson omitted from the 1556 edition of his translation. For more on the politics of patronage during this period, see John King, "Print, Patronage, and Propaganda," in King, *English Reformation Literature,* 76–121.

4. See Lupton, *Utopia,* 19.

5. See King, *English Reformation Literature,* 111. See also, pp. lxxi–lxxii of Lupton's introduction to his edition for more on the letters and Robinson's relationship to Cecil.

6. See *Utopia* (London: Abraham Vele, 1551).

7. See Lupton, *Utopia,* 18–19.

8. See Lupton, *Utopia,* 18, where Robinson discusses the possibility of his having ruined the "grace and pleasure of the eloquence" of More's Latin and thereby damaged the "frutefulnes of the matter," too. Nevertheless, Robinson's desire to be, as he puts it, "acqytte and discharged of all blame" (19) is suggestive of more than stylistic anxieties.

9. See *Utopia* (London: Abraham Vele, 1556), ii–iii.

10. See *The Workes of Sir Thomas More,* ed. William Rastell (Richard Totell, John Waly, and John Cawod, 1557). The following excerpt is from Rastell's dedication of the work to Mary:

> I truste this boke shal be most acceptable, both for that . . . it being read of many, as it is likely to be, shall much helpe forwarde your Maiesties most godly purpose, in purging this your realme of all wicked heresies.

11. See Collins, *Utopia,* 139, where Raphael in his peroration contrasts a "ryche gold-smythe or an usurer" with "poore labourers, carters, yronsmythes, carpenters, and plowmen."

12. For information on Thomas Chaloner's life, see Clarence Miller's introduction to his edition of Chaloner's *The Praise of Folie,* Early English Text Society, no. 257 (Oxford: Oxford University Press, 1965), xxix–xlv. The reference to Chaloner's funeral is quoted from Miller's introduction, p. xliv. It is originally from Camden's *Annals.*

13. See Miller, *The Praise of Folie,* 3.

14. See Lupton, *Utopia,* 17. See also Sidney's distinction between the errors of More the "man" and the "absolute" way of patterning a commonwealth that More adopted in *Utopia* (Sidney, *A Defense of Poetry,* ed. Jan Van Dorstein [Oxford: Oxford University Press, 1966], 73).

15. See Lupton, *Utopia,* 18–19.

16. See Collins, *Utopia,* 115.

17. See the Yale *Utopia,* 110.

18. See the Yale *Utopia,* 146.

19. See Collins, *Utopia,* 43, and the Yale *Utopia,* 102.

20. See Lupton's introduction to Robinson's translation of *Utopia,* p. lxxiii.

21. See Elizabeth McCutcheon's "Denying the Contrary: More's Use of Litotes in *Utopia,*" in *Essential Articles for the Study of Thomas More,* ed. Richard Sylvester and G. Marc'hadour (Hamden, Conn.: Archon Books, 1977), 263–75. See the Yale *Utopia,* 38, and Collins' edition of Robinson's translation of *Utopia,* p. 250. "Homely, playne, and simple speche" is Robinson's translation of "neglecta simplicitas."

22. Collins notes this difference on p. 183 of his edition of Robinson's translation. See also the 1556 *Utopia,* 45.

23. The validity of the term "commonwealth men" has been challenged by G. R. Elton in his "Reform and the 'Commonwealth Men' of Edward VI's Reign," in *The English Commonwealth: 1547–1640,* ed. Peter Clark, Alan Smith, and Nicolas Tyacke (Leicester: Leicester University Press, 1979). Elton's point is that "commonwealth men" is a name devised by modern historians to denote a group of moralists—Hugh Latimer, Robert Crowley, and John Hales, among others—who had little in common besides

relatively incoherent goals. Elton is perhaps right to argue that the "commonwealth men" did not form a political "party" in the modern sense of the word. Nevertheless, the populist rhetoric of figures such as Crowley and Latimer and the patronage afforded to such populism by government officials—that is, Cecil and Somerset— gave them more of a coherence than Elton is willing to admit. Helen White, while not relying on the term "commonwealth men," has grouped figures such as Crowley and Latimer together and has associated them with the "age-old protests of the have-nots against the haves" (*Social Criticism,* 110). The Renaissance evidence for the validity of the phrase "commonwealth men" is slender but telling. In a letter of the aggrieved gentryman, Sir Anthony Aucher, to William Cecil, Aucher expresses a fear of "these men called commonwealths and their adherents," and he suggests that "under the pretence of simplicity and poverty there may rest much mischief" (September 1549; *State Papers Domestic, Edward VI,* vol. 8, no. 56). John King avoids the whole question by calling the "radical reformers" of the Edwardian period "gospellers" (*English Reformation Literature,* 15), but I have retained "commonwealth men" because this phrase indicates the undeniably social implications of their evangelical message.

24. Arthur Ferguson, *The Articulate Citizen and the English Renaissance* (Durham: Duke University Press, 1965), 250.

25. For an account of Cecil's complex maneuvering during this period, see the second chapter of Conyer Reed, *Mr. Secretary Cecil and Queen Elizabeth* (New York: Knopf, 1955). See also Pollard, *England under Protector Somerset,* 238–314.

26. See the "proheme" to Cooper's *Bibliotheca Eliotae* (London: Berthelet: 1548). This proheme reappears in the 1552 and 1559 editions of the *Bibliotheca Eliotae,* but it is put in a much less prominent position.

27. See Collins, *Utopia,* 16.

28. See the Parker Society edition of *The Sermons by Hugh Latimer,* ed. Rev. George Corrie (Cambridge: Cambridge University Press, 1845), 110.

29. Quoted from *Sermons and Remains by Hugh Latimer,* ed. Rev. George Corrie (Cambridge: Cambridge University Press, 1845), xx–xxi.

30. See *Sermons by Latimer,* 106.

31. See *Sermons by Latimer,* 66–67.

32. Collins, *Utopia,* 16.

33. See *Sermons by Latimer,* 86.

34. See *Sermons by Latimer,* 135.

35. On the social dissatisfaction common to both the rebels at Norfolk and Cornwall, see Barrett Beer, *Rebellion and Riot: Popular Disorder in England during the Reign of Edward VI* (Kent: Kent State University Press, 1982), 63–70.

36. See Alexander Neville's *De Furoribus Norfolciensium* (London: Binneman, 1575), 130, 137.

37. See Barrett Beer's reproduction of this manuscript account in " 'The Commoyson in Norfolk 1549': A Narrative of Popular Rebellion in Sixteenth-Century England," *Journal of Medieval and Renaissance Studies* 6 (spring 1976): 73–101. The reference to the prince's "commandment" concerning enclosures can be found on p. 80.

38. See John Cheke, "The Hurt of Sedition" (London, 1549). Unfortunately it is only sporadically paginated.

39. See *Holinshed's Chronicles of England, Scotland, and Ireland* (London, 1808), 3:966.

40. See Neville's *De Furoribus Norfolciensium,* 50.

41. See the Yale *Utopia,* 106–7, for More's articulation of similar views.

42. For more on the perception that the rebels were misusing political nomenclature, see Neville, *De Furoribus Norfolciensium,* 120, where the king's herald advises the rebels to pay more attention to "res sua publica"; note the way in which "sua" separates "res" from "publica"—"de qua omni in sermone non perinsusle minus, quam nefarie, impieque gloriari solerent" [concerning which in every discourse no less foolishly than nefariously and impiously they were accustomed to exult].

43. See Sir Thomas Smith, *A Discourse of the Commonweal of this Realm of England,* ed. Mary Dewar (Charlottesville: University Press of Virginia, 1966), 105–8, 126–29. To be sure, the reference to Utopia occurs in the context of a discussion of the advisability of devaluing the English coinage—a solution that Pandotheus rejects as Utopian. The reference may be to the Utopian practice of using gold in demeaning ways (Yale *Utopia,* 156–57), but it also serves the broader purpose of suggesting that, his name notwithstanding, Pandotheus' ideas offer no imaginary or "castle-in-the-air" solution to England's woes.

44. Annabel Patterson's *Censorship and Interpretation: The Conditions of Writing and Reading in Early Modern Europe* (Madison: University of Wisconsin Press, 1984), 57.

45. Lupton, *Utopia,* 15–16.

46. Collins, *Utopia,* 39–40.

47. Collins, *Utopia,* 31.

48. See Lucian, *How to Write History,* trans. K. Kilburn, in *Lucian,* 8 vols., Loeb Classical Library (London: Heinemann, 1913–1967), 6:3–9, where he describes himself as surrounded by hack historians. But Lucian is satirizing this multitude of writers whereas Robinson seems to be taking the learned men writing on behalf of the commonwealth more seriously. See also Guillaume Bude's *Opera Omnia,* vol. 3 (Basel, 1557; rpt. Westmeat Farnborough: Gregg Press, 1966), 2–4, where Bude uses the Diogenes topos as part of his preface to *Annotationes in Pandectas.* In Bude's version he is not so much surrounded by hack writers as inept readers, who will misjudge his efforts. See the prologue to Rabelais' *Tiers Livre,* which addresses the issue of the writer's function during war and his relationship to his public but not the "vocation" of learning.

49. See Collins, *Utopia,* 63.

50. See Max Weber, *The Protestant Ethic and the Spirit of Capitalism,* trans. Talcott Parsons (New York: Scribner's Sons, 1958), 72–92, 204–10. The notion that the advisory role and "calling" of the learned and that of other kinds of laborers may even overlap is also expressed in the preface to Smith's *A Discourse,* 12:

> Therefore I would not only have learned men (whose judgment I would wish to be chiefly esteemed herein) but also merchantmen, husbandmen, and artificers (which in their calling are taken wisely) freely suffered and yea provoked to tell their advice in this matter . . . [i.e., the grievances of the commonweal]

Accordingly, in Smith's *A Discourse,* although Doctor Pandotheus takes the lead, a knight, husbandman, and merchant also participate in the process of giving advice. The king is only one possible audience for their counsel. To be sure, Robinson's busy workers also have a "degree" as well as a "vocation." But note that this degree seems to be a function of what they do rather than an inherited privilege.

51. See Latimer, *Sermons by Latimer,* 65.

52. See Collins, *Utopia,* 124.

53. See Collins, *Utopia,* 10.

54. See Collins, *Utopia,* 12. For the Latin, see the Yale *Utopia,* 60.

55. See Collins, *Utopia,* 15.

56. See Penry Williams, *The Tudor Regime* (Oxford: Clarendon, 1979), 324–26.

57. Robert Crowley, *An Information and Peticion against the Oppressours of the Pore Commons of this Realme* (London, 1548), in *The Select Works of Robert Crowley,* ed. J. M. Cooper for the Early English Text Society (London: Trubner, 1872), 156.

58. See Crowley's *The Way to Wealth* (London, 1550), in *The Select Works of Robert Crowley,* 142.

59. See Collins, *Utopia,* 16.

60. See Crowley's 1550 *Pierce Plowman,* fol. cxvi.

61. *Sermons by Latimer,* 250–51.

62. See *A Dialogue Concerning Heresies,* ed. Thomas M. C. Lawler, Germain Marc'hadour, and Richard Marius (New Haven: Yale University Press, 1981), pp. 412–13.

63. See Collins, *Utopia,* 125.

64. Collins, *Utopia,* 125:

> He, as sone as he was baptised, began against oure willes, . . . to reason of the Christes religion; . . . and began to waxe so hotte in his matter, that he did not only preferre our religion before all other, but also did utterly despise and condemne al other, calling them prophane, and the followers of them wicked and devilish, ... When he had thus longe reasoned of the matter, they layd holde on him, . . . and condempned hym into exyle; . . . as a sedicious persone, and a rayser up of dissention amonge the people.

65. See Collins, *Utopia,* 125.

66. Collins, *Utopia,* 124:

> But after they harde us speake of the name of Christe, of his doctryne, lawes, myracles, and of the no less constancie of so manye martyrs, whose bloude willynlye shedde brought a great number of nations . . . into theire secte; you will not believe with howe gladde minde they agreed unto the same.

> Robinson uses the word "sect" repeatedly in his discussions of Utopian religion. See, for instance, the discussion of Utopian prayers in Collins, *Utopia,* 134.

67. See Collins, *Utopia,* 127, and the Yale *Utopia,* 222.

68. Quoted from James Gairdner, *Lollardy and Reformation* (New York: Macmillan, 1941), 3:179.

69. The replacement of the Mass by Communion began with the 1548 *Order of Communion,* which provided an English form of administering Communion in both kinds to be used in conjunction with the Latin Mass. In the 1549 Book of Common Prayer the "Supper of the Lord and Holy Communion, commonly called the Mass" replaced the Missal. In 1552 "communion" is no longer "commonly called the mass" but replaces it altogether. See John King's *English Reformation Literature,* 140–42.

70. See Miller's edition of Chaloner's translation of *The Praise of Folie,* 4–5.

71. Chaloner, *The Praise of Folie,* 34.

72. See ASD 4.3:110–11. See also Chaloner, *The Praise of Folie,* 45.

73. Chaloner, *The Praise of Folie,* 28.

74. Chaloner, *The Praise of Folie,* 39–40.

75. See the Yale *Utopia,* 160. The Utopians debate whether *felicitas* consists in virtue or pleasure, and, according to Raphael, they lean too much in the direction of the faction that asserts the primacy of pleasure (i.e., Epicureanism).

76. See Chaloner, *The Praise of Folie,* 87.

77. Juan Luis Vives, *De Communione Rerum,* in *Opera Omnia,* 8 vols. (Valencia: Benedicti Montfort, 1784; rpt., London: Gregg Press, 1964), 4:477. The translation is my own.

78. See LB 2:424B.

79. See John Foxe, *A Sermon of Christ Crucified* (London: John Day, 1570).

80. For more on the context of this sermon, see William Haller, *Foxe's Book of Martyrs and the Elect Nation* (London: The Bedford Historical Series, 1963), 99–102.

81. See the introduction to Lawrence Sasek, *Images of English Puritanism: A Collection of Contemporary Sources* (Baton Rouge: Louisiana State University Press, 1989), 3. For more on Foxe's own complex relation to the national church that he helped to establish, see also Jane Face, "John Foxe and the Defense of the English Church," in *Protestantism and the National Church in Sixteenth-Century England,* ed. Peter Lake and Maria Dowling (London: Croom Helm, 1987).

5. Utopia and Faerie Land

1. See Ben Jonson, *Works,* ed. C. H. Hertford and Percy Simpson (London: Clarendon Press, 1925–52), 1:137.

2. For the Elizabethan tendency to assimilate different historical instances of radicalism, see "A New Interpretation," in Brents Stirling, *The Populace in Shakespeare* (New York: Columbia University Press, 1949), 97–151, and, more recently, Annabel Patterson, "The Peasant's Toe: Popular Culture and Popular Pressure," in *Shakespeare and the Popular Voice* (Oxford: Basil Blackwell, 1989), 32–52. Neither Stirling nor Patterson, however, emphasizes the assimilation of Utopian polities to such accounts of English radicalism.

3. See Peter Lake, *Anglicans and Puritans? Presbyterianism and Conformist Thought from Whitgift to Hooker* (London: Unwin Hyman, 1988), 81–85. Lake's first chapter, "What Was the Admonition Controversy About?" (13–71) makes the case for the nature of the visible church as the central issue of the debate. See also Donna Hamilton, "The Elm and the Vine," in her *Shakespeare and the Politics of Protestant England* (New York: Harvester Wheatsheaf, 1992), 1–29.

4. See Marprelate, *Oh Read over D. John Bridges* (1588), in *The Marprelate Tracts {1588–1589}* (Leeds, U.K.: The Scolar Press, 1967), 37. See also p. 34, where Marprelate writes that the bishops are afraid that "the common people should learne that the only way to salvation is by the word preached."

5. See Marprelate, *Oh Read over D. John Bridges,* 8–10.

6. Hamilton, *Shakespeare and the Politics of Protestant England,* 8–15. See Gabriel Harvey's "An Advertisement to Pap-Hatchet, and Martin Mar-prelate," in *Pierces Supererogation or a New Prayse of the Old Asse* (London: John Wolfe, 1593; rpt., Menston, U.K.: Scolar Press, 1970).

7. Marprelate, *Hay Any Worke for Cooper,* in *The Marprelate Tracts,* 16.

8. Marprelate, *Oh Read over D. John Bridges,* 39.

9. See *A Transcript of the Registrar of the Company of Stationers in London 1554–1640,* ed. Edward Arber (London, 1875), 816.

10. See Harvey, "Advertisement for Pap Hatchett . . . ," 33.

11. James Nohrnberg, *The Analogy of The Faerie Queene* (Princeton: Princeton University Press, 1976), 683, as well as Debra Belt, "Hostile Audiences and the Courteous Reader in *The Faerie Queene,* Book VI," *Spenser Studies* 9 (1988): 107–35.

12. See, for instance, David Miller, "Abandoning the Quest," *English Literary History* 46

(1979): 173–92; Richard Helgerson, *Self-Crowned Laureates: Spenser, Jonson, Milton, and the Literary System* (Berkeley: University of California Press, 1983), 97; Clare Regan Kinney, "The Ends of Questing, the Quest for an Ending: Circumscribed Vision in *The Faerie Queene Book VI*," in her *Strategies of Poetic Narrative: Chaucer, Spenser, Milton, Eliot* (Cambridge: Cambridge University Press, 1993), 70–122; and most recently Elizabeth Fowler, "The Failure of Moral Philosophy in the Work of Edmund Spenser," *Representations* 51 (summer 1995): 47–76 and, in particular, p. 51, which posits the "unraveling" of ethics and politics in the final books of *The Faerie Queene*. The shared source of their approach to book 6 is Harry Berger, "A Secret Discipline: *The Faerie Queene*, Book VI," in *Form and Convention in the Poetry of Edmund Spenser*, ed. William Nelson (New York: Columbia University Press, 1961), 35–75, and reprinted in Berger's *Revisionary Play: Studies in Spenserian Dynamics* (Berkeley: University of California Press, 1988), 215–43. I will also be making use of Berger's article, but I will be doing so to offer a different reading of book 6 than that of Spenser's "private" and "interior" journey through his own poem.

13. For purposes of comparison, see "Donne and the Conditions of Coterie Verse," in Arthur Marotti, *John Donne, Coterie Poet* (Madison: University of Wisconsin Press, 1986), 3–25.

14. See George Edelen's introduction to *The Folger Library Edition of Richard Hooker's Works* (Cambridge: Harvard University Press, 1977), xiii–xiv. This problem was a familiar one to More as well. See John Headley's notes on More's *Responsio ad Lutherum* (New Haven: Yale University Press, 1969), 867.

15. See Marprelate, *Hay Any Worke for Cooper*, 14.

16. Marprelate, *Oh Read over D. John Bridges* (the epitome), 5.

17. See John King, "Was Spenser a Puritan?" *Spenser Studies* 10 (1989): 6.

18. Marprelate, *Hay Any Worke for Cooper*, 8–9.

19. Marprelate, *Hay Any Worke for Cooper*, 12.

20. Jean Brink, "Who Fashioned Edmund Spenser? The Textual History of the *Complaints*," *Studies in Philology* 88 (spring 1991): 153–68.

21. See Harvey's 1592 *Four Letters and Certain Sonnets*, ed. G. B. Harrison, Elizabethan and Jacobean Quartos (New York: Barnes and Noble, 1966), 15–16:

> Mother Hubberd in the heat of choler, forgetting the pure sanguine of her sweet Faery Queene, willfully overshot her malcontented self . . . if mother hubberd in the veine of Chaucer, happen to tell one canicular tale, father elderton and his sonne Greene, in the vaine of Skelton or Scoggin, will counterfeit an hundred dogged fables.

Harvey's distinction between the "vein of Chaucer" and that of Skelton does not quite work because Spenser's persona Colin Clout himself recalled the vein of Skelton.

22. The Fox, to be sure, is only a "disguised dog," but this disguise, like the others that the Fox and Ape assume, is a surprisingly fitting one.

23. See *Pap with a Hatchet*, in *The Complete Works of John Lily*, ed. R. Bond (Oxford: Oxford University Press, 1902), 400.

24. See Harvey, "Advertisement to Pap Hatchet":

> but had I bene Martin, (as for a time I was vainely suspected by such madd copesmates, that can summarize any thing for their purpose, howsoever unlikely or monstrous) I would have beene so farre from being mooved by such a fantasticall confuter [i.e., Lyly] that it should have beene one of my May-games . . . to have driven officials, Commissaries, Archdeacons, Deanes, . . . Bishops, and Archbishops, . . . to entertaine such an odd, light-headed fellow for their defence. (74)

25. Nashe, *Have with You to Saffron Walden,* in *The Works of Thomas Nashe,* ed. R. B. McKerrow, 5 vols. (Oxford: Basil Blackwell, 1958), 3:49. For more on Harvey and Nashe, see Alexandra Halasz, *The Marketplace of Print: Pamphlets and the Public Sphere in Early Modern England* (Cambridge: Cambridge University Press, 1997), 82–114.

26. See the published Spenser-Harvey correspondence in *Spenser: Poetical Works,* ed. J. Smith and E. Selincourt (Oxford: Oxford University Press, 1912), 610–41. See p. 621 in particular. For more on the Harvey-Spenser correspondence and its pertinence to *Mother Hubberds Tale,* see Annabel Patterson, "Still Reading Spenser after All These Years?" in *English Literary Renaissance* 25 (1995): 432–45.

27. R. B. McKerrow argues that the issue of libel hinged upon a poem included in the Harvey-Spenser correspondence. The poem, *Speculum Tuscanismi,* was able to be read as an attack upon the Earl of Oxford. See McKerrow's introduction to *The Works of Thomas Nashe,* 5:73. See also p. 71, where McKerrow argues that Harvey must have been recognized as holding Puritan views in order for Lyly to accuse him of being Martin Marprelate.

28. Harvey, "Advertisement for Pap Hatchet," 94–95.

29. See Harvey, "Advertisement for Pap Hatchet," 98, 100, 101. See also Harvey's linking *Four Letters,* p. 54, where Harvey castigates satirical wits and in so doing makes reference to the canicular Mother Hubberd:

> they can lash poor soules and spurgall asses mightily, they can tell parlous tales of bears and foxes, as shrewdly as mother hubberd . . . they will be as egregiously famous as ever was Herostratus, or Pausanius, or Kett, or Scoggin: Agrippa and Rabelais but ciphers to them.

30. Harvey, *Four Letters and Certain Sonnets,* 29.

31. Harvey, *Four Letters and Certain Sonnets,* 29.

32. Harvey, *Pierces Supererogation,* 58.

33. Marprelate, *Oh Read over D. John Bridges,* 23.

34. D. M. Palliser, *The Age of Elizabeth, 1547–1603* (London: Longman, 1983), 75.

35. Harvey, *Pierces Supererogation,* 8.

36. See the "Preface to the Curteous Buyer," in *Spenser: Poetical Works,* 610.

37. On the subject of the surplus of educated aspirants for a limited number of government positions in Tudor England, see Mark Curtis, "The Alienated Intellectuals of Early Stuart England," *Past and Present* 23 (1962): 25–44; Lawrence Stone, "The Educational Revolution in England, 1560–1640," *Past and Present* 28 (1964): 41–80, as well as his "Social Mobility in England, 1500–1700," *Past and Present* 33 (1966): 16–55.

38. Harvey, "Advertisement for Pap Hatchet," 77, 106.

39. Thomas Cooper, *Admonition,* ed. Edward Arber (London: English Scholar Library, 1882), 159.

40. See Cooper, *Admonition,* 148.

41. With regard to the denial of lordship that Cooper ascribes to Martin, see also E.K.'s etymology of the word "lord" in the notes to the July eclogue. E.K. traces this word to the "tyrannie" of the Danes over the Britons.

42. Thomas Smith, *De Republica Anglorum,* ed. Mary Dewar (Cambridge: Cambridge University Press, 1982), 144.

43. Smith, *De Republica Anglorum,* 50.

44. Harvey's marginalia includes a similar reading of ideal republics. See *Gabriel Harvey's Marginalia,* ed. G. C. Moore Smith (Stratford-upon-Avon: Shakespeare Head Press, 1913), 197:

Vivimus in Smith Rep; non in Mori Utopia; aut Platonis; aut regno Xenophantis Phantasticarum Rerumpublicarum Usus tantummodo phantasticus.

45. See this poem in *Spenser: Poetical Works,* 637–38.

46. Thomas Chaloner, *Praise of Folie,* ed. Clarence Miller, Early English Text Society (Oxford: Oxford University Press, 1965), 34. Sidney applies to poetry this distinction between ideal commonwealths and the kind of manipulations displayed by Menenius Agrippa in Sidney, *A Defense of Poetry,* ed. Jan Van Dorstein (Oxford: Oxford University Press, 1966), 41. According to Sidney, Menenius Agrippa eschewed "far-fet maxims of philosophy (especially if they were Platonic)" and chose instead the "homely and familiar" manner of a poet.

47. The rivalry of Plato and Xenophon has its origin in Aulus Gellius 14.3, but interestingly a text reconciling the two was available to Spenser in Sidney's *Defense* as well as in Sir Thomas Smith's *De Republica Anglorum.* Indeed, Spenser here has taken Sidney's *agon* between poetry and philosophy, and he has made Xenophon and Plato the representatives of each side. Thus, Xenophon implicitly practices "doctrine by example" whereas Plato teaches "by rule." Yet, although Sidney praised Xenophon for bestowing a "Cyrus upon the world to make many Cyruses" without mentioning Plato, Sidney also, substituting More for Plato, classifies the "methods" of designing ideal commonwealths and those of educating a ruler under the same poetic rubric. Thus, Sidney asks, "[W]hat philosopher's counsel can so readily direct a prince, as the feigned Cyrus in Xenophon; . . . or a whole commonwealth, as the way of Sir Thomas More's *Utopia? . . .* for that way of patterning commonwealths was most absolute, though he perchance hath not so absolutely performed it." In other words, Spenser could have followed this passage from the *Defense* and made the "patterning of commonwealths" and Xenophon's *Cyropedia* similar rather than opposed "methods" of imparting doctrine.

48. Of course, in addition to tempting Redcrosse with heavenly bliss, Despair also tries to convince him that his sins are so great that he cannot be saved.

49. *The Folger Library Edition of the Works of Richard Hooker,* 24.

50. See James Nohrnberg's *The Analogy of the Faerie Queene,* 615:

> Agape is not, as might first be supposed, a mistake for Philia. The analogy between the divine love and brotherly feeling is a New Testament commonplace, and Agape brings up her children to love one another as she has loved them. The ecclesiastical community is a fellowship; its members are urged to "love brotherly without feigning" (1 Peter 1:22) and to forgive and forbear mutually on the Lord's model. (Colossians 3:13)

But, as Erasmus had shown, the church had progressively fallen away from this model.

51. I think that Annabel Patterson misses the point here when she sees Theseus' rejection of the "Battle of the Centaurs" as the eschewal of a "learned, humanist" entertainment in favor of the more populist performance of Bottom and the mechanicals. For despite its being sung by a eunuch, the "Battle of the Centaurs," which took place during a nuptial, is the extreme of class strife that Theseus wants to prevent the visit of the mechanicals to his wedding from becoming. See *Shakespeare and the Popular Voice,* 63.

52. See *Shakespeare's Ovid, Being Arthur Golding's Translation of the "Metamorphoses,"* ed. W. H. Rouse (New York: W. W. Norton, 1961), 242–45.

53. Lily, *Pap with a Hatchet,* 397.

54. On this issue, see Kenneth Borris' " 'Divelish Ceremonies': Allegorical Satire of

Protestant Extremism in *The Faerie Queene* VI.viii.31–51," *Spenser Studies* 8 (1990): 175–211.

55. See, for instance, the proem to book 5.

56. See Virginia Stern, *Gabriel Harvey: His Life and Marginalia* (Oxford: Oxford University Press, 1979), 186.

57. Berger, *Revisionary Play,* 218.

58. See also book 2.9.25. In Alma's house, which explicates good government at the level of the body, the tongue exercizes the function of porter, excluding "utterers of secrets," "babblers of folly," and "blazers of crime." As porter, the tongue can sound a "larumbell" but never "out of time." Spenser's Blatant or "babbling" beast is all that the porter of Alma's house is meant to counter, but, as a babbler and blazer, the Beast also emerges out of the description of the porter's function.

59. See *The Works of Edmund Spenser: A Variorum Edition,* ed. Edwin Greenlaw, Charles Grosvenor Osgood, and Frederick Morgan Padelford, 11 vols. (Baltimore: Johns Hopkins University Press, 1932–57), 6:265.

60. See CWE 29:259–60.

61. For this genealogy, see 6.1.7–8. For an alternative genealogy, see 6.6.9–11.

62. Nashe, *Summer's Last Will* in *Thomas Nashe: The Unfortunate Traveller and Other Works,* ed. J. B. Steane (1972; rpt., London: Penguin, 1985), 185–87.

63. For the argument that the Giant may represent Kett, see Merritt Hughes, "Spenser and Utopia," *Studies in Philology* 17 (1920): 132–46. Hughes, however, is so anti-Giant that he actually finds Talus a sympathetic character. For readings more sympathetic to the Giant, see Fowler, "The Failure of Moral Philosophy in the Work of Edmund Spenser," 62 and Annabel Patterson's "The Egalitarian Giant: Representations of Justice in History/Literature," *Journal of British Studies* 31 (1992): 97–132. Both Fowler and Patterson connect the Giant to Spenser's experiences in Ireland. There was also, however, an English context for the Giant's topicality and equivocal character in the 1590s.

64. Ann Imbrie, " 'Playing Legerdemaine with Scripture': Parodic Sermons in *The Faerie Queene,*" *English Literary Renaissance* 17 (1987): 142–55.

65. More, *Responsio ad Lutherum,* 534.

66. See John Headley's annotations on *Responsio ad Lutherum,* 959. My own references to the text of Esdras will come from The Anchor Bible: I and II Esdras, trans. Jacob M. Meyers (New York: Doubleday, 1974).

67. See Harvey, "Advertisement for Pap-Hatchett," 129. Here, Harvey may be responding to Marprelate, who, like other Puritans, had attacked the inclusion of the Apocrypha in the Bible. Marprelate links the confusion of Apocrypha and holy scripture with the attempt to "mingle heaven and earth together":

> The last lent there came a commaundement from his grace into Paules Churchyard / that no Byble should be bounde without the Apocrypha. Monstrous and ungodly wretches / that to maintaine their owne outragious proceedings / thus mingle heaven and earth together / and would make the spirite of God / to be the author of prophane bookes. (*Oh Read over D. John Bridges,* 37)

Note that for Marprelate mingling heaven and earth together means corrupting something that should remain pure—that is, scripture. For Harvey, however, the mingling of heaven and earth means attempting to purify what must be, in part, corrupt—i.e., human government, whether of church or state.

68. Nashe, *The Unfortunate Traveller,* 211–13.

69. DeWitt Starnes and Ernest Talbert, *Classical Myth and Legend in Renaissance Diction-aries* (Chapel Hill: University of North Carolina Press, 1955), 91. See also Boccaccio's *Geneologia Deorum,* 5.35 and Nicolas Perotti's *Cornucopiae.* I examined 1532 editions of both works.

Epilogue

1. Gilbert Burnet, "A Sermon Preached Before the House of Commons" (London: John Starkey and Richard Chiswell, 1689), 15.
2. *Utopia,* trans. Gilbert Burnet (London: Richard Chiswell, 1684), 198.
3. See the *Second Treatise* in Locke's *Two Treatises of Government,* ed. Peter Laslett (Cambridge: Cambridge University Press, 1960), sect. 124.
4. See C. B. Macpherson, *The Political Theory of Possessive Individualism* (Oxford: Oxford University Press, 1962).
5. Preface to Burnet, *Utopia,* unpaginated.
6. Burnet, *Utopia,* 59.
7. See Collins, *Utopia* (Oxford: Clarendon Press, 1904), and the Yale *Utopia,* 104.
8. See Macpherson's *The Political Theory of Possessive Individualism,* 138–42.
9. On the Levellers and their alleged Utopian scheme of leveling as well as a more general picture of the Utopian eruptions of the Civil War period, see Frank Manuel and Fritzie Manuel, *Utopian Thought in the Western World* (Cambridge: Harvard University Press, 1979), 332–67.
10. See *Gerrard Winstanley: Selected Writings,* ed. Andrew Hopper (London: Aporia Press, 1989), 10–11.
11. Burnet, "A Sermon Preached at the Coronation of William III and Mary II . . . Westminster, April 11, 1689" (London: J. Starkey and Richard Chiswell, 1689), 20.
12. Burnet, *The History of the Reformation,* ed. Rev. E. Narres (London: J. F. Dove, 1830), 3:43–47.
13. Burnet, *Utopia,* 177.
14. Milton, *Eikonoklastes,* in vol. 3 of *Complete Prose Works,* ed. Don M. Wolfe (New Haven: Yale University Press, 1953–1982), 337.
15. Milton, *Areopagitica,* vol. 2, *Complete Prose Works,* 562.
16. Milton, *Areopagitica,* 561.
17. Milton, *Areopagitica,* 521.
18. Milton, *Areopagitica,* 565.
19. Appendix to Milton, *The Ready and Easy Way to Establish a Free Commonwealth,* ed. Evert Mordecai Clark (New Haven: Yale University Press, 1915), 178.
20. Milton, *Ready and Easy Way,* 180.
21. Milton, *Ready and Easy Way,* 26.
22. Milton, *Ready and Easy Way,* 179.
23. Milton, *Ready and Easy Way,* 177.
24. Milton, *Ready and Easy Way,* 25–26.
25. Milton, *Areopagitica,* 526.
26. Milton, *Areopagitica,* 549.
27. Milton, *Areopagitica,* 555.
28. Milton, *Areopagitica,* 532.
29. Milton, *Areopagitica,* 549.
30. Milton, *Areopagitica,* 547.
31. Milton, *Areopagitica,* 536.

32. Milton, *Areopagitica,* 556.

33. Milton, *Areopagitica,* 535, 558.

34. *John Milton,* ed. Jonathan Goldberg and Stephen Orgel (Oxford: Oxford University Press, 1991), 64.

35. Milton, *Areopagitica,* 544.

36. See for instance Mark Rose, *Authors and Owners: The Invention of Copyright* (Cambridge: Harvard University Press, 1993), 29:

> Throughout *Areopagitica* it is the individual author who is portrayed as the source of authority and value. Texts are of authors. Thus Milton speaks of "a good book" as "the precious lifeblood of a master spirit."
>
> Milton is concerned with authorial dignity rather than authorial property. Yet he uses commercial metaphors, which anticipate the commodification of writing.

See also Abbe Blum, "The Author's Authority: *Areopagitica* and the Labour of Licensing," in *Re-Membering Milton,* ed. Mary Nyquist and Margaret W. Ferguson (London: Methuen, 1987); and Christopher Kendrick, *Milton: A Study in Ideology and Form* (New York: Methuen, 1986).

Index